The 265 days portrayed in this book,
The AFRICAN DREAM, are a testament
to the strength of the love and concern
that connected two people.
Day after day facing unknown perils
yet relishing the spirit of adventure!
No greater love hath a couple than to
risk it all, knowing they can accomplish
almost anything, together!

This book, these stories,
are dedicated to the memories of;
Pat's son
Ronald Jerry Patterson
March 20, 1961 - December 12, 1979
who had dreams unfulfilled.
Pat's brother
Charles Jerry Patterson
April 15, 1941 - July 29, 1960
whose dreams took him afar, in the US Navy
and
Terry Tintorri
Realtor, Partner, Leader of the Band
March 15, 1943 - March 10, 2002
We didn't always see eye to eye but we always stood shoulder to shoulder.

Book One of *Bicycling Beyond Boundaries*

The African Dream

By Pat and Cat Patterson

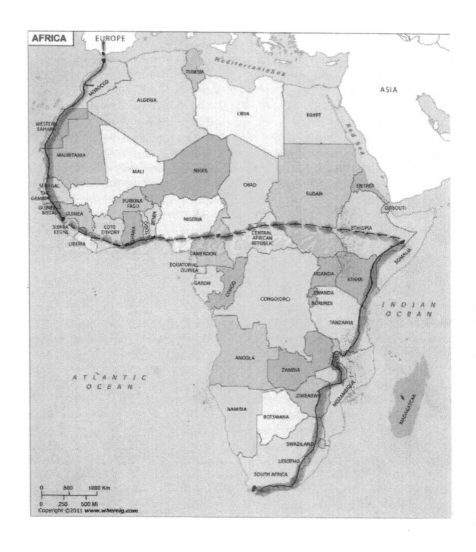

AFRICA was nothing like we thought it would be...
AFRICA was everything we had hoped it would be!

Africa on Bicycles? You must be CRAZY!

Since the beginning of our dream to ride
bicycles through Africa, I always laughed
when my wife Cat worried about wild animals
roaming the roads. Cat got the last laugh!

CAT TRAX Day 165 Mikumi National Park, Tanzania, Africa Under cloudy skies that threatened rain we got a glimpse of the sign, "Entering Mikumi National Park, Dangerous Animals Next 50 Kilometers!" Almost instantly, we encountered baboons. We'd wondered about how they might react when confronted by cyclists on their road. Stories told of aggressive baboons rushing cars, climbing on them, even opening the doors. Perhaps they'd never seen cyclists, but as we rode toward them they scattered into the jungle and simply stared back at us through the leaves.

Our next exciting encounter was a family of wart hogs. When they caught our scent, they turned tail and ran. We laughed aloud at the way they waddled, butts swinging as they trotted away on their stubby legs. Not far off the road, herds of giraffe and zebra grazed contentedly in the tall grass. This was the Africa we had dreamed of, the real Africa!

A truck driver blared his klaxon horn and yelled "Tempo!" We didn't understand. We rolled over toward him and he shouted again. It sounded Swahili. Cat questioned, "Elephants?" He shook his head up and down vigorously, "Yes, yes, Tempo on road!" Rounding the corner we came face to face with the biggest thrill of all. A thrill that left us shaking in our cycling shoes. We were sharing the road with elephants, two adult females tending three young calves. As we stopped, one of the adult guardians turned toward us and pinned her ears back, expressing anger.

Fight or flight? Fight seemed a joke and flight to where?

1

Elephants are quick, she'd be on us before we could get turned around. Sitting there wasn't a good option, either. Could she smell our fear? I made the decision to make noise to see how four tons of elephants would react. I held my front wheel brake. It squeaked as I rocked back and forth. The big adult on the road snorted and looked agitated. We were preparing to turn and high tail it when the other elephant turned toward her calves. They spun around and she followed, crashing through the brush. The old girl guarding us made a fantastic decision: she grunted, turned, and followed. *Whew!*

Rain drops that had been sprinkling down, now turned into a downpour. As we entered the Mikumi Park gate, a French couple in an SUV pulled up. He said, "You look like drowned rats. Did you see any animals, on the road?" We told him about our elephant encounter. Then he asked, "Did you see lions?" When I said no, we didn't think they'd venture out onto the road they laughed. He said, "We've seen them out there, several times. Just three days ago we saw an entire pride walking leisurely along the highway." Oh, my God, we didn't need to hear that.

How Death Changed my Life

We can't blame him, he was only eighteen, and Lord knows he didn't want to die. Ronald Jerry, my first born, a son, my ticket to immortality, the one who'd carry on my name. Or, so I'd been taught. Ron had dreams of a successful career, owning a sprawling ranch in the Santa Ynez Valley. Ah, the best laid dreams of mice and Ron. It was the silent killer, an aneurysm, that got him. Perhaps it was congenital, an  arterial weakness since birth; or brought on by the way he bounced 400 pounds off his chest when bench pressing; maybe even caused by a hard hit, while playing high school football. The why will never be known. However, the event changed my life forever. He was gone, and cry as I might, he wasn't coming back. Nope, not his fault, but a stark reminder to me of The Impermanence of Life. His formative years, and those of my daughters Lori and Stephanie, had been mixed-up with two divorces. Victoria was my third wife. A large part of my previous two failures had been my drive to succeed. I'd invested countless hours in my career, all too often

2

ignoring the things of true importance. Work was a huge part of my life for most of my life. In retail I worked six days a week and every Sunday and holiday, going for the double- and triple-time wages. In my real estate career, I was driven to sell more, earn more, and have more—large houses, expensive cars. Now my son was gone, and my world imploded. I wanted more, not more *things*, but more *life!*

Ron was smart and street-wise. I knew that many of his ideas had been transferred to his friends, his sisters and his step-brothers! He was a great teacher of lessons. Those lessons would be remembered, he would be remembered.

My Theory of Immortality, Confirmed On an African Road

CAT TRAX Day 98, Kandiafara to Boke. The Cat and I had already endured one hell of a day. Ups and downs in extreme heat, several creek crossings, and a jungle fire. It was 5:00 p.m. when a guy we'd seen earlier pumping the tires on his car, pulled up. Cat asked him how far it was to Boke. He pointed to red letters painted on a mud hut, "PK 26", and told her that meant twenty-six kilometers. Fatigued, she asked if we could ride with them, then turned to me and said, "We can't possibly make it before dark, I'm tired and tired of roughing it." When he asked for the

equivalent of $6.00 US, she quickly agreed. It was okay, we had a deal, I'd agreed that anytime Cat felt our health or safety were threatened she could make the call to stop. We grabbed the ride.

Some of our bags were jammed into the trunk, our bikes laid atop them. Cat and I sat in the back seat with our other bags packed in around us. The little car was so overloaded we felt every bump in the road, and progress was painfully slow. Our driver pulled up in front of a hut with red letters, PK 16. Damn, a flat tire, and we'd only come six miles. We

3

had to remove most of the bags from around us, simply to get out. Then we took the bikes and bags from the trunk. I thought the man was digging out his jack and spare tire. Nope, no spare or jack, just a lug wrench and a tired old hand pump. As the usual crowd gathered, the driver borrowed the long pounding pole a woman was using to crush millet in a pestle. His helper dragged a big rock over and they struggled, trying to lift the car enough to slip the rock under.

We sat roadside, like spectators observing the struggle. My thoughts drifted back to memories of my first car.

June, 1955 During my high school days I bought my first car, an old '46' Ford. She suffered terribly from my heavy foot. An ominous _clank, clank, clank_ rang out when I missed a speed-shift while drag racing. With no money for a mechanic, I began tearing her apart. In order to reach the transmission, I had to remove the rear axle. The jack wouldn't lift her high enough. Dad came out and shared an idea. He found an eight-foot-long two-by-six board and had me fetch a log that was cut but not yet split for our fireplace. He placed the log at the rear of the car and used the board on the pivot to easily lift the rear of the car. "This little trick is called lever and fulcrum," Dad explained. Then he boasted, "I could move the earth using the moon as a fulcrum, if I had a long enough lever."

Speaking of the moon, it was rising above the African trees. I took the stick from them and pushed the rock up under the edge of the car. At first, they seemed irritated that I'd butted in. Then a light went on in the driver's big brown eyes as I pressed down on the lever. It was bending, the driver borrowed another lever from a woman pounding grain. We all pushed down, and _voila_ the wheel rose off the ground.

I returned to my spectator seat and watched as they patched the tube. As they struggled, I reflected on one of my theories I call "The path to immortality." This lever-and-fulcrum thing that Dad had gotten from fellow mineworkers during his days underground had just been channeled through me _into_ those African guys. They will never know my father or the miner that had taught him. They would soon forget me, too. However, they'll never forget this lesson. Hopefully, they would share it with others, thus ensuring the continuation of the idea. The ongoing transfer of thoughts and ideas was my theory about how to achieve immortality.

So, my belief was that Ron's wisdom and lessons would continue to influence others for eternity.

Chin, A Kid in China who Changed my Life

Back in 1985, my former wife Victoria and I began taking time away from business. It was part of our slowly growing success. When it was my turn to choose, I saw an ad for China Passages, a bicycle tour. At that time, China had only been open to tourists for a couple of years. We joined nineteen hardy riders and became some of the first foreigners cycling on China's countryside roads in more than forty years.

I've been asked hundreds of times, "Why bicycles? Why riding a bike around the world?" My response was, "That kid in China, the one walking next to me into the commune." I was pushing my bike when he said, "Ni Hao."

I responded, "Ni Hao" then said, "Hello."

He smiled and slowly said, "He-llo."

"You speak English?" I questioned quickly.

"No" he said, shaking his head.

"You do", I cried out.

He seemed wary when I asked his name. "Chin," he answered then asked mine.

"You live here, Chin?"

"Yes, where live you?"

"USA," I said and he frowned. "America," I added. He broke into such an excited rapid babble, I only understood a few words.

We were nearing our lunch stop. I'd caught a small peek into his life and he mine. The woman at the gate of the Commune Cafe shooed him away.

As he retreated he called out, "Goodbye Mr. Pat, America!"

In that moment, I felt the something I'd been searching for, the something I thought could bring meaning to my life. Bicycle touring was it. Adventure in strange and unusual places, and meeting people, real people like Chin. No more tour groups, I yearned for the open road. I could do that. Imagine all the wonderful moments like I'd just experienced. Untold adventures awaiting me.

It wasn't until days later in Hong Kong that I got the courage to bring it up. Victoria had arranged a stay in one of the world's plushest hotels, her kind of travel. "Are you crazy?" she fumed.

"Riding bicycles in foreign lands, strange languages, bad food, and carrying our own bags? We've got a business to run and bills to pay and lots more vacations to exotic places to take."

The conversation had ended. Finished, dead! Yet, in my mind, I couldn't get beyond that kid and his voice as he shouted, "Goodbye Mr. Pat, America!" She was hooked on what I called saran-wrapped plastic bubble tours. Freedom of the open road wasn't her idea of travel. Thoughts of adventure and the allure of the seldom-traveled roads of the world became my dream, her nightmare. I'd found that something unique and different. By 1988, I was prepared physically and financially to travel the world, and I wanted to do it on a bicycle.

How I Found The Cat and How She Hooked Me

In 1989 Victoria and I set off, first riding across the southern US. She didn't like it. I loved it. She felt our friends were laughing at us. I didn't care. She said, "I know you, once you're committed, even if you hate it, you'll keep going!" Once I began I did feel driven to complete the trip. She said, "You're obsessed!" Yes, I think I was and I thought I could convince her. Riding through Texas, Louisiana, and Mississippi, I was already dreaming of Europe, India, and China.

On a cold day in Yugoslavia with snowflakes in the air she sobbed, "I can't take this, I'm going home." I wanted her to stay, but it was hard for me to express that I loved her, yet didn't want to stop my traveling. Her decision to leave was understandable. We did go home, together. And, during that short time I got permission to cycle across the Soviet Union.

We had grown up and grown together. She was my first true love. It heartened me when I got permission to cycle across the USSR. She was excited and decided to come along. We were the first foreign cyclists allowed. It wasn't easy. The Republics were far less developed than either of us had imagined. Victoria had cried many times during that first cycling year, but her tears in the Soviet Union were even more frequent.

She departed Tashkent, Uzbekistan, USSR, to join a Bicycle Touring Company in France. I was jealous. The owner was younger than I, and a successful lawyer. We held each other, both weeping, then she flew away to the west, and I continued cycling east. We made many expensive long-distance phone calls. On a cold wet day in China I scribbled this note:

Colors of the Ag and CB
(Pet names for Victoria and Pat)
White hot, like lightening, suspended in time,
Surrounded by red, green, silver and gold, Christmas in The City.
Orange, sun, sand, a beach at Hanna in Hawaii.
Slow dissipation of heat to a white glow of truth and trust.
Ever-present, shimmering, a guiding star in our nest of love.
Red Embers, discontent, flared to a ball of flame, roaring with anger.
Fueled by feelings, that neither could control.
Flammable comments and actions.
They sat, amazed, where had the WHITE GONE?
Black—shadows of doubt, distrust. Felt on both sides of the world.
Black—mourning, the death of the best friendship and love affair,
Either had ever known.
A cool grey goodbye. The spectrum blurred.
The Colors ran, like tears.

Victoria later expressed her feelings in a letter. "We became best friends and fell madly in love. I admit you are the best friend I ever had. We lived a life like Camelot. We knew great wealth, great poverty, incredible journeys, horrific personal and family tragedies. It took five years to get divorced. God knows why, we didn't have anything to fight about."

The bicycle adventure I had dubbed "Voyagers Two" was a catalyst, however, we also had other gnawing issues. We had loved, laughed, learned, and cried, oh how we cried! My first true love and I split and divorced. Having suffered so, loved and lost during that first voyage I felt sure I'd never find a woman who'd want to cycle and share my life. I became a Lonely Voyager.

Cat and I met in a bar, not just any bar, but a Private Dining Club. In the midst of divorce and mired in feelings of lost love, I was adamant that I'd pursue no more close relationships—and definitely no marriage.

I glanced down the bar and saw two gals sipping and laughing. One caught my eye and smiled.

Her story goes like this:

Cat said, "I met that guy before, he's in real estate."

7

"You should go say hello," her friend Carole urged.

"No way, look he's with a couple of women, he doesn't need another."

Her friend pressed, "C'mon girl, what's a little competition? I know you like to dance, are you afraid you can't keep up with him?"

Irked, Cat accepted the challenge. Walking down the bar, she searched inward, looking for that self-assurance she'd once known. Looking me in the eye, she felt a moment of doubt, a second of hesitation, then, struggling for words, she blurted out, "We're going to dance!"

My friends were shocked. I thought, "This gal is gutsy." However, I answered, "I'm with someone." Summoning up all the attitude she could muster, Cat said, "Hey, I didn't ask you to marry me, I just asked for a dance."

I took her hand and we whirled onto the dance floor. The trio played songs, fast and slow, and we danced three straight. I felt the fit. She enjoyed the moment. I was re-living dances of the past. She was dancing toward a future of recovered confidence. Oh, how we danced! We were completely hooked.

Cat was on the mend, too. Her marriage had ended and their business was bankrupt. They, too, had had it all, the Mercedes, the Porsche, a waterfront home and boats. Her Ex had borrowed a large sum from her brother. They went on a business/golf trip. While there, the Ex told her he loved another. Devastated and embarrassed, she had been avoiding social events.

Dating immediately, within a short time we moved in together. A few months later, we found a larger place. Along with furniture, I moved in my memorabilia of Voyagers Two. Digging through my box of video tapes, Cat asked, "How are they cataloged?" Her organizational skills demanded that we view and list them chronologically. At about the same time, I left my corporate position and we formed Patterson & Tintorri, Inc. Realtors. It was hand-to-mouth for the first years. I managed sales, Cat covered administration. We vehemently shared the feeling that we'd never marry again. Of course, eventually, we did.

My dream had been to cycle through Africa. After viewing the videos, Cat expanded, "Why not just ride south through Mexico and South America, then fly to Africa and ride north?" I couldn't afford another failure. This had to be the final love of my life! We settled on a plan to ride across the USA, to get a feel for the road and see if she liked it. Make sure she could adjust to the hardships of the strange lifestyle that Victoria had hated.

How did you afford to take off for 4 years?

I applied for early Social Security. We sold our real estate company, and those monthly payments, combined with my SS payments, became our tickets to the world. Once on the road we never looked back. Our four-year Odyssey took us through 57 countries. After hearing our plan to cycle around the world most people said, "You must be crazy!" Then, almost in the same breath, they questioned, "How did you find a woman willing to do that?"

To Go or Not to Go, That's Cat's Call!

On a sunny spring day in April, we set off on our bicycle adventure. We chose a send off from our former office attended by family members, friends, and our associates. Our five-year-old granddaughter Aubrie grabbed my leg and cried, "Please don't go Papa." Cat's eighty-five-year-old Dad stepped in front of me, grabbed my handlebars, and in a trembling voice said, "You take care of my little girl!" With our emotions flowing, we pedaled away into the world.

In a few days, we became accustomed to our heavy loads. Camping was something we did if we had to or wanted to. We had to several times between Ventura and San Francisco. Riding on highway 80 near Truckee, California, Cat took our first bad spill. Luckily, she swerved into the guardrail and not traffic. That evening she called her parents. When her Dad heard about the spill he bellowed, "Abandon the trip, abandon the trip!"

We didn't, never even gave it a thought. However, after two months calls and e-mails flooded in. Our fifty-eight-year-old realty partner Terry Tintorri had died. Another silent killer (Pulmonary Edema) brought the big-hearted guy down. We immediately stored the bikes, returning to be with his family and our friends. Two weeks off, and beyond the first shock of loss, we headed back to the road. That was the only time we returned home during the entire four years.

Near Salt Lake City, Cat sank down to the hot pavement. After a week recuperating from heat exhaustion and dehydration, she felt roadworthy. Up and over the Continental Divide we rolled out onto the great plains. None of it came easily, but it was now our life!

Canada, our first International crossing, provided our first change of language. Luckily, Cat had studied French, and the Eastern Provinces spoke a sort of French. Cat understood about half of the French-Canadian conversations. Even saddled with language difficulties we found many new friends.

An expensive decision led us to find a way to get to Greenland and the Polar Ice Cap. Also, our first brush with death. A young girl hiking with her boyfriend Ruud from Holland, drowned as they were crossing a river. Tragic, we became his family until her father arrived. We later visited him at his home in Den Haag, Netherlands.

Europe was a cinch. Wonderful people, many of whom spoke English. Scandinavia, Russia, Poland, Germany and France. More new friends and wondrous experiences. We loved Portugal, Spain, and warmer weather. I was hit by a truck in Portugal. Scary, but no lasting scars. Also in Spain, I broke a tooth and Cat experienced heart palpitations. Both were treated inexpensively at local facilities.

In August, 14 months after beginning our Odyssey, we climbed to the Top of the Rock of Gibraltar. There we met the famous Macaque monkeys and glimpsed Africa through the haze. That night we lay awake, counting our blessing and new friendships. Reminiscing about successes and wondering, worrying about what lay ahead. Fear and trepidation? You bet!

CAT TRAX ... Tracking our progress. It's impossible to report all the difficulties of cycling 50 - 60 miles or more daily. Ups and downs, heat and cold. Leaving Spain for Morocco we'd ridden our bicycles 14,738 Ks, that's 9,158 Miles.

Every DAY began as a MYSTERY.
All we had to do to solve it was PEDAL!
*Life is a journey, we each choose our own path. For me and now
Catherine we chose a Bicycle Path. We chose the Bicycle Path less taken!*
Our thanks, to Robert Frost

Chapter 1 Cycling in an Islamic Kingdom

Morocco was "Africa Lite" and "Islam 101"

CAT TRAX Day One, 2 Ks, Ferry to Tangier. The rattle of the gangplank chains sent a tremble through the Tangier Ferry. It hit African soil with a crash. The crewman signaled for us to go ahead of the trucks and cars.

The eyes of the crowd, anxiously awaiting the throng of tourists and their money, focused on us. We shivered, remembering warnings and stories of horror. "They will push you down...strip your bikes...take everything of value." I thought of Cat's Dad as he grasped my handlebar that first day of our Odyssey, "You take care of my little girl!" What had I done, would I be able to protect her? My sister had sent a daunting e-mail, "All Muslims want to kill Americans."

Being cycling tourists set us apart from the typical. Riding down the ramp we were met by the crowd of the customary hucksters. Shouting and showing their wares, they parted and made a pathway for us, then began to cheer. Even the other tourists took a moment from their fears and anxieties to express admiration. We believed they should be wary, everyone knew those lambs came loaded with pockets of coin. Tourists wanted to steal bargains and the few bad apples among the locals wanted to steal their coins. Perhaps because

we looked like tramps we were immune at least for that moment.

Morocco proved to be more European than other North African Countries yet there was an immediate difference. Food, accommodations, and religion had all changed. We had a lot to learn about Morocco and Islam.

That first afternoon we decided to walk the streets of Tangier. Exiting the hotel, a young well-dressed boy began to talk with us. He had a name tag associating him with our hotel as an official guide. We told him we didn't need a guide, but he persisted, "You do not have to pay, this is my job." He continued to grind us down until we relented-then, he opened windows and doors

11

to a world we couldn't have known without him.   Entering   the Kasbah, he paused and asked, "You have been to Spain?" When we told him we had he posed another question, "What is the difference between Morocco and Spain?" Thinking he wanted a political answer I philosophized, "In Spain, half the men were named Jesus. Here in Morocco half, like you, are named Mohammed." He smiled and the tour continued. Of course we loved him. When he left us at "The best restaurant in the Kasbah," we slipped him $10.00 US. He was delighted, and we were pleased to be able to share.

After dinner, we walked to our hotel through darkened streets. Mohammed had pointed out landmarks to help us find our way. In that maze of narrow alleyways were interesting-looking people, wisps of faint conversations between family members, and the smells of spices being blended in dinners behind closed doors. Always vigilant, we never felt threatened.

CAT TRAX Day Two, 60 Ks, Tangier to Asilah. Visual changes, Arabic street signs, men and women in robes. And the smells-not bad smells, just different. The streets were teeming with cars, trucks, and humanity. The further south we cycled, the more primitive it became. Overloaded donkey carts and old trucks chugged past us, stacked high with freight.

Young kids came running from the fields, hands extended and shouting. We thought they were yelling. "Hello." Several were pushy, insistent that we give them something. Eventually Cat figured it out, "They're saying Cadeaux, gift in French." It was tough to see little ragamuffins and not have a gift for them. It was there that we developed our rule for dealing with beggars, "We can't give to everyone, therefore we will give to no one."

Teenage boys stood in groups calling out for cigarettes. We began yelling back "Pas de fume, don't smoke." To emphasize our point, we'd cough and choke, and they would chuckle.

Many friends, and of course our family, were nervous about our plan to cycle through Islamic regions. They reminded us about how some Muslims had said, "It is the duty of every Muslim to kill an American." We had to remind ourselves of our philosophy that "98% of all people, Muslim or not, are good people. Our challenge was just to avoid that 2% fringe."

CAT TRAX Day Three, 90 Ks, Asilha to Moulay Bousselham. Two girls we met from the States told us they loved Morocco but wouldn't return unless accompanied by a guy. They said young Moroccan boys were constantly touching them and crowding their personal space. They'd been told that women traveling alone were considered whores. Some urged Cat to wear a scarf and long dress- she wore cycling shorts and a short sleeved bike jersey, as it was hot.

A row of produce stands lined the road. A young boy ran out and offered Cat a melon. We stopped and thanked him, then tried to tell him we didn't have space to carry it. He became angry and raised the melon as though he would throw it. I grabbed his arm, but he wrested it away. An older man came to the rescue. He insisted we take the melon, even helped me get it under my cinch strap as he scolded the teenager. A short way down the road Cat stopped and said, "That boy grabbed my shoulder and pinched then pushed me."

CAT TRAX Day Four, 86 Ks, Moulay Bousselham to Kenitra. Cycling into Kenitra was less than welcoming, especially to my sinuses. Men collecting leaves in eucalyptus groves stirred up dust. Also clouds of acrid smoke roiled up from the piles of burning plastic in the fields. The smells sickened us and roadside food had our stomachs gurgling.

Hotel D'Europa looked like our best bet. The staff was moving bags under Cat's direction as I checked in. While signing the registration a voice from behind asked, "I own this place. How are they treating you?" Shocked to hear perfect English I turned and said, "We've only been here five minutes but so far so good."

Abdallah introduced himself and said, "I learned English during school in England. I also lived and worked in Maryland and New Jersey." We told him about our trip and it would have ended there had he not asked the desk clerk to give us his business card. He wrote his cell and home phone numbers on it then shook my hand and said, "Call when you arrive in Rabat, I shall have you visit my home for tea."

CAT TRAX Day Five, Sick in Kenitra. As a young guy I worked in grocery stores. My buddies and I often went out drinking, and coming to work with a hangover was fairly common. Jokingly we called our symptoms the "African Guff-Guff." What was often called "Montezuma's Revenge" back in California-diarrhea that drained our energy-became known between us as the African Guff-Guff.

Surviving diarrhea had become second nature, however throwing up was something I had dreaded since childhood-I'd almost rather eat poop than vomit. Leaping out of bed to avoid soiling the sheets my bottom barely hit the cold porcelain when *whoosh*. Then, as I sat draining from the backside, the urge to purge welled up in my throat. Fortunately the room was sick-friendly. Seated on the toilet, I just had to lean to the right to hang my head in the sink. I filled both. My ups and downs kept Cat awake most of the night.

Still woozy on the third day, we wanted to ride, but didn't like the idea of riding to Rabat searching for a hotel. An SOS call to Abdallah and he set us up at a hotel he called moderately priced and good. Then he reminded me that we must visit his home while in Rabat.

CAT TRAX Day Six, 40 Ks, Kenitra to Rabat, the Capital City. At our good hotel we met a group of Fulbright Scholars. A couple of them, well-versed in Moroccan History took us along on a sightseeing tour. First stop was Hassan Tower, built in 1195 AD. It was like stepping into the *Arabian Nights.* We witnessed the changing of the guards, saw soldiers in colorful costume on horseback. Hassan Tower had been the tallest tower in the Muslim world for centuries, but only pillars now remained of the once-impressive mosque. The father and grandfather of Mohammed VI, were interred there. They are all direct descendants of The Prophet Mohammed.

Chapter 2 Lessons of Islam, Taught by Abdallah

CAT TRAX Day 8, Rabat; An Informative Visit with Abdallah and Family. Abdallah picked us up in his chauffeur-driven

Mercedes. He spoke of his good fortune as we rode. "I was a poor boy in Kinetra when I received a scholarship that led to an education in England. I met my first wife, an American, while in school." As we pulled into his drive, he continued, "Like most immigrants I worked long and hard eventually owning restaurants in Maryland and New Jersey. After we divorced, I began to long for Morocco."

His home looked western. He and wife Sue had two adorable young kids, Ahmed and Alba. Danny, Abdallah's son from his first marriage, also lived with them. They were a progressive Muslim family. Though they didn't drink alcohol, they offered us wine. Sue set their cocktail table with traditional Moroccan hors d'oeuvres.

A bit of religious history offered by Abdallah: "When you hear of customs or the cultural ways of Muslims they seem backward, antiquated when compared to today's Christian world. You must remember Islam is a very young faith, 700 years younger than Christianity. If we use that comparison we find Christians under Queen Isabella and King Ferdinand persecuting, even executing Jews and Moors during the inquisitions, beginning in 1483."

The treatment of Muslim women was an issue for many in the US. We reminded Abdallah that just a scant eighty years ago women in the USA finally won the right to vote. (Many times since that evening we've marveled at the significance of our happen-chance meeting. Abdallah opened a conduit, allowing information to flow to and from us. Our new friend was worldly-wise and open minded, providing a peek into the world of Islam.)

Leaving was difficult, as we felt like family. Hugs from the little kids and Sue and a hand shake from Danny then a long hand shake followed by a hug from Abdallah. He insisted we call his sister when we arrived in Casablanca. This was the first of many introductions Abdallah provided. He opened doors and proved supportive throughout Morocco and beyond.

There are times when you know instantly that you've found a new friend. You hear it in a voice, see it in a face or smile, and recognize true concern in the eyes of a stranger. Pat & Cat

CAT TRAX Day 9, Rabat to Casablanca. 95 Ks (60 miles) We cycled ups and downs along spectacular cliffs overlooking the Atlantic Ocean. Getting from Rabat to Casablanca was a good days' ride when healthy-after several days of African Guff-Guff, it was quite a challenge. Casablanca was nothing like we had envisioned. Modern glass buildings lined the main street. It was a modern city, a place that Humphrey Bogart (star of the 1950s film "Casablanca") would have had a tough time recognizing!

CAT TRAX Day 10, to- Day 14, Exploring Casablanca. After cycling in, we phoned Fouzia, Abdallah's sister, to introduce ourselves. We suggested meeting for lunch in a day or two. "No, no," she said, "I will come pick you up now!" Within thirty minutes we were in her car, on a whirlwind tour of Casablanca. We drove past the imposing Mosque Hassan II, then through interesting picturesque neighborhoods. Once again we imagined Humphrey Bogart, Peter Lorre, and that song. "You must remember this, a kiss is just a kiss, a sigh is just a sigh!" Fouzia knew the manager of a nice hotel. She drove by, introduced us, and arranged an ocean-view room.

Fouzia lived in an upscale, high-rise condominium. We joined her and three women friends around a table filled with a huge platter of couscous. Thinking that was lunch, we ate heartily. Then Fouzia's maid delivered a  leg of lamb embellished with French fries.

Being surrounded by Moroccan women led to interesting conversation. We wanted to know about their lives in the Muslim Kingdom. Surprise, we found that Fouzia was a divorcee. Her friend Samira had been widowed and remarried. Two cute young girls Nezha and Bouchra were single, independent career girls.

Cat asked if any of them wore hijad, the head scarf. None did, however Bouchra said, "Most women wear a scarf when praying."

Cat said, "We've heard that fathers and mothers often choose

16

their daughter's husbands."

Bouchra quickly replied, "This is customary only in small villages. In cities, we choose the one that we will marry."

"We've heard that King Mohammed VI recently said, since we have but one heart, men should love only one wife," I said, then asked, "Do men here still marry more than one wife?"

They all smiled as Fouzia said, "According to our men, they may marry more than one wife." The others laughed. Bouchra chimed in, "Yes, but the Quran also says that the man must be loyal to each wife, that is impossible. There are places where men still marry more than one wife, however only if the first wife agrees to the arrangement."

Bouchra continued, "I am very happy to be 29 years old, working at a good job, enjoying my freedom and being single." She and Nezha both smiled and nodded positively while blushing slightly. This prompted a rapid-fire conversation amongst the girls in French. Cat thought they were discussing Nezha's boyfriend but only caught part of the chatter.

Fouzia asked "Have you read the newspaper today? Young twin girls were caught with explosives strapped to their bodies in the Rabat Supermarket liquor department." We were shocked-we'd purchased wine there. "You've probably heard of the bombing in Casablanca two months ago that killed thirty-two people?" Very scary for us, being western foreigners.

Chapter 3 A Tour of Hassan II, with Najate

Omar, our friendly English-speaking breakfast waiter introduced us to another customer, Najate. She taught linguistics, spoke four languages, and was a tour guide at Mosque Hassan II. We made an appointment with her to visit the mosque.

CAT TRAX Exploring Mosque Hassan II. Najate boasted, "I am first woman, now only woman, permitted to guide tours of the mosque. I have been guiding tours for four years." She explained, "Hassan II is very new and modern. We accommodate 25,000 worshipers inside and additional 80,000 in the outdoor square. It is named for our past King who ruled Morocco from 1962 until his death in 1999. That huge door at the far end, and the walkway down the center of the two waterways in the main prayer room are reserved for our current King, Mohammad II, when he is here to worship."

The best came as we began asking Najate about customs and traditions of Muslim worship. She was very open to our questions even adding comments to expand them. "Ninety-eight percent of Muslims in Morocco are Sunni, more moderate and progressive than the Shiites. Women cover their heads for prayer and pray in a separate section away from the men."

When Cat asked if the women wore veils, Najate quipped with a sly smile, "Only the ugly ones!" Shifting quickly back to her teaching mode she added, "There is no religious connection to the veil, just an old custom." Cat told her that women in the Catholic Church and some other Christian Churches cover their heads during services. Najate turned her head and softly said, "I know nothing of Christian customs."

Then she led us down into the bathing area. "Here the faithful wash three times daily as did the Prophet Mohammed." Leading us into the Hammam hot bath area, Najate said, "Men and women bathe separately, men are required to bathe at least monthly. Both men and women are required to bathe after sexual experience," She said, turning away slightly as though to express modesty, "Women must also bathe after menstruation."

Najate was wonderful, providing a great personal experience for us. We spent the afternoon walking, talking, and window shopping through small back alleys and souks. We suggested getting a snack, but she said, "Sorry I cannot, I am one of twelve children, my sister and I are the only ones working. We also cook for our family." She called her sister to tell her she'd be late. Yes, she had a cell phone.

When we asked what we owed she did the age-old, "You pay as you wish." We loved her ability and frankness. We put our heads together and decided we should pay at least California minimum wage. Figuring $8 per hour we handed her $40. She was so excited, she grabbed Cat and did the kiss-kiss thing on her cheeks. Then in typical Najate style she asked Cat, "May I also kiss Pat?" She did, then we did a heartfelt group hug.

Chapter 4 The Road South, Cyclist Down

CAT TRAX Day 15, 81 Ks, Casablanca to El Jadida. The only sound more sickening than screeching tires is impact, collision, the sounds of metal bending, glass breaking, and bones being crushed. Along with our fears about some political fanatic with a gun or knife, we were always mindful of the hazards of the road.

We were lulled into complacency by the warm sunny Moroccan morning when, suddenly, a car slammed on the brakes. We were shocked to see a teenage boy fly off the hood and onto the side of the road, still clinging to his bicycle. He tried to stand, then sank down and sat staring. He'd ridden into the path of the speeding car. It hit him square, his backside crashed through the windshield. The impact bent the roof of the car.

A crowd gathered. The boy was bleeding from the left side of his face, his left arm, and leg. We guessed he had internal injuries. The driver of the car jumped out, yelling. It sounded like she was blaming him for ruining her car. A guy in a Mercedes, perhaps a doctor, stopped and ran to the boy. He checked his eyes and pulse, then called for help on his cell phone. The boy's mother came running, crying and screaming. Some in the crowd held her back. We were amazed that the boy didn't cry or moan. He just sat staring. He did try to speak, but the people talking to him seemed to be telling him to save his strength. We felt helpless, there was nothing we could do. So we cycled cautiously onward, hoping he would be okay.

It was a graphic reminder of how fragile we are. You're riding along enjoying the morning sun one minute and the next you're a hood ornament. It made us pause and reflect on the impermanence of life. Yes, we were vulnerable, but careful.

El Jadida is a city inside a walled area they called the Medina. The walls of the Medina were thick and brown like so many things there-the fields, the animals, even the people all came in varying shades of brown.

The Cistern Portuguese was the grand feature of El Jadida. The water reservoir of Roman design it was built in 1541. (Morocco fell under Portuguese authority in 1513, and they controlled it for more than 200 years. Morocco became the "protectorate" of France in 1912, and finally gained independence in 1956.) We fell in love with the building and the effect of the sunlight playing on the water as it reflected the pillars. It was awe-inspiring. Several movies had been shot there including Orson Welles' "Othello."

CAT TRAX, Days 18 - 19, Train to Marrakesh. Why would anyone come to Morocco and miss Marrakesh? Once we saw how close it was to Safi, we'd been singing our own version that old Crosby, Stills and Nash song, "Don't cha know we're ridin' on the Marrakesh Express, it's takin' us to Marrakesh."

Train tickets bought, Cat went on-line to book a hotel. No rooms in Marrakesh. Why take a train if you couldn't book a room? As a last resort, she tried the Sheraton Resort, the kind of hotel we usually avoid. Wow, 1250 Dirham $125 US per night! Ya wanna go to Marrakesh, ya gotta pay the piper.

We met a gal, Leila from New York City. She said, "The first train from Safi to Benguerir is a nightmare. Old wooden cars that also carry cattle and sheep." To us that sounded interesting. We were disappointed, no cows, goats, or sheep. We had the eight-person cabin to ourselves. It was neat, clean, and the air-conditioning was a treat.

There was an hour and a half layover in Benguerir, a dusty desert military outpost. As the train pulled in, we were thrust into a pushing, shoving, crowd-all trying to board. We jammed into a full compartment. A couple from Australia made the crush interesting. They spoke English, well, English Aussie-style. They were heading for a trek in the Atlas Mountains.

Yellow street lights cast an eerie glow in the Marrakesh Station. The main road could have been Scottsdale, Arizona. Row upon row of brand name hotels. The check-in process was unlike any Sheraton we'd ever visited. As in the train station, people were cutting or elbowing into the line. Our room was so distant from the main hotel they drew us a map. Who'd guess $125 would put us in the cheap seats? The pool was busy with people splashing off the dust of the day. It was 9:00 p.m. and still ninety degrees.

We needed food. They had several restaurants but most required dressy clothing. Pasta by the pool was the only dish within our price range. The stuffy maître d' passed us by several times. Our loud complaint brought a wonderful server. The pasta was tasty, the wine expensive. All our anti-upscale feelings aside, the king-sized bed felt great!

The next morning, the cost of dinner had left a bad taste in our mouths. Bitter, we looked at the expensive breakfast menu. Our decision was to walk into town. At the door, we were attacked by a horde of pushy taxi drivers. Despite their warnings, we smiled, waved, and walked. We began to feel sorry for tourists hustled in, bussed to bustling souks, fleeced, then hustled back to the Sheraton. They went home with a memory stick full of inane photos taken from a bus window. No real experiences. The boulevard was wide and picturesque. The morning sun hadn't yet scorched through the cool night air. It was half a mile to the massive 12th century gate. Passing beyond the tall Minaret, we felt that we'd stumbled into centuries past. We found a clean place, serving pastries and rich aromatic coffee. Breakfast for two was a bargain at $5.00, US. We fell in love with the place, the staff and local patrons.

The main square, Djemaa el-Faa, was wild. We encountered snake charmers, who lured us in by placing a snake on my shoulder. Playing their flutes they began to mesmerize the cobras. We took pictures and enjoyed the moment until one got in my face demanding 500 Dirham. I pushed back, "No way, Jose, that's fifty bucks!" I handed him 50 Dirham and we walked away. They yelled what we assumed were profanities. Fortunately, we didn't understand.

The souks were so interesting that I, who hate shopping, spent two hours exploring with Cat. Interesting stalls, merchants, and items for sale. The colors, the spices, the people and foods kept us wandering through the meandering alleyways.

A veiled woman selling clay water vessels approached. I asked for her photo. She resisted so I told her I'd pay for a pitcher. She posed and, oh, those eyes. I paid, then handed the pitcher back. Her big brown eyes twinkled. A guy nearby motioned for me to show him the photo. He looked and scolded her. Then in gruff English he growled, "You take picture me!" I told him he wasn't pretty enough. His friends laughed as he scowled.

There were several fine restaurants on Djemaa el-Fna. Restaurant Marrakchi was the only one that served wine. The square at dusk was awe-inspiring. Our window table on the fourth floor overlooked the surging, pulsating crowd. The food was okay, the wine was the best in town. A local duet in crimson robes played as we dined. Their throbbing rhythm was accented by a tambourine. The tambourine player was a showman. He'd rise up and roll his head, causing the tassel on his fez to twirl in time with the music.

Walking back through the darkened market was bizarre; the crowd moving around us was nearly invisible. The gas lamps glowed like fingers reaching out into the black desert night. The road back to the Sheraton was serene. Our two-day excursion to Marrakesh was definitely worth the cost and time spent.

At breakfast in town, we met Mandy and Asesha from London. They loved trekking the mountains and Marrakesh but would never return without a male companion. They had been hassled even by their guide. Young guys tried to grope them. Asesha, of Indian decent said, "I think the boys have been influenced by Bollywood movies. They believe women all have loose morals." She added."I think the boys here are sexually repressed. They're separated from girls at a young age, that's not healthy."

CAT TRAXDay 21, 126 Ks, Safi to Essaouira. Essaouira was a picturesque fishing village with a small harbor. The old walled city looked straight out of the middle ages. It was also an international surfing Mecca. Fresh fish daily, and surfers wandering amongst the fish mongers.

CAT TRAX Day 23, 72 Ks, Essaouira to Tamanar. There is no better cycling motivator than a pack of snarling dogs. They gave chase, nipping at our heels. We cranked up, leaving all but one behind. Our tongues were hanging out further than that damned dog's. We pedaled and panted in the afternoon heat. Tiring, I gave him a shot in the face from my water bottle. That stopped him in his tracks. He'd probably never seen water hanging in the dry desert air then hitting him in the face.

Rumor had it we'd find a hotel in Tamanar. Happiness was rolling downhill into the village. Joy faded when we found the deserted hotel. The gendarmes were less than friendly. We asked permission to set out tent in their yard and the Commandant said no. Then, in French, he told Cat, "Go to the Co-op, across the street." As we crossed, a busload of German tourists was pulling away. A pretty young woman waved and yelled, "Auf Wiedersehen." Turning she asked in French, "Do you want to tour our Co-op?"

Cat began explaining our quandary in French. The girl stopped her and said, "I speak English." Amazing how simple that made communication.

Cat said, "We need a place to sleep tonight. The gendarme sent us to you?"

She smiled and said, "You want to stay my house? I have big house."

Could we trust her, would we be safe? Cat hesitated a moment, then nodded, "Yes."

The girl said, "Okay, follow me, we must first make aware the gendarme." So, when she rented a room she had to register with the police. That brought our level of confidence way up.

The gendarme handed us a registration form, then asked for our passports. We were reluctant. The girl, Kadijah, who also had to sign, said, "It is for you protection, you get back tomorrow morning." Perhaps that was meant to give both us and her family a feeling of security?

Kadijah locked the Co-op doors then led us through the dirt streets of Tamanar. Kadijah was twenty-one years old. She lived in a nice-looking house with her family. She was one of eight children, four still living at home.

Her father, Abdullah, was seventy-five, his wife was younger. She was shy. Though the family spoke Arabic and French, she spoke only Berber. Kadijah's two sisters, Latifa and Ilhame, were typical teenagers. The oldest, Latifa was assigned to be our guide and helper. She gave us a tour of their home, speaking faltering English. They had ten bedrooms. She showed several rooms then said, "You sleep here, Kadijah's room."

Two brothers and several other people came in, introduced themselves, then disappeared. Kadijah's room was upstairs. A stairway off a small balcony went down into the courtyard. Chickens, rabbits, and a duck wandered around waiting to eat or to be eaten.

The only bathroom was in the courtyard. It had hot and cold running water, a toilet and shower. I remembered as a kid our family of six shared one bath. There was always a lineup. We pictured ourselves waiting in line for the toilet or shower.

Abdullah prepared vegetables and goat meat in a huge tajine (a dish named after the clay pot it's cooked in). One of the brothers fried a big pan of boney little fish. Our greatest joy was enjoying Latifa and Ilhame's company. They spoke enough English to carry on a halting conversation and translated Abdullah's French for us.

In restaurants, even small roadside cafés, we had been given forks and knives with tajine. Here Abdullah served Moroccan family style. Crowded around, we used a piece of wonderful tasting bread and our fingers to scoop from the tajine. It gave breaking bread a new meaning. Folded bread was folding us into their culture. We sat on carpet in the courtyard scooping tajine smothered in conversation.

Kadijah and her sisters enjoyed dressing us in robes for dinner. They plopped a little hat similar to a Jewish yarmulke on my head. After dinner, the girls brought out a tired-looking tape player that poured out traditional Moroccan music. As they swayed, Cat was drawn into their dance circle. Abdullah and the mom came to the door and watched. Cat convinced the girls to make the high pitched warbling sound well-known among women in Arabic lands. They taught her how to quickly move her tongue back and forth while forcing a falsetto scream. The girls said she sounded like a native.

Later we sat with Abdullah, Kadijah, and her brother, Abdullah Jr. He was thirty, college-educated and like so many young there, unemployed. He sits sipping tea and talking with friends all day in a local café.

Abdullah was retired, and we never understood what his work had been. We think they were saying he was a carpenter. The family seemed loving, especially for its size. Abdullah Jr. received a cell phone call. We wondered how he afforded the phone. The family seemed upscale, they had things. We decided that the old house had been in the family for generations. Perhaps, as Cat thought, they were running a prospering bed & breakfast.

Sipping sweet tea, I ran the pictures on our computer for them. Abdullah Sr. said, "Look at that old man," when his picture came up on the screen. Abdullah Jr. asked if we could make copies of our pictures. I told him we couldn't but I would put them on a CD. He said, "There is an internet café in the village where I can print copies." It was 10:00 p.m. by the time our heads hit Kadijah's pillows. Lying in the dark, we agreed we had been very lucky to have met Kadijah and spent time with her family.

CAT TRAX Day 24, 81 Ks, Tamanar to Taghazout. The Imam began his call to prayer at sunrise. As his singsong voice boomed over the speakers, the village dogs began to bark, the donkeys brayed, roosters crowed, and the hens began to cackle. We loved the

25

spontaneity of the moment, a symphony of the sounds of Moroccan life. Luckily, we'd prayed for an early start. We ate breakfast with part of the family. They served a hot white liquid similar to a thin porridge. The mint tea and bread with argan-nut butter and honey was wonderful. Kadijah had rushed off to work which limited conversation to fractured French.

We all posed for a picture at the gate. Our new family waved and shouted encouragement as we cautiously rode down the steep rocky road. First stop the gendarmerie to retrieve our passports. The Commandant greeted us and asked if we'd slept well. Passports in hand we went across to the Co-op to say our goodbyes. Kadijah insisted we take a tour. Argan nuts were sorted by hand, then pressed until the oil oozed out. The argan tree, native to the area, produces nuts that look and taste like almonds. The oil extract is used for cooking and salads, the pulp for animal food, but the lucrative part of the operation is oil exported for a variety of cosmetics applications. The co-op provided income and independence for more than 50 women.

We'd spent the final moments of pillow talk last evening trying to decide how much to pay Kadijah. Rooms had been cheap even with private baths. Food, too, was inexpensive. However, experiences like we'd had were priceless. We decided on 400 dirham, $40 US. She absolutely beamed as we handed it to her. We could sense the pride she felt in having earned it for her family. She was a very bright and industrious girl.

Another moment of sweet sorrow. After the customary cheek-cheek kisses, we hugged. Walking out the door we were misty-eyed. We cycled out of their lives but they would always be a part of ours and we would hold them in our hearts.

(After returning home, we received an e-mail from a guy in Holland purportedly Kadijah's cousin. He was angry and said the pictures on our site had insulted his family. He insisted we take them down. Fearing he would retaliate against her I told him we couldn't make changes and asked for her telephone number. When the phone connected a girl's voice answered. She sounded distant but said the pictures were fine. Then click, and once again Kadijah was out of our lives.)

We had just left town when we saw a tree full of goats, climbing on branches, munching on the leaves. We'd read of the phenomenon but it was such an anomaly we had to stop. As I pulled out the camera the herdsman smiled and waved us toward his goats. Half his herd was high in the tree. It was easy to see why. The parched soil didn't support grass or any other plants.

CAT TRAX Day 25, 20 Ks, Taghazout to Agadir. When we told a gal in France about our plan to cycle Africa she said, "I have a wonderful friend, Luis, who lives in Agadir. He would love if you contact him. He could be very helpful." Seeking a comfortable and affordable hotel, we called Luis, who proved patient and helpful. He drove us from hotel to hotel and we struck gold at Hotel Tivoli. A resort with a pool we wouldn't use, a large clean room with cable TV for 640 Ds, $64 US. We had landed.

Chapter 5 Southern Morocco

CAT TRAX Day 28, Feelin' Nifty, Cat turns 50, in Agadir. Cat decided against a camel ride for her fiftieth birthday. Becoming concerned as we traveled southward, she wanted malaria pills instead. The doctor in Agadir prescribed a six-month's supply and suggested we start taking them right away, to assure they'd be effective. We choked them down with breakfast. Stepping out to the pool area was like arriving in a Russian resort. By 10:00 a.m. all the chaise lounges were filled and the vodka was flowing. Snow birds from the frozen steppes of Siberia.

We celebrated Cat's birthday with dinner at a nearby restaurant. A trio was playing current music, so I asked them to play Happy Birthday for her. We joined in singing a duet at the microphone. The crowd loved it and joined in, too. They spoke Russian but knew Happy Birthday in English. I lifted a glass to Cat's continued health and cycling success. They all joined in the toast.

CAT TRAX Day 29, 99 Ks, Agadir to Tiznit. Sometimes, when writing our memories, I forget we were riding bicycles. The road to

Tiznit was long, straight and flat. Soon, our legs began to tire and our butts were burning. We both had knee pain. Cat blamed being off the bikes for too long. It was a ninety-nine kilometer ride, maybe she was right. She just wasn't one to sit around.

The lonely road wondered through open space and rocky farmland. We shared the tarmac with plenty of trucks and cars, but they gave us adequate riding space, plus cheers, honks, and thumbs ups. We could see the mud brown buildings of Tiznit from five Ks out, and easily found Hotel Idou Tiznit, the only game in town. A typical bland brown exterior but our room was nice and a value, at 460 Ds. ($46)

CAT TRAX Day 30, 67 Ks, 1059T, Tiznit to Bou-Izakarn. The Atlas Mountains form a barrier across Morocco. The range in this area is called the Anti-Atlas or Tail of the Atlas. The grade pitched up six to eight percent. Ambassadors of good will, we waved at trucks. It paid off as they passed us repeatedly, coming and going, all the way to Mauritania.

Entering Bou-Izakarn we encountered a gendarme at a roadblock. We'd cycled past several that had waved us on. He pulled us over and began questioning in French, "Where are you going?" When Cat said Mauritania he took our passports and asked more questions, "What was your father's name? What was your mother's maiden name?" He directed the questions to me, ignoring Cat. After licking his pencil, he would carefully write down each answer.

When he finished I asked a guy that spoke English, "Does the gendarme radio this information ahead to let others know we are coming?"

He said, "It is for your protection, we like Americans but not your government!"

The gendarme stopped a Gran Taxi. He got in and said, "You follow."

Nervous, we did as told. We were pleased when he led us to the decent-looking Hotel Anti Atlas. We thanked him, then another surprise the clerk quoted "80 Dirham." ($8.00 US.) The bargain room turned out to be a lot like camping. No water in the crusty toilet, no shower. The functioning facilities were at the other end of the hallway. Cat made a trip to the squatter toilet before dinner and reported seeing a huge cockroach. She flushed it down the drain. When I visited at bedtime he was back. I left him undisturbed. All living things, even cockroaches, are Sacred.

CAT TRAX   Day 31, 40 Ks, Bou-Izahkarn to Guelmim. Our guidebook suggested a couple of hotels in Guelmim. Lost, we gave up and stopped to ask. A young guy standing on the corner spoke to me in French. When I said I only spoke English, he got excited and told us he taught English and had a cousin in New York.

Boushabe chatted as he led us down the street to Hotel Bahich.

"I have girl friend in Kentucky. She have been married and have two-year-old baby. We met on Internet." He and I talked as Cat checked us in. When he'd finished his tale of love he had to go but suggested we have tea later.

Asked about food, the hotel waiter said, "We finish serve lunch, follow I show where you get food." He led Cat down the street. She came back and said, "We're eating at a café with no AC but there's a

nice guy seated there who joked with me and spoke good English."

Habib had studied English at hotel school. He was an unemployed waiter and a character.

We bought him a coke and chatted as we ate. Cat asked, "Is there a place here that sells wine?" Habib said, "There is only one store in town, that sell alcohol. It owned by Jewish man but he closed, Friday and Saturday." When we expressed our disappointment, Habib roared with laughter, "Muslim can't to drink and to selling alcohol is forbidden. The Jew he closed to celebrate Sabbath. The Moroccan guy next shop sneak into the Jew guy's shop on such days. The police look other way on days Jewish guy closed. The Jew and Muslim they like brothers." Again he burst into laughter.

He offered to walk with us, "I sure you not find this place." What started out as a quest for wine became a guided tour of Guelmim. When we reached the alcohol store we knew he was right, we'd never have found it. The Moroccan guy ducked through a door into the Jew's shop. He returned with two bottles of red, no white wine. We bought them and a small bottle of "Water of life," a schnapps drink made of distilled fig and anisette, for Habib.

He volunteered to take us to a good place for dinner. A café that served barbequed camel. We were delighted. He confessed, "I Muslim but I am like many who like red wine."

At 8:00 p.m. we were hungry and waiting for Habib at the hotel when Boushabe showed up. He had another guy Hammoui with him who worked at a restaurant. We gave up on Habib and followed. On the street Habib mysteriously showed up. He seemed upset, "Why you don't wait?" I said, "You were late, we were hungry." We asked him to join us, and, of course, he did.

Dinner was fun, but there was a definite rivalry between Boushabe and Habib. After Boushabe went back to work Habib said, "He is not teacher, he work in tourist shop." He warned, "Many things aren't as they appear, in Morocco." Boushabe was probably getting a commission from Hammoui for taking us to his restaurant, which meant Habib had been beaten out of one.

With Habib's help we ordered a camel-meat brochette and our second lamb tajine of the day. The camel tasted like beef. Hammoui had promised wine and he delivered, probably sending a runner to the Moroccan guy while we waited. He presented a full liter bottle of a cheaper red, then came to the table, glass in hand, and poured for himself without asking. An interesting evening with new friends.

Boushabe came back and cornered Cat in conversation about his Muslim beliefs. I was glad I had Habib to talk with. He told me, "I have plan, to own restaurant one day. I know of place, I trying to find money." He also said, "With economy in Morocco I have good life if making 1,800 Dirham each month. ($180 US)

The guys wanted to continue the party. We were tired and opted for bed. After goodbyes they scattered. We made a date to meet Habib at 8:00 a.m.. He seemed pretty happy about the idea of guiding us to the camel market.

Entering our room, I opened the armoire to check the bags. My heart sank, our black case was open-someone had been in the room. The computer was there, but they'd jammed and broken the bag's zipper. Cat checked our toiletry bags-sure enough, the bumbling burglar had scored. He'd found and made off with our 100 Euro stash. That was the only thing we found missing.

We went to the front desk and complained. The clerk denied it could have happened. I was angry and showed him the broken zipper. I demanded he call the police. He went into his office, returned and said "I have called Patron, you will wait please." We sat on the stairs for almost an hour. No "Patron." At last the clerk confessed he thought the Patron was sleeping. I insisted he call the gendarmes. He said "I have call commissar, he out, be back tomorrow."

I was so pissed I went out looking for a policeman. In the dark, the faces all looked sinister. Was everyone watching me? Did they know what had happened, and were they involved? Paranoia was setting in. I found a gendarme and tried to tell him I needed help. When he found I couldn't speak French he shrugged and walked away. I was really pissed.

Sleep was our best option-we'd deal with the problem in the morning. I rigged up straps to secure the door. We knew someone with evil in their heart had a key to our room.

CAT TRAX Day 32, 100 Ks Bike, 30 Ks Van, Goulmime to Tan Tan. Habib hadn't shown by 9:00. We wondered if he was involved. Had his dream to own a restaurant brought him to a life of crime? The Patron failed to show. The girl at the desk couldn't reach him and said, "Police are not coming." She wanted us and the problem to go away. In the spirit of, "Always do the right thing," we backtracked up Blvd. Mohammed V to the gendarmerie.

A guy at a typewriter attempted to ask questions. We tried to understand. I wrote our story down to save time. We learned he was typing something that had nothing to do with us. Cat was anxious, we had a long ride ahead. When we told him we were leaving he took us into a windowless room. A guy there looked familiar. Oh, it was the Patron. So, he'd gotten the word we were there and showed up.

A young officer who spoke English said, "It is our job to learn all we can about this problem." They took our passports. Cat really got nervous. Then he added, "Thees man owns hotel, he say ees not

31

posseeble, what you say."

Cat jumped in, "Do you think we would ride our bicycles here to tell a lie?"

I added, "We know we'll never see the 100 €uro or get the broken zipper fixed. We just wanted to tell you what had happened."

Again The Patron mumbled something and the cop said, "He denies everything, this cannot happen in his hotel!"

We were getting tired of the game. I asked the English-speaking one to ask Patron, "If this did happen would he want to know about it? Would he want to know someone in his hotel would rob a guest?"

The young cop translated that or so we assumed. Patron mumbled and the policeman said, "He say thees is not posseeble in ees hotel."

We demanded our passports and they released us on our own recognizance. My parting words were, "Now it is your problem!"

The road passed by the camel market. It was late but we had to see what was purported to be the last active camel market in Morocco. Ah, those unfortunate beasts. They were cruelly mistreated. Six guys would grab one by the tail and head then bend the neck until it looked like it would break. Once it was forced to the ground, they hobbled one leg. Back upright, the beast was off balance and hopped around.

Those were the camels that had already been sold.

We pushed up to the herd and into a herd of German tourists. Then a strange twist, Hammoui our server at the restaurant was the German's guide at the camel market. He was aloof until we began talking with the Germans. When I pulled out our cards, he said, "Yes, you can give cards to these Germans," as though he had to authorize it.

32

Putting two and two together, we remembered that Hammoui had been with Boushabe when they led us to the restaurant. As we pushed the bikes through the camel dung and dust, a small voice called out, "Cat and Pat." Our suspicions flared wider than the nostrils of the poor camels. It was Boushabe. He was leaning against a pickup truck but made no move to come talk with us.

Movin' on, we rolled onto the highway and into a 130-kilometer day. The road surface was fair and flat. Roadside varied from sand to hammad, or hard-packed soil. Cat was a little shaky. We thought it was due to the nerve-wracking police experience. We needed food. A tajine helped.

At 3:00 p.m. we were only half the way to Tan Tan. Then came hills so steep we had to walk. We'd come 80 Ks, when we crested a hilltop. Bad news, in the distance we could see the road snaking up the side of another steep hill.

Tired and thirsty, we had soft drinks at a café then pressed onward. The next hill was another big push. Cresting out on a curve at the 98 K marker we decided to ride around the corner and check out the terrain. Ahead, more hills and a sun quickly setting. At marker 100 Ks Cat pulled up and said, "We need to find a ride."

Just as I blurted, "We'll never get a ride," a small Suzuki van careered around the corner.

Cat threw her hand out and the guy stopped. She spoke with the driver, then he got out and opened the back. The van was crammed with luggage. There was another guy, a woman and baby inside. I

didn't think we'd fit.

Mohjoui, the driver, wore a typical Moroccan robe and loose turban. He indicated we could put the bikes on the roof and our bags inside. His brother and sister-in-law began shuffling their bags. Ours filled every bit of remaining space. Mohjoui and I strapped the bikes to the van top as the last rays of sun sank behind the hills.

The van's battery was dead. The brother-in-law and I pushed, ran and jumped in. Though he was a good driver, Mohjoui pressed the little vehicle to its limit. Cat was squished between me, the Mom and baby. I held onto the handle above the door and closed my eyes. The little van hurtled through the darkness. He passed trucks on hills, leaving my heart in my throat. I imagined what might remain of us in a head-on crash with a truck.

We pulled up at a police roadblock. A husky gendarme shone his light into the van. Mohjoui spewed words. All we understood was, "Tan Tan." The Policeman turned the light onto our faces and asked "Where from, you?"

Our stock answer of California brought the word "America" to his lips. Then he said, "You come."

We reluctantly left the van and followed him into his lean-to office. He put us through the paces we'd experienced in Bou-Izikarn. Father's name, mother's name, etc, etc, etc. All the while Mohjoui kept the little engine running. Finally, once he'd flipped through every page of our passports and looked with wonder at our Russian visas he let us go. Another gendarme appeared out of the darkness.

He asked, "Where you go?" in English.

"Tan Tan."

"Where you stay?"

We answered, "hotel."

He said, "Stay Hotel Sables d'Or."

Cat thanked him in French then we dashed back to the van and Mohjoui's revving engine.

It was black as pitch. The others wore heavy clothes. Mohjoui had the van's heater turned up full blast. We wondered if they could smell us, ripe from cycling (four days since our last laundry).

The baby was squirming and fussing. Mohjoui said he would drop them first. The sister-in-law asked Cat if we wanted to stay with them. We both needed a good night's sleep and privacy. We shook our heads no, then thanked her in Arabic, "Shukran" and French, "Merci Beaucoup!"

After dropping family off, Mohjoui drove to the hotel. I ran inside knowing he had to keep the engine running. The room was clean, spacious, and had a nice bath. An official-looking guy started grabbing bags and stacking them on the walkway. We pulled the bikes off the top in minutes. Obviously Mohjoui was anxious to get home. Cat and I had decided we would give him 300 Ds (30 Dollars US) for his kindness, as well as wear and tear on his aging van. He turned to Cat and asked, "Can you give 100 Dirham for petrol?" I handed him a 100 Dirham note through the van window. He was saying thank you in both languages when I handed him the other 200 and said, "Pour les battery." Astounded, he took the bills, folded them and tucked them away. He shook my hand vigorously then touched his heart. We liked that nice gesture men make, touching their hearts as thought to say, "From my heart!"

It was 9:00 p.m. and the restaurant closed at 9:00. The chef waited. I had told the desk clerk we needed food. The cafe was in the basement and had no windows, though it did have flies. Seated, we sweated and swatted. I asked if he would turn on the Casablanca fan. The chef went two tables away and pulled the cord. We felt not a breath of air, so we picked up the place settings and made a move. When he returned, he asked if we wanted him to stop the fan. Must have been that desert legacy thing. We loved the cool air blowing down and it kept the flies at bay.

CAT TRAX   Day 33, 25Ks, Tan Tan to El-Ouatia (Tan Tan Beach). It rained during the night. The street was wet, the dust was mud. Riding to Tan Tan Plage sounded better than staying put—going to the beach rather than a day off in another simple town. We were tired physically and mentally but the next day was my birthday. We deserved a day on the beach.

Loading the bikes, we discovered one of our cinch straps was missing. Damn, we'd have to find a rope to tie the bag down. Tires squealing, the little white Suzuki van came racing down the street, horn blaring. Mohjoui, strap in hand, waving his arm wildly. Another "faith in humanity" moment. He'd driven all the way back because he thought the strap was important.

The ride to the beach wasn't an easy twenty-six Ks. It was a long, grinding uphill pull. At three Ks we began pushing. It took two hours to climb the fifteen miles. Cycling in, we passed a western-looking guy. Stopping, Cat asked for directions in French. He returned a few words, then broke into English laced with a thick Irish brogue.

Patrick worked with a major fishing company, with boats and processing plants all over the world. He visited Tan Tan monthly, to check on the operation. He suggested the Equinox Hotel and told us, "I'll meet you there after my walk." We went directly to the hotel, hoping for a big lunch and two nights lodging. Big lunch, no problem. A French couple owned the place. Cat asked about a

35

room. Madam said, "We have only for this night. A group in private areoplanes have book us for tomorrow. They fly Aero Postal Route France to Senegal then back to Toulouse, France." Patrick joined us and suggested the adjacent Hotel Bellevue. He had stayed there before. He also took our bag of laundry to his housekeeper.

Cat whispered, "Did you see that mouse run up the wall behind Madam? I'm almost glad we're not staying here!" The guys next door were friendly. The room had a double bed but the window looked out onto the hallway. We wanted beachfront for a romantic birthday. The only room with a view had tiny twin beds. *Hmmm.* We winced, but chose the view.

Cat pulled back the covers exposing dead bugs on the sheets. *Arggh.* They hadn't been changed since the previous guests had vacated. She marched down to the front desk. The manager came up, agreed, and brought clean sheets. The shower ran hot, the toilet ran constantly. He suggested, "Turn water on, for flushing." A small annoyance, worth it to hear the pounding waves and enjoy the scent of sea air.

CAT TRAX Day 33, Birthday Off (Tan Tan Beach). The tiny town had nothing to do—which drove Cat crazy-but Patrick invited us to his house for birthday lunch. Samdi, his housekeeper and cook, prepared a tasty luncheon. She also had our laundry folded. We quietly  slipped her $5.00, she quietly accepted. Patrick and Samdi were wonderful 64th birthday gifts.

The streets of Tan Tan Plage were dirty and littered, but the beach promenade was a different world-pristine and beautiful. The pilots were in at the Equinox, seventy men from France, Germany, England, and Ireland. The pilots were re-creating the trip author/aviator Antoine de Saint-Exupery (author of *The Little Prince*) had made and documented in his book *Vol de nuit* (*Night Flight*).

CAT TRAX Day 35, 101 Ks, El-Ouatia to Sidi Akhfennir. Up and out early, we faced a sixty-mile ride and were determined to finish before dark. The pilots at the Equinox were on the promenade

36

in force. They clapped and cheered. Fielding questions in several languages made us feel like celebrities.

They bid us adieu and boarded minibuses. At the top of the hill I heard the ping of a spoke. Damn, there went our early start. Two broken spokes, we'd never make 100 Ks with a wheel in that condition. I asked a passing guy about a bicycle mechanic, and he signaled for us to follow. The shop was a dirt-floor shack. Several grungy-looking young guys were working on a rusty bike. They stopped, questioned our "nationality" and said something about Osama, then set to work repairing the wheel. In order to pull the gear cluster, they fashioned a tool from an old spark plug. Their tired old grinder's plug was two bare wires. One of the kids gingerly inserted the two wires into a 220 volt socket. Yikes! Risky, but he probably did it every day. Mohamed broke the rear axle loose, using the modified spark plug. After replacing three spokes and re-installing the wheel he said, "Shiite!" (Obviously, he knew some German). Another broken spoke.

As we waited, the "crazy young men in their flying machines" buzzed the beach. It was 11:15 by the time we rolled out of town. The road hugged the coast-the sparkling Atlantic was to our right, stark desert on the left.

At a checkpoint, Ali the gendarme pored over our passports. He couldn't get past my name "J. R. Patterson" on my passport and drivers license. He kept saying, "I never see thees name, GEE AIR before, never!" Once freed, we found a tiny store and bought two tins of sardines, bread, and Cokes. Locals drifted up, squatted and talked among themselves as they stared.

Approaching three service stations, we thought we'd arrived at Sidi Akhfennir. I gulped down another Coke. It tasted musty. At last sip I felt something mushy. I spit out the remains of a mouse (left in the bottle before it was filled?) Argh, just what my queasy stomach needed. Then, more bad news, it was still twenty-five Ks to town.

With a brisk tail wind on a slight downhill, we flew in to Sidi Akhfennir. Ali the gendarme took the usual info. When we asked for a place to camp, he said, "You stay Auberge Yves. Turn left at gendarmerie." We figured Le Auberge had to beat camping.

The Auberge was dark. Mogdah, the young proprietor said, "Power comes, 6:30." On time, the lights flickered on and the water-heater kicked in. *Apres* showers, Mogdah sold us a bottle of wine. Sitting in the comfortable living room, we got a few minutes of CNN news before the power failed. He was cooking and it smelled great. We asked if we could eat there. "No, some gendarmes, they coming. You eat, Café France, across highway."

We used our headlights to cross the highway and a car flashed its lights as a warning. It was Ali the gendarme. He asked, "You go to dinner, Gee Air? Come, I know owner, he good man." Ali not only introduced us, he and the owner Mohammad took us into the kitchen and they helped Cat choose the freshest fish. I told Ali we needed a bicycle mechanic due to more broken spokes. He said "We meet at gendarmerie, 8:00 a.m.."

CAT TRAX Day 36, 103 Ks, Sidi Akhfennir to Tarfaya. We awoke in darkness. Oh, no electricity until 6:30 p.m. Mogdah served hot coffee and toast. When we got to the gendarmerie a gendarme gestured for us to follow. He took us to two bike repair guys. They didn't have the tool needed to pull the gear cluster. They tried the modified spark plug tool, but it broke. They tried to fashion another and failed. So, they bent the broken spokes, pulled them out, then bent the new spokes and pushed them through the holes. They trued the wheel and we were ready to roll.

It was 11:00 a. m. Another incredibly late start, another incredible distance to ride. The good news was our friend the wind. It blew up our backsides all day, giving us the push we needed. The road drifted away from the coast into sand dunes, some crossing the highway.

Paranoia set in, we could have sworn a Land Rover was tailing us. Then a dark blue Mercedes followed, stopping often. We hoped they were just good guys with a bad engine problem.

At a café stop, we caught a couple of gendarmes sipping tea. Cycling away, we saw the lurking Mercedes begin tailing us again. Cat wanted to turn back and tell the gendarmes. Then as the car slowly passed, surprise, a gendarme sat in the passenger seat-they were escorting us.

It was thirty Ks from the drink stop to Tarfaya, a town off the highway. The blue Mercedes was waiting at the turnoff. The gendarme, Mohamed, told us he would lead us to the hotel. The dirt streets had no signs-without help from our new friend we'd never have found the place.

The usual tribe of kids crowded around asking for food or money. Mohamed pushed his finger on the hotel manager's chest. We felt he was making it clear that we should be treated well. The word "Americans" mingled with Arabic as he poked and spoke.

Several young guys helped carry our bags and bikes up the narrow stairway. The ten by twelve foot room barely accommodated us and our things. We were requested to meet back in the dingy little office. The desk clerk quoted a rate three times higher than Mohamed had indicated. We complained, and he mumbled then reduced it.

A guy in a white silk robe spoke English. Well educated, he appeared wealthier than the others that sat and listened. He asked about our journey, we outlined the route.

The toilet was a filthy squatter in the hallway. The shower had only cold water. The clerk suggested we bathe at the nearby *hamman*. He assured us we'd have the place to ourselves. Reluctantly, we accepted, gathered our clothing and towels, then walked around the corner. The layout was similar to the *hamman* at Mosque Hassan II. That was where the similarity ended. The first room was cool for dressing and undressing. The middle room was tepid, for a cool down. The third was steamy, the bathing room. The walls were slick with mold. The water, in an open tank with fire below, was boiling hot. We used a hose to cool the water before splashing ourselves.

Refreshed, we exited into the dark eerie street. A guy wearing a *jellaba* with the hood up was hunched over a little table listening to a small radio. He sold cigarettes, by the pack or singles. He looked like a Halloween ghoul in the glow of his lantern. Cat noticed her hairbrush was missing, and ran back inside the *hamman*. Eureka, she found it-as well as thousands of scurrying cockroaches when she flipped on the light.

Later, in dark streets with shadowy figures lurking, we found a cafe. It was crowded with men sipping tea and watching soccer on a small TV. All turned and stared as we entered. The soft drinks and chicken tajine were tasty but it was uncomfortable being the focus of the crowd. Back in our tiny concrete cell with barred windows, I locked the flimsy door then leaned the bikes against it as an early warning system. The small twin beds had dirty linen. We took out our sleeping bags. At 9:00 p. m. we thought we were in for the night and tomorrow Tarfaya would be just a strange memory.

We'd just dropped off to sleep when someone pounded on the door. I could see the feet of four guys under the door. They began rattling the flimsy door then pounded, *boom, boom, boom*. One said, "Open the door" in French.

"What do you want?" Cat asked, in French.

A different voice said, "We want peace!" In perfect English.

I moved quietly to the door, shifting the bikes and piling on some bags for a little more security then forcefully said, "We want peace too-go away, and let us sleep!"

They talked among themselves for a few minutes, shuffled their feet, then left. We lay in the dark listening, still shaky from the event. We decided they were the young guys full of mint tea and strong feelings from the cafe downstairs. Most likely, we convinced ourselves, it had taken all the nerve they could muster to come to our door. Their attempt to frighten the Americans had worked. We hoped they were back downstairs sipping their tea, bragging about how they'd scared us.

I worried. We were trapped in the tiny space without a phone, and no way to reach out for help. It was one thing to put myself at risk quite another putting Cat in harm's way. Remembering my promise to her Dad I dug out our Swiss Army knife and the aging cylinder of Mace. I lay them and the headlight on the floor next to my bed. I would defend her as best as possible.

We had just begun to relax when running feet came up the stairs again. *Bang, bang, bang*, they pounded on the door, but said nothing. I got up, weapons in hand, and assumed a defensive stance. Cat whispered, "Don't answer them." I stood in the dark, prepared to hold the door with my body. Failing that, to spray mace in their faces. Thankfully, the shuffling stopped and the shuffling steps retreated back down the stairway.

We were pretty shook up. Would they continue these hourly assaults? Would their boldness increase with the waning hours? Would more tea or whatever they were smoking or drinking bolster their courage? Would they come back, pounding and kicking, trying to bring the door down? Were they motivated by Muslim extremists' call to kill Americans? We lay in the dark talking in whispers and waiting. Sometime after midnight, we dozed off into light sleep.

Sleepless was the best way to describe that night. Adding insult to injury I awoke at 5:00 a.m. frantic with the urge to purge. Yep, diarrhea, and no idea who might be outside the door. In a panic, I began to tear down our security wall. Immediately, it was clear I wouldn't be able to get to the squatter. The urge turned to a surge, leaking down my leg. We had slept in our cycling clothes, now mine were soiled. In a panic, I pulled the shorts down and hoisted my fanny onto a little corner sink in the room. WHOOSH, the sudden release filled the sink. I had to plunge the brown chunky sludge down the drain with my hand. It was an icky smelly job.

Cat who'd tried to help, now had to go pee. The sink was too high so she used one of our empty water bottles. As bad as I felt, as bad as the mess was, we were both relieved at not having opened the door in the darkness. After wiping off my shorts, I pulled them back up and lay on top of the sleeping bag. Adventure travel has its moments-some more smelly than others.

Another hour and a half of fitful sleep, then in dawn's early light we began preparing to ride out of that hell-hole. Dawn broke at 7:00 a.m. and we quickly carried the bikes and bags down. The office and tea room were empty. Moving everything down wasn't easy but we were motivated.

CAT TRAX Day 37, 115 Ks, Tarfaya to Laayoune. Children on the way to school swarmed us, "You give *stilo*, you give pen?" We were in no mood, but tried to be pleasant. A fat old man waddled up watched then asked for a "stilo." We shook our heads no then he asked for Dirham, money.

Down the street we found a tiny place for breakfast. My stomach wasn't ready for greasy eggs but I definitely needed protein. As we sat locals staring, the old guy we'd said no to hobbled up. Standing in front of us he held out his hand, begging. I

41

saw he had a long pointed fingernail on the pinky of his right hand.

I finally forcefully said, "No, no baksheesh, no Dirham," loud enough that the waiter heard and confronted the old man. He resisted and they scuffled. The old guy was no match for the young waiter, except the beggar put his finger nail into action. He gouged the waiter's wrist so deep that it bled. The waiter recoiled, then screamed at the beggar kicking him in the behind as he waddled away. We talked about how bad that could have been had he severed an artery in that isolated place. We discussed adding long fingernails to our arsenal. Riding away we felt elated. The tough night made cycling 100 Ks away from Tarfaya seem simple.

A herd of wild camels led by a big male sauntered along beside us in the head wind. Even thorny local fauna seemed to dislike the blowing sand. It took us more than an hour to ride back to the highway. Interesting, we felt safe cycling among friendly fish trucks and Gran Taxis. We waved and they honked. The road swung southwest, giving us the boost of tailwind.

At thirty kilometers, the blue Mercedes stopped and the driver waved. He was talking with a woman in the back seat and pointing toward us. Perhaps telling her about the two crazy Americans. We shouted a hello as we flew onward with the wind.

Another roadblock, another smiling gendarme. We felt he knew who we were yet he asked the questions, anyway. Cat had taken Ali's suggestion and written down the answers. He looked at the paper, put it aside, and continued asking the same old things. Feeling weak and queasy, I took a seat in the shade, letting Cat sort out the details.

CAT TRAX Total miles cycled in Morocco, 1,544 Ks (960 miles)

CAT TRAX Total miles cycled since beginning our Odyssey 16,282 Ks (10,095 miles)

Chapter 6 The Western Sahara

The Western Sahara was controlled by Spain until 1975, when Mauritania attempted to take over, but lost to local rebel forces, the

Polisario. On November 6, 1975, by decree of King Hassan II, 350,000 Moroccans flooded onto the southern desert (an event called the Green March). Most were unarmed civilians, who soon made up the population of the tiny villages. A soft state of war had existed between Morocco, The Polisario, and Mauritania for more than twenty-five years.

CAT TRAX Day 38 through Day 41, in Laayoune, Western Sahara. Cycling into The Western Sahara thrust us into the middle of the remnants of war. Conflict, constant conflict had continued despite the presence of the United Nations. The UN had worked tirelessly to stop the violence and bring the warring parties to the negotiating table.

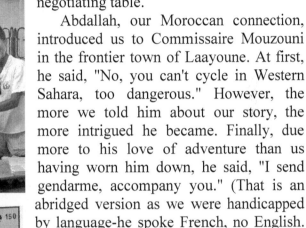

Abdallah, our Moroccan connection, introduced us to Commissaire Mouzouni in the frontier town of Laayoune. At first, he said, "No, you can't cycle in Western Sahara, too dangerous." However, the more we told him about our story, the more intrigued he became. Finally, due more to his love of adventure than us having worn him down, he said, "I send gendarme, accompany you." (That is an abridged version as we were handicapped by language-he spoke French, no English. Most of the conversation was using sign language but it worked.)

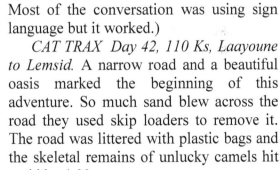

CAT TRAX Day 42, 110 Ks, Laayoune to Lemsid. A narrow road and a beautiful oasis marked the beginning of this adventure. So much sand blew across the road they used skip loaders to remove it. The road was littered with plastic bags and the skeletal remains of unlucky camels hit by trucks. We entered Lemsid by 4:00 p.m.

CAT TRAX Day 43, 76 Ks, 1654T, Lemsid to Boujdour. We heard a *ping* as we rode out onto the highway-another broken spoke, but on the outside, so it was easy to change. A beautiful day, blue sky with puffy little clouds. We rolled up to a checkpoint near Boujdour. One gendarme checked out our passports as two others asked Cat about our troubles in Guelmim and Tarfaya. They seemed to know everything. The first gendarme said, "You follow!" and led us to a four-bedroom guest house that we had all to ourselves.

Mohamed, a good-looking young guy said, "I am your security in Boujdour." Due to the number of Mohamed's he suggested we call him Mohamed C. He left, then in a few minutes two guys, one in military fatigues, the other in *jellaba,* came pounding on the door.

We were nervous and told them to leave. Mohamed C returned and introduced them. The guy in *jellaba* was Mayor of Boujdour District. At the gendarmerie we met Chief Hassani of the Royal gendarmes. Mohamed C drew a map of our route for the chief, showing our route and where we would stop each day.

Mohamed C took us shopping, bought lamb shanks, then returned and cooked. As we ate he said, "I am 34 years, engaged to girl 21 years." He was pleased when Cat told him I was 14 years older.

The food was great, Cat said, "She's a lucky girl, that marries a good cook!"

They posted the guy in fatigues as night sentry, which seemed like overkill. I told Cat most police I knew were always at the ready, prepared for the worst.

CAT TRAX Day 44, 140 Ks, Boujdour to Labouir. Cat slept well, I stirred with every little sound. Paranoia even with a security guy. At 8:00 a.m. Mohamed C was there, waiting. He counted the bags then said, "Because you ride today 140 Ks, too much load on bicycles. Mohamed B, the Mayor, he bring bags to Labouir this afternoon."

A team of two gendarmes lurked behind as we rode. We stopped for lunch, they pulled over about 300 meters back. Cat had to pee, so I shielded her from the road with the bikes while she squatted. As she finished and was squirming back into her sweaty shorts the gendarme drove up. They almost caught her with her pants down!

The gendarmes honked, waved, and turned back, leaving us in the solitude of the Sahara. It felt good to be on our own until another car began lurking. Was it gendarmes or bad guys? As they passed I caught the glimpse of a uniform, we were in good hands again.

Flies and butterflies seemed to be everywhere, even the most desolate of places. Flies buzzed around like a black cloud until the wind shifted enough for us to brush them away. At times a dozen butterflies flew in front of us like dolphins leaping ahead of a ship.

A small herd of camels grazed near the road. The big bull raised his head and snorted then turned and ran parallel to the highway. The others followed, then the entire herd swerved left, crossing directly in front of us. Two excited cyclists were paced by a pack of the once mighty "ships of the Sahara" now doomed to the butcher's block.

Mohamed S, wearing a Nike cap, walked up as we arrived in Labouir. He was chief of this region. The Sahara Petrom service station was our home for the night. A garage bay with steel door and no windows, it was also home to a swarm of flies. We sipped soft drinks, swatted flies, and watched as Mohamed S drew a new map of our route for the next two days. He was fun and funny. He bid us adieu saying, "I will come to you, in morning at 8:00 a.m."

We set the tent up inside the bay to avoid the flies. The noise of locals laughing and talking, and cars coming and going were no bother. We were sound asleep before 9:00 p.m.

CAT TRAX Day 45, 140 Ks, Labouir to Aarich. We loaded the bikes inside rather than let the neighbors see our worldly possessions. There was a bevy of gendarmes including Chief Mohamed S, all in uniform having breakfast. The same swarm of flies buzzed and dove, trying for bites of our food. As a show of appreciation we bought breakfast for the gendarmes, all of 80 Ds. ($8), so we thought it was a good investment. They took our bags to the office and locked them inside. The plan was that Mohamed S would accompany us to the local boundary, then return and send the bags on the 1:00 p.m. bus. They felt sure they'd arrive in Aarich ahead of us.

Mohamed S was our security. He pulled ahead and waved.

Then, just a few minutes later, Mohamed B pulled up in his big white Range Rover. He asked about the other Mohamed, then drove off to catch him. Soon Mohamed S drove by, headed back to his base. He stopped and said, "Bon chance, someone waiting for you at local agency border."

We thought we'd seen the last of Mohamed B, but there he was with two uniformed gendarmes. He had our bags and was transferring them into the gendarme's Jeep. We had dreaded they might want us to load them on the bikes. Previously the gendarmes had refused to accept responsibility for our bags in their vehicles. Mohamed B. had become very interested and involved in our journey. We think he didn't like the idea of our bags being on the bus unguarded. He actually hugged us and posed for a picture. What a wonderful guy.

The new gendarmes stuck to us like glue. They'd spurt ahead, wait until we passed, then move ahead again. The sun was high in the sky and it was hot. I felt spent, we were both burned out by the

time we reached Aarich and the Service Station. Yep, another service station accommodation. Fighting fatigue and slight nausea we drank Sprite and mango juice. We pitched the tent inside again, fending off flies and bugs. There was no shower. The guys at the station café heated a pot of water. We stood in the toilet, straddling the squatter, and took spit baths. Pretty stinky, but it felt good to wash off the sand and sweat.

Cat caught the African Guff-Guff again. She made two quick trips as we set up camp. For dinner we had mutton tajine! Three local guys tried to stare Cat down as we ate. A dozen dogs circled, licking their chops, hoping for a taste of the tasty mutton. We sat in the café staring back at locals until our eyelids drooped. We built a bicycle barrier in front of the un-lockable door and were in the tent, with lights out, by 9:00 p.m..

CAT TRAX Day 46, 65 Ks, Aarich to La Dakhla. I awoke at 6:30 with an extreme need for the toilet. I was in trouble. I began to un-stack our bikes. The strain of moving them took a toll. I wasn't able to hold it. What a *crappy* way to start the day. The café wasn't open, so I poured our bottles full of pee over the fence, filled them with fresh water, and used them to clean up the mess. My cycling shorts were a real problem as there was not enough water to get them clean. They would have been terrible to wear all day. Luckily I had a pair of regular shorts. We bagged the crappy shorts and I used Handi-Wipes to clean up. If this is too explicit, sorry, but it was a memory we'd never forget. All too often we dwell only on the pleasant.

Al Dakhla was in sight, out on a peninsula. We left the highway and circled out around the bay. Tired to the bone, we were like old horses headed for the barn. The road was bumpy and hilly. Our legs were burning, but we were motivated to get to Al Dakhla for a bath and good bed. Our guardians recommended the Sahara Regency.

Our personable personal gendarmes stood curbside at the hotel. One, Abdessamad, shook my hand and placed his hand on his heart as men there often did. I put my hand on my heart then on his chest and said, "Thank you, from my heart to yours." He seemed embarrassed then asked, "Can I leave my e-mail with you?" We were pleased to learn that he had an e-mail address.

The Sahara Regency would be our home for a couple of days. The shower was lukewarm. No matter, it felt great to get the sand and crud off. We lounged until 7:00 then went down for dinner and our first glass of wine in five days. Dinner was just okay, and the wine was expensive but essential. We were in the big bed by 9:00 p.m.

CAT TRAX Day 47 and 48, Rest, Dakhla. The hotel manager was on the telephone as we approached the front desk. He set it down and asked, "You want to pay?"

"No," I told him, "I want to know if we have a message from the gendarmerie?"

He looked confused then called to a guy coming through the door and asked if he spoke English. He said, "Yes, I speak English, what do you need to know?" When I told him I wanted to see if we had a message from the gendarmerie he said, "We are gendarmes." Wow, three of them, the chief of the gendarme (the one who spoke

English), the chief of military police and the chief of security police. We were in safe company.

The military chief said, "It is not possible to ride bicycle to border, too far and too dangerous. You cannot camp on the desert, too dangerous." As he spoke, I got a piece of paper, drew a map of the route and told them we'd pay to have a truck come with us. The captain was emphatic, "You will not pay!" When they saw the logic of my idea, to take the bikes back to the cross roads and start there, they put their heads together. Soon we were drawing a map that included an eighty-eight kilometer ride from the cross roads to a service station where we would sleep. They agreed to take us back to where we turned off the highway and chaperone us to the border. The captain kept saying, "You no worry, you safety my responsibility, you have no problems."

CAT TRAX Day 49, 90 Ks, Dakhla to Punta Bolsa. Younes, the hotel manager, drove his uncle's Mercedes. We loaded the bikes in the trunk, then set off, retracing our route across the flats looping around the seashore. It was hazy, almost foggy.

Younes talked as he drove, "I am the product of a cross-cultural marriage. My father met my mother while studying in Paris. She is from Ireland, he Morocco. They fell in love, the rest is history." I asked whether his mother being Catholic and his father being Muslim created problems for him. He said, "My father isn't religious, it was never a problem for me." I asked about Ramadan, he spoke almost under his breath, "God, I hate Ramadan, it is so strict, and people watch each other to make sure they  don't eat or drink, during the day. Even though we don't practice religion, we are careful about eating or drinking in public. It would cause problems with our help, and our business."

The chief of the gendarme was waiting at the crossroads. An old Renault and two uniformed gendarme sat waiting. As we off loaded the bikes, the chief introduced the two, Hachad and Hajib. They took charge of the bags, putting them in their trunk. The *capitaine* bid us a formal adieu with handshakes and a slight salute. Younes stood awkwardly for a moment, then grabbed my hand, shook it vigorously, touched his heart and said, "Remember me!" I put my hand on his and told him he would always be in our memories and our hearts. He stood in front of Cat for a moment then took her shoulders did the cheek to cheek kiss-kiss then reiterated the *capitaine*'s warning, "You will be riding the longest distances between places and, in the most dangerous part of the region." It was a poignant moment as he drove away.

We cycled, Hachad and Hajib followed, as Cat put it "Like flies on you know what." El Aargoub was directly across the bay from Dakhla. A few drops of rain began to make little dust clouds as they hit the parched earth. We stood, collecting drops on our shoulders as we discussed our trip and provided the usual info at a military police roadblock.

We were in El Aargoub in just two hours. Amazing how fast we could ride when not burdened by bags. Asrgoub was a military outpost. The adjacent village had the look of hastily constructed row houses and small businesses. Cycling toward town as the rain increased, we decided to have a soft drink and take cover. Our guide/guards found a small café. We left the bikes in the rain. Cat couldn't control her laughter as we stepped through the door. There was as much rain pouring through the roof as was falling outside.

The place was dimly lit. Several guys sat sipping tea and staring. One nice guy sidled over and said, "I study English, I forty year old." Wearing a sport shirt and baseball cap he sported a very western look. After a brief explanation of our trip, he continued, "I have come here with army for three year ago. I married have two girl one boys. They all young, attending school." He drew a deep breath then added, "I dreams of being near to my home in Marrakesh. I must be staying here two years more." He walked with us as we exited into the thinning rain, held out his hand to catch a few drops, then said, "This first rain, since three year I be station here."

We pushed through mud back to the highway. Onward, southward, we rode. Dakhla was now barely visible across the water. There would be no sun that afternoon but at least the rain stopped. The wind didn't-we pedaled hard into it. The gendarmes were staying close. We sent them ahead so we could take a toilet break roadside.

Somewhere along the route we had unceremoniously crossed

the Tropic of Cancer. There were no signs or markers. We knew from our map it was thirty-five kilometers south of El Aargoub. Amazing, just seven months earlier we'd set off from Vaasa, Finland, 200 Ks south of the Arctic Circle. We were becoming impressed with ourselves. We'd come a long way, baby!

As the wind calmed, my rear wheel began to wobble. Argh, two broken spokes. We rode in to Punta Bolsa past a new community. Hachad told us, "This built for the gendarme. I and Hajib stationed here, lives here." Below the cliff, near the ocean, we could see a collection of shacks. Hachad said, "For fisherman."

We were given the room where the Atlas Service Station manager and his assistant usually slept. We assumed Hachad and Hajib would go home for the evening. "No, we stand guard," Hachad said, with an air of authority, "You safety, are my duty." Thinking they meant sleeping in the car we told him we would set the tent and they could sleep in the room with us. We threw the rain fly over the top for privacy then invited them in to take a look. They laughed and called the Station Manager. He, too, laughed then tucked his bedroll under his arm and walked away shaking his head. Hachad told us, "We sleep with manager." The room was ours alone.

No bath again, so we stood in the stinky toilet area sponged off then joined the gendarmes at the café. They had satellite TV, and the manager continually flicked from channel to channel. Finally, he landed on Arabic  news. They watched with interest then talked among themselves. They said nothing to us, it meant nothing to us.

I found a broken screwdriver and used it to secure the door. We stacked the bikes in front as our early warning system, again. The sleeping bags felt warm and cozy.

CAT TRAX Day 50, 140 Ks, 2165T, Ponta Chica to Lamhiriz. A skillet full of overcooked eggs, a loaf of flat bread at least three days old, and we were on the road. Sameness as far as scenery for as far as we could see. There was no wind, it was eerily still. Drops of rain began to spatter then thicken to drizzle. The skies darkened and it poured. Second rain in three years!

Early lunch in the back seat of the gendarme cruiser. Soaked to the bone, Cat shivered as we ate. We delayed for a little, then stepped back into the deluge and rode on. Cold rain fell the rest of the afternoon.

At 5:30 we called a halt to the madness. Sorry, dear gendarmes, we were done for the day. The kilometer marker read 165 K to Nouadhibou. Our plan was back track to the highway tomorrow then make the final push to the Mauritanian border. Hajib estimated it was twenty-five kilometers to the motel and another eighty or so to the border.

We stuffed the bikes into the too-small trunk, then loaded bags in around them. The remainder filled the back seat on the driver's side. That door didn't open, lots of things didn't work, and the car was running ragged.

The sun was on the horizon by the time we got to Motel Barbas. It was, without doubt, a far-flung outpost. We thought about leaving the bikes on the car. The manager Hassan told the gendarmes, "The only guests and people at

the restaurant are locals, known to me." He added, "We have 24-hour security." I felt uneasy as the cast of characters began to gather round. Hachad made the final decision. "You take cycles to room, I lock bags in trunk."

Cat was chilled to the bone. She shivered all the way to the room, then wrapped herself in a blanket. Hassan came to tell us, "Bad news, have no hot water." Having been in that situation before, we asked Hassan to provide a bucket of hot water.

Water began dripping into the room through the ceiling light fixture. Cat called the girl who was sweeping the deck, to take a look. She immediately moved us, bag and baggage, to the next room. Water and electricity didn't mix any better there than they did on the other side of the world.

I went to the bar and arranged a cup of hot tea for the cool Cat. Hot water arrived in a huge plastic tub. We took turns splashing inside the cold ceramic shower. The water was so hot we had to pour in some cold. What a treat it clouded the shower room with steam. Warming up and washing down felt great. Cat dallied in the warmth for so long it was after 8:00 p.m. by the time we got to the patio area for dinner.

We sat talking with Hachad, Hajib, and a guy named Marino who spoke a tiny bit of English, "I construction foreman." I told him the roof leaked, he replied, "Yes, yes, I know, it very hard to get material." Hachad asked about a truck. Once Marino understood he called someone then said, "Truck to bring you to highway, come 7:00 in morning. Truck goes to Dakhla, he drop you, then he go."

Better for the bikes than cramming them back into the Peugeot. A great Hachad idea.

CAT TRAX Day 51, Lambriz to Nouadhibou, 110 Ks, 60 Ks in Van. Anxious to get on down the road we were up and ready before 7:00. They'd have the truck drop the bikes at Kilometer 165 and we'd cycle back then have breakfast. I told Hachad we would ride in the truck, no need for them to follow that short distance. He  shook his head vehemently and said, "Pat, this most dangerous of all road in Sahara, we must to go!" Hachad drove the car, Hajib rode in the truck keeping an eye on the bikes. The fog was thick and the windshield wipers didn't work. With only twenty feet of visibility Hachad drove with his head out the window.

The truckers handed the bikes down, wished us well and disappeared into the pea soup fog. The twenty-five Ks were under our wheels in an hour and twenty minutes. Breakfast omelets, toast, juice and coffee. Fuel to finish our "Tour du Maroc." Hachad got the grocery store clerk out of bed just for Cat, who was worried we might have to spend the night at the border waiting for a ride in the "No Man's Land." We might need food for the evening and next morning. We got canned meat but the store was sold out of bread.

Excited, we were off to Mauritania, the next leg of our journey.

We got a picture with Hachad but Hajib refused. Most of the gendarmes had been camera-shy. Hachad was our favorite, we wanted a keepsake photo to remember him. He posed with three locals. It was 10:30 by the time we got back out on the road.

The fog had retreated and the sun was bright, we hoped it was a good omen. After ten Ks we hit the mountain Hachad had warned of. Not really a mountain, more a downhill through a dry riverbed, then back up. The terrain became a valley of rocks. Cat liked the change of scenery.

It looked like someone had spent a lot of time stacking rocks artistically along the road. As we took pictures our companions pulled up. Cat asked about the stacked stones. Hachad's answer shocked us, "The Army make this rock, it mark safe area. All past, are with *land mines*! This are war zone." The conflict had persisted for more than twenty years. The Polisario and Mauritania the losers, wouldn't give it up.

Here's an aside about the good in people. Our gendarmes passed, followed by SUVs from France. We thought the French pulled over for another roadblock, then we realized it was locals in one of the cars. They had found and brought fresh bread. Again Hachad was thinking ahead and the others were kind enough to drive all the way there just for us.

Eating sardines from the cans, we shared fresh-baked bread with our gendarmes. Finished, they threw their can into the gutter. Cat told them about our anti-litter laws back home. They had heard of them but thought there was so much desert space that it wasn't a problem. I dug a small hole with my shoe and buried our trash.

At 3:30 p.m. we arrived at the Moroccan Border. There was a gendarme checkpoint. We passed that test easily, then moved to the next. This one was rock shacks with a heavy cable strung across the road. Oh, the pavement ended there, too. Ahead lay No Man's Land, and Mauritania.

Hachad had mentioned something about an autobus that would take us across to Mauratania. A clunky van stopped. We'd seen it at the first checkpoint. Cat whispered, "Thank goodness we won't have to ride with them."

The gendarmes and soldiers talked and laughed. Then the bad news: we would be riding in the clunker van. The Mauritanians had agreed to take us. Hachad told Cat, "They will charge you nothing."

Then another of those worst moments of our journey, the goodbye. Goodbyes often overshadowed the excitement of the adventure. It was hard to believe how attached we had become to those two standoffish gendarmes. We hadn't gotten to know Hajib well, maybe the language barrier or perhaps he was a quiet person. As Hachad shook my hand I said, "You will always be in our minds and in our hearts." He pulled me closer and I hugged him. Cat hugged him and they exchanged cheek kisses. We both began to well up and get that familiar lump in our throats. It was time to go!

CAT TRAX Total Ks cycled in Western Sahara 696 Ks (431.5 miles)

Chapter 7 Mauritania: A Rough Landing in an Islamic Republic

CAT TRAX Moroccan Border to Nouadhibou, Mauritania. 60Ks in Van. When Hachad and the Moroccan border guards spoke with the van driver he seemed to object, then gave in. The van was full of furniture and produce. Hachad and Hajib helped hoist our bags and bikes inside and boosted us up atop the load. We crawled in and sat uncomfortably atop the bikes. The only comfort was knowing it was only sixty Ks to Nouadhibou. Less than forty miles. We knew we could endure an hour or so.

Reports we'd read about the bad road were an understatement. From rough rocky places to soft sand that had our driver gunning the engine and fishtailing. We'd only driven a mile when we encountered the first road block.

The van stopped abruptly. Through the slit window in the rear door, we could see a dozen soldiers gathering. Our driver spoke with them, and we assumed he was explaining how we became his passengers. He opened the doors and one of them waved an AK 47 in a non-threatening way, indicating I should get out. I stood on the bumper looking down at the sea of brown and black faces. A strange sight, as we'd seen very few blacks in Morocco. He said,

"Passports." I handed them down, he held them up, surveying my picture and face then peered further into the van giving Cat the same once over. He asked a few simple questions in French. Cat gave simple answers. Country of origin, father's name, mother's maiden name, etc.. Then with another wave of his assault rifle we were officially in Mauritania.

Another slow bumpy mile, another military outpost. Cannons covered with camouflage were aimed toward Morocco. The buildings were stacked rock, their tin roofs covered with the same camouflage netting. Again, a dozen soldiers gathered, spoke to the driver then he opened the door. They ordered us out and ushered us into one of the shacks. Most waved AK 47s carelessly. The Commanding Officer had us sit as he reviewed our passports and visas. He stared, glared and asked, "Where do you go?" in surprisingly good English.

I said, "We are going to Nouadhibou."

"How you get there?" He sort of snarled.

"We're riding with this man," I said, pointing toward the van driver.

"This man say Morac gendarme make him take you, he drops you here," he declared, staring daggers that almost cut right through us.

"We thought he was taking us to Nouadhibou," I responded.

"You must pay him," he said arrogantly.

"And if we chose not to pay?"

"You stay here," he said, in a threatening tone.

Cat was nervous, she whispered, "We can't stay here!"

"How much money do we have to pay this man," I asked.

The officer, checking our papers without looking up, said, "One thousand Dirham." (Roughly $100 US for a forty-mile ride!)

I said, "That's a lot of money!"

Cat spat out, "Pay him!"

The negotiation complete, that left us pretty much penniless until we could find an ATM or Bank. Fortunately, they didn't require payment then and there. Our driver smiled ear to ear as the officer explained the deal. He handed our passports back and motioned for us to go. We had made it through Immigration's scrutiny. Back in the cramped quarters of the van we felt our confidence growing. The van was our sanctuary.

Another thirty minutes of bumps, grinds, and dust. Another heavily armed military post, customs office, another wave of an automatic rifle. As we crawled out, several young guys pressed in, asking where we were going. Hustlers wanting to help us find a hotel. Hachad had recommended Hotel Palmiers, but the boys were obviously paid by Hotel Al Jazeera. The guard shooed them away with his rifle, then pointed it toward me. Cat interpreted "He wants only you to go inside." I started to complain. Not wanting to rock the boat she said, "If I have a problem I'll scream."

Reluctantly, I backed toward the door, watching as the soldiers stepped away from Cat. The rock shack had no windows. The light from the door diminished as I came through. As my eyes adjusted, a large imposing black man gestured for me to sit. Another took our passports as he opened an official-looking book. He then lit a small candle and held the passports up in the flickering light. He asked in English, "What is your job?"

"Imobilier, Real Estate," I said, proud of using French.

Then, he stared directly into my eyes and asked, "Do you bring a gift for me?"

Composing I took a deep breath and said, "I didn't know I should bring a gift." He smiled, so I continued, "What gift should I bring for you?"

As if to intimidate me, he waved to the other big guy who moved to the table, leaned down toward my face and said, "100 Dirham."

I accepted the challenge and told them, "I have no money. I have to pay the driver all of the money we have with us."

The big guy leaned even closer as the seated one furrowed his brow and said, "What car you have?"

"I have only a bicycle, no car," I told him.

"Imobilier no car?" He sighed and said, "You must not be good Imobilier!"

"Do I have to give you a gift?" I asked, trying to ascertain whether his request was legal.

"It would not be nice, if you don't," he again sort of threatened.

I opened my wallet containing 320 Dirham, took out the 20 D bill and put it on the table. He asked if we were taking the train or driving back. I hated to lie, but under pressure, as I shielded the 300 D from him, I said, "We'll be back in four days." That's what might be called "creative truth." He objected telling me that was his day off. Then I extended an olive branch, saying we'd be in town why not stop by our hotel, and I would buy him tea and we could talk. He seemed to like the idea. I asked his name. Amazing, he said "Bill" then even spelled it B-i-l-l. I shook his hand and retreated to the safety of our basic, albeit expensive, transportation.

I filled Cat in on the graft as we bumped along. She was upset that I'd given money, even $2.00. I reminded her how quickly she had volunteered $100 at the Immigration shack. I decided not to tell her that Bill might come visiting.

Much of the time there was no road. A dry creek bed almost stalled progress. The van bogged down but the driver was able to back up, gun the engine, then swerve and sway through. Once on solid ground, he pulled up, came around and opened the door. He said something unintelligible, we assumed an invitation to use the bushes. He joined the two women and baby on their knees. They prayed as we selected a private spot, hoping that local snakes were busy praying, too.

Soon, the van began lunging and bumping along again. Darkness set in, along with feelings of trepidation. I assured Cat I could whip the little guy if I had to. She said she didn't doubt that if he wasn't armed. As we worried, there was another lurching stop and flashlights shone through our slit window. We could see another group of soldiers talking with the driver. They held up their flashlights, trying to see in. We hunkered down, attempting to avoid the prying lights. They waved him on!

Now in total darkness, our minds played tricks with our emotions. We envisioned him stopping at home and the two of us being overwhelmed by family. Would our world journey end there in violence? Would we be stripped of our possessions and dumped into the dark wilderness? This was the longest thirty-eight miles we'd ever endured; we could have cycled faster. Also on our minds, the $100 (300 Dirham) question, were we actually going to

Nouadhibou?

Jolting along, we began to see signs of civilization. Lights in windows of little houses. Camels standing in the eerie yellow glow of a streetlamp. Another stop-it was too late for prayers, ours or theirs-so we girded for action, hoping for the best, trying to prepare for the worst. The driver pounded on the door. Would he order us out? Would we have to fight for our lives?

He struggled with English then got out three wonderful words, "Hotel or camping?" We wondered whether he heard our sighs of relief as we sang out in unison, "Hotel." He urged the aging van back to life. More street lights fighting back the blackness. What a welcome sight the tree-lined drive of Hotel Al Jazeera. Cat stood guard. I went in hoping they had a vacancy.

The young desk clerk spoke English. He assured me they had a room; I asked to see one. He grabbed a handful of keys and we went on the hunt. The building was rundown and each room he opened had some problem. No hot water, no water in the shower, broken furniture, etc. Finally one with all plumbing and furniture functional, but slightly dirty. I thought it would work. The clerk began filling out the registration form. I said I wanted my wife's approval. Back at the van, Cat was standing ready to unload. I told her the situation, and she sang out, "Take it!"

She handed me a bag, then the driver jumped in and started helping. I carried the first bags in and confirmed we'd take the room. The struggle of off-loading bags and bikes felt great. Our muscles were stiff and sore after the torturous cramped five-hour ride.

I grabbed the camera and went out to pay the driver. He'd fought that old van through rough terrain for hours, and waited patiently as we were interrogated and intimidated at all the checkpoints. Now that we were safe, we felt obliged to pay. He and his family would need money to keep the old rust-bucket on the road, hauling necessities for family, friends, and occasionally cycling aliens.

CAT TRAX Days 51 - 56, Nouadhibou, Hotel Al Jazeera. It was 9:00 p.m., by the time we settled in. Fortunately, the clerk didn't't ask for cash, as they didn't accept credit cards. The 300 Moroccan Dirham (about $3.00 US) was our total net worth. The fourteen-hour day had taken a financial, physical, and emotional toll. We needed food.

There were still a few people sitting and sipping tea in the restaurant. We wondered what they thought of two sweaty, stinky, crusty, dusty foreigners. The only item available at that hour was spaghetti. Not very tasty, but we wolfed it down with gusto.

Steaming hot showers loosened our tight muscles and washed away the sweat and dust. We'd survived, so sleep was easy to find.

 At breakfast we met Emad and his secretary Dagmara. Both Dutch citizens, he was born in Egypt, she Poland. They complained about the food, but for us the coffee, juice, and croissants were fantastic. We signed our second tab.

Emad owned a wholesale seafood company and was there buying prawns. He and Dagmara were sick of Nouadhibou, they'd been there ten days. He confirmed that there were no ATMs in Mauritania and the banks wouldn't advance cash on credit or debit cards. "I wait for money coming on Western Union," he added. That put a knot in our stomachs and almost ruined breakfast.

We told Emad about our dilemma: credit and cash advance cards, but no cash. He offered to loan us enough to get by. We declined, thinking we had enough stashed Euros, but a thorough search turned up only one 5 Euro note and the 300 Dirham. We walked the dusty streets to the internet café hoping to get an SOS off to Base Camp Charlie. The cafe owner wasn't supposed to change money, but was happy to see the crisp Euro note. He converted it to 250 Ouguiya and we hit the keyboard. The only way to solve our problem was have Charlie wire funds via Western Union.

Who was Charlie, of Base Camp Charlie? He was the most honest, straight-forward person I'd ever known. A good real estate agent, he became property manager of our firm. As we planned our departure, he agreed to take care of our ongoing business. We made him signatory on our bank accounts-that's complete trust, as he could have dipped into our savings. He'd been managing all our monetary affairs, making payments and deposits in our name, since we'd been on the road.

Message sent, we lounged at the hotel then walked back to the internet cafe at 6:00 p.m. They only sold internet time in one hour increments. We explained our quandary, and the clerk agreed to allow us to pay for the hour and use half then and the other half the following morning.

There are few words that express our relief at receiving Charlie's message. He had already sent $700. Walking back, we talked about our feeling of helplessness, comparing it to what a homeless person must endure daily. Whether in Mauritania or New York City, being broke is a totally demoralizing situation. Thanks be to Base Camp Charlie!

The cast of characters at dinner were Russians, there refurbishing ships. They'd been there more than a month. They knew the waiter and loved joking with him-delighting in ordering things they knew were never available. Knowing there was no ice cream, they each took a turn ordering a different flavor.

Jiyed, the amiable assistant manager, was dressed for a party, a political party. President Taya running for his third four-year term was going to attend. He'd led a bloodless coup in 1984. Mauritania had been a Democracy since 1992-Taya won the first election and continued to run unopposed.

They had a traditional tent set behind the hotel. Persian carpet covered the dirt. A row of large chairs lined one side. They were occupied by local leaders awaiting the strong man's arrival.

Cat had insisted on beginning courses of chloroquine, the malaria pill, a month earlier. I had scoffed at the idea. We were in a desert, no mosquitoes there. That night I was glad she'd won that argument. Desert or not, we had mosquitoes in the room. There were holes in the screens, an open invitation to those blood-sucking critters. The buzzing was as annoying as the bite. We sprayed noxious smelling Deet on our clothing and the bed linen. The fumes helped abate the little buggers buzzing but we wondered about the effect on our lungs.

Emad was angry enough to curse at breakfast. The money to get his shipload of prawns moving was there but the bank wouldn't release it. They couldn't tell him why. That jangled our nerves as we, too, were on money watch. He offered again to loan us money, and we accepted. Strange how strangers often step up with acts of random generosity.

The DHL office manager Mr. Hady confirmed Base Camp Charlie had also sent supplies. However they wouldn't arrive for a week. He directed them to Nouakchott the Capital City.

We weren't homesick, just sick of the food at the hotel. Visits to both Super Marche's located across the street from each other netted canned corned beef, Swiss cheese, and bread. We ate in the hotel lobby while soaking up Al Jazeera news. Good food, not good news. Wild fires were blazing in several areas of Southern California. More than 20 dead and 2,300 homes destroyed. The only good news, they hadn't threatened our home or families.

Late in the afternoon, Jiyed offered a different room. The shower had hot water and there was a tiny air conditioner. It could cool the room just enough to allow us to keep the windows closed. No more mosquitoes, no more Deet-soaked sheets!

Breakfast was a lonely affair. Ramadan had begun. All good Muslims adhered to the "No food between dawn and dusk" tenet.

Our opulent taxi ride (40 cents) to the Western Union led to good news and bad. Our $700 was available but Western Union's exchange rate was 256 Ouguiya to $1 US. We had been counting on the street exchange-over 300 Os to $1. We'd have 16% fewer Os than we'd been counting on. The bank manager walked us to a teller's window, pushed aside two guys and stuck his arm through the opening in the bullet proof glass. He handed the clerk the Western Union check. The clerk began stacking bundles of bills. The two guys mumbled something as several others gathered round. We began to get nervous. Suppose we got the money, then lost it to robbers. When the teller pushed the stacks through, we grabbed them and counted. We became the center of attention for all the men loitering in the bank.

We confirmed 179,934.40 Ouguiya then stuffed the bills into

money belts under our shirts. The bulges looked like we were wearing colostomy bags. Exiting the bank, I wanted to get as far away as quickly as possible. A Mercedes taxi pulled over. I jumped in as Cat began bargaining with the driver. His fare to the hotel was

200 Os. Cat scolded him, saying we'd only paid 100 to get there. He objected, "100 is for little cars." The crowd was thickening, I got Cat's arm and pulled her inside. She was upset until it sank in that 200 Os was only 80 cents. We laughed at how we lose track of value and reality during times of stress.

The next challenge: transportation out of that Allah forsaken place. Our original plan to cycle included the dangers of having to backtrack through "No Man's Land." Plan #2, taking the coal train to Timbuktu was "derailed" when Jiyed told us the train had jumped the tracks and would be out of service for two weeks. Plan #3, he suggested his friend with an SUV would take us to the highway for $600 US. He said, "The road is very bad, very dangerous and near the border."

Emad said, "Why not fly?" Amazing, he called a friend Abdi who worked at the airport and booked two tickets for only $80. With excess weight for bikes and bags the price doubled, but was still a bargain. Emad spoke with the front desk, and they issued the tickets right there. We were so happy, we paid back the loan and bought his lunch.

Good news, we were booked; bad news the 3:00 p.m. flight was fully booked. They put us on the 6:00 p.m. plane. Emad called his friend again who said, "We'll try to get them on three o'clock flight." Emad covered the phone and said, "Grease his palm if he gets you on." We needed bags to pack for the flight. Emad and his buddies took us shopping. The large plastic bags we wanted were 1000 Ougiyas. Emad began the bargaining at 200. Eventually we bought several for 500 Ouguiya about $1.95 each. He asked if we needed anything else. Cat said, "I want a whistle, like that policeman is using. It would be good to have if we get in trouble or need help."

Visiting shop after shop we found none. Cat mentioned the

gendarme on the corner was directing traffic, often using his whistle. Emad had a Mauritanian approach the officer. Smiling he returned and asked, "Would you pay 1000 Ouguiya?" Cat got her whistle for less than $4.00 US. And the gendarme was a happy guy. We all roared with laughter as the Mauritanian told and retold the way the scene had played out!

Parting with Emad for the last time was difficult. We shook hands then he pulled us both into a big bear hug. Another of our "Friends In Deed!"

Cat argued with the young hotel desk clerk when he added tax to our bill. They'd said it was included. I refused to pay and asked to see the manager. The clerk said, "Manager not here, sick." We knew the manager lived in the hotel. It only amounted to $35 but we still needed to be cautious money-wise. Also, there was the principle involved. As we prepared to pay, the clerk sheepishly told us, "I have remove tax."

We pushed the bikes to the airport. There, we put our panniers into the plastic bags. Several guys lurked hoping to earn a tip. One muscled in, and started to help break the bikes down. He knew what he was doing, and we had them ready to fly in no time. I gave him 200 Ouguiya he beamed. How did those people make a living? He spent half an hour helping us with the bikes, then helped carry our bags and bikes to the check-in counter, all for 80 cents.

Emad's friend Adib looked in the bags then had our helper tape them. They threw everything on the scale and he said, "65 kilos, okay?" He took me into his office and pushed buttons on the calculator. The total was $46. I asked if that included getting us aboard the 3:00 p.m. flight. When he said yes, I put the required Ouguiyas down then added some grease. He smiled and slipped it under his book.

The waiting room was full of guys on their knees observing afternoon prayers. Our prayers were answered when the plane taxied up to the gate on time. As passengers lined up, Abdi escorted us onto the runway. Inside, the flight attendant told us to sit anywhere. At takeoff, the plane was about half full. Okay, we'd been hustled, but it felt great to see Nouadhibou slip under the plane's wings and into our past. We'd survived a harrowing five-day stopover!

CAT TRAX Day 57, Nouadhibou to Nouakchott. The Boeing 727-200 was almost new; it felt good to be inside something made in Seattle. The flight was smooth and we arrived in Nouakchott, the  capital city, in just forty-five minutes. Exiting, a young guy tried to take our carry-on panniers out of my hands. Fearing theft, I clung tightly and pushed him away. The room was full of young guys pushing, shoving, and trying to help with baggage. I accepted his help despite Cat's objection. Another choice made based on the feeling I could out run or whip him. Cat had booked us in the Novotel Hotel, the one the Southern Mail pilots in Tan Tan recommended. It was the highest-priced hotel in Nouakchott but we needed pampering.

A guy in the terminal held up a sign-a divine sign-"Novotel welcoming passengers." Our helper introduced us to the driver. He sorted out the wanna-be porters. As our bags and my bike came in another rush of people began. Once all the baggage was in the terminal, our Novotel driver ducked under the low door looking for Cat's bike. He came back empty-handed. An agent in flowing *daraa* said, "It is in Nouadhibou." I got in his face.

"That's BS, we saw them load it onto the plane," I spat out. We insisted he call Abdi. He did, then let me talk with him. Abdi confirmed both bikes were put on the plane. Mr. Daraa told us to come back at 8:00 p.m. it must be on the other plane." Then he said, "If it's lost, we have insurance, you can buy another."

With translation from the Novotel guy I retorted, "They are special bikes, it would take a month to get another built and shipped. We are not leaving without that bike." Then I started making a scene. I shouted, "gendarme, gendarme!" Mr. Daraa

64

turned away waved his arm and said in French, "You find one."

Every gendarme had disappeared. Maybe because of the ruckus. Just as I shouted again, three guys came through the front doors carrying Cat's bike. They'd somehow been able to steal it over a ten-foot wall from inside the secure baggage area.

Two of them carried the bike, the third had his hand extended toward us-they wanted a tip! I was pissed. The larger one said, "5 Euro" and the rag-tag crowd began to press in. I pulled out a 500 Ouguiya note, stuck it in his hand, and grabbed the bike. The crowd laughed as the three guys began to argue. We felt certain they were about to attack so I asked the Novotel driver what they were saying. He chuckled, "No, not angry, they argue how to split 500 Ouguiya three way."

As we loaded the van a tall, gaunt, dirty-looking guy reached out hoping for a hand out. As he pressed I pushed him away and said, "La la." (No, no) It was easy after what we'd just been through. Poverty is terrible but we can't give to everyone, especially pushy beggars. I felt no guilt. We headed for heaven, the Novotel, in a cloud of dust.

CAT TRAX Days 57-60, Nouakchott, Mauritania. As we checked in, Manoel the Belgian manager introduced himself. We told him we hadn't had wine in eight days. He said, "I love wine, too." We invited him to stop by our room for a glass. He replied, "I'd love to, but I gave it up for Ramadan. I'm no Muslim, I do this for the staff." We suggested he slip in and sneak a sip. He smiled, but said, "I make a promise and a promise is a promise!"

Manoel had wine sent to our room. That was the beginning of spending. The daily rates combined with costs of food and vino were astronomical. But since Heaven was located in the midst of Hell and a 'No Credit Zone,' we couldn't complain. Fortunately, the Novotel accepted American Express. They ship the charge slips to Paris to bill to our account. Of course there was an "Add on Charge" for the service. Manoel quietly violated company policy allowing us to charge 10,000 Ouguiya ($40 US) to our Amex Card for extra cash.

We lounged rested ate, ate, and ate. I put the bikes together. DHL delivered the package from Base Camp Charlie. We now had a West Africa Guide Book, Michelin Maps of West Africa, and DVDs for our camera, enough for 3,000 photos.

Ali, the chef, came to us at lunch and asked if we were the famous cyclists. He insisted on preparing a fabulous evening meal especially for world travelers. Lobster bbisque followed by camel steak and paella. Royal treatment that came at a royal price. This would be our most expensive stay in any country when the $100 ransom for the van ride and five days at the Al Jazeera were factored in.

Our three nights in paradise came to an end, as all good things must. We hated to leave the Novotel, however our odyssey wasn't about staying in one place. Manoel exerted sway with the gendarme. He learned there was no lodging between Nouakchott and the border town of Rosso. However, we could camp at the gendarmerie in Tiguent, a tiny village about 100 Ks south.

Another wonderful meal, then as we packed, we both began to feel the pangs of African Guff-Guff. A holdover from Al Jazeera? We couldn't believe it could be the product of Chef Ali's fine cuisine. No matter, it had us running for the toilet several times that night.

CAT TRAX, Day 61, 104 Ks, Nouakchott to Tigueant, With toilet paper on board and on weak legs we pedaled away from paradise! Main Street quickly transitioned into terrible areas. Dusty streets gave way to highway Rue du Rosso. Two large trucks blocked an intersection-even donkey carts couldn't pass. We cautiously pushed between the trucks around the curious crowd and onto the highway. The city quickly gave way to desert and

desolation, with a few scattered shacks. Rue du Rosso was straight and flat. Road kill was numerous and large. Camels, donkeys, cattle, and goat remains ranged from fresh carcasses to skeletal. Most must have taken broadside hits from trucks careering down the highway.

Tiguent was nothing but a few shacks and tents. Manoel's feeling that people would crowd around wasn't the case. A gendarme in fatigues lay on a cot in front of the gendarmerie. He was barefoot, his shirt open, and his trusty AK 47 leaned against the mud hut wall. His name was Albere. Cat couldn't understand his French. He seemed impressed by his power. He barked out an order and a young boy appeared from behind the hut. Another shouted order sent the kid running. He came back with a young man in tow.

Karim spoke good English and began translating. Albere called him "Le Professor." Karim told us Mr. Albere was chief of the gendarme. We believed he was the only gendarme at the lonely outpost. We told Karim that the gendarme in Nouakchott had said we could set our tent near the gendarmerie. He posed that to Albere then said, "Mister Albere likes your glasses." Albere took them off my head and put them on. When we asked about staying Karim said, "Mr. Albere say, you cannot stay there, he has a room for you."

They led us across the roadway to a cement block building. Karim said, "Mr. Albere say you stay in this little room. You pay 6,000 Ouguiya. ($24 US) Mr. Albere say owner allow gendarme use for storage." The place was full of sand and bedding. Perhaps they slept or did Allah only knows what else there.

I asked, "How much is the room rent, if I trade glasses with Albere?" He immediately reduced it to 5,000. His glasses were cheap. I didn't want his deal, however he had the AK and authority. I complained that the place was dirty and full of sand. Albere shouted orders. A couple of young guys appeared and began stirring up the dust.

It was a far cry from the Novotel but we had a room for the night. Karim asked a woman in a tent behind the gendarmerie about food. She agreed to fry chicken and potatoes for 2,500 Os. That made our tab for the night $30.00 US plus my sunglasses. That, too, was a far cry from the Novotel.

Karim's attempt to flag down a ride to Nouakchott finally paid off. We hated to see him go. He was our lifeline of communication with Albere. As a parting shot, Albere spewed something in Arabic. Karim said, "Mr. Albere asks your nationality." When I said, "USA," Karim told us Albere said, "I like Americans, they protect the world." It was hard to tell if he was being facetiousness.

67

President Maya and Mauritania had been allies with Saddam Hussein and Iraq during the Gulf War. Yikes!

Tired and weak, we pulled our bags off the bikes and sat on them. It felt like we were in a dungeon awaiting our last meal. We walked across to check on the food, and caused a stir. The woman's six kids clung to her, fearful of foreigners. A second uniformed guy came out of her tent. In rough French he said they would bring food in half an hour.

I began to worry about being locked into the cement block cell. Probably a flashback to that terrifying night in Tarfaya. I used one of our bicycle lock cables and wound it around the outside hasp, making it difficult to put a lock through. We waited to set the tent until after eating so Albere wouldn't see it. Finally at 8:00 the woman and her eldest baby brought fried chicken and chips. Grease ran down our throats into our churning stomachs.

We'd just started setting our tent when Albere pounded on the door. He wanted in. I told him we were eating and didn't want to open the door. He stuck his arm between the bars on the little window trying to reach a pile of blankets. I handed them to him but he dropped them back saying "Rouge Torch." Cat figured out he was asking for a flashlight. I shook the blankets and a red flashlight fell out. He took it. Cat thanked him in French for providing security as he vanished into the darkness. We hoped and prayed that was his last trip to our cell block.

We fell into troubled sleep, but awoke with every little noise or gust of wind. We both began coughing due to the dust. Neither of us had diarrhea, but both needed to pee during the night. I just went out the window and Cat squatted over a plastic bottle that we'd cut the top off.

At break of dawn, Cat went to the woman who'd cooked dinner asking if she had coffee or food. She was lying on the floor while one of the kids braided her hair. Not moving she just said no. We ate the two bananas and bread we had on board. As we prepared to leave, a fresh-pressed officer came to the doorway asking if we were okay. Then Albere waved, as he walked away wearing my sunglasses. So he was just the Night Chief. Hey, we'd slept, albeit fitfully, we were safe and would live to ride another day.

CAT TRAX Day 62, Tiguent to Rosso, 97Ks. Back to the road of carcasses. The flora began changing to small clumps of trees, the

fauna was skinny camels who ate the sparse leaves. By late afternoon we were fading. At last after eight and a half hours we completed our second 100-plus kilometer day, riding into Rosso.

Manoel had recommended Hotel Union. Asking at a service station, the staff stared and shook their heads. A tall Senegalese man speaking French pointed up the street. There was a pink building with the sign Hotel As Asmaa. We needed a toilet, food, and bed. They had all three. We took a ground floor suite big enough to handle the bikes. It was worn and dirty. The Clerk said, "Chaud eau, no." (No hot water)

We turned both ACs up and it was soon so cold Cat put on her jacket. I lay resting on the couch. As my eyes adjusted to the dim light I saw trash on the floor and other evidence the room hadn't been cleaned. Back to the desk to complain. I was greeted by a tall handsome guy named Mostopha. As I tried to communicate in

French he said, "Do you speak English?" He followed me to the room and said, "This is not as it should be!" He brought the desk clerk and cleaning lady in and pointed out the trash. Mostopha was the new hotel food manager.

As I returned a mouse ran across the floor and under the couch. I hated to tell Cat, but felt it was better she know than be surprised. I assured her we'd be okay if we kept our food in closed containers. She feared they'd crawl on us during the night.

I asked Mostopha for a bucket of hot water for bathing. He brought a bucket but the water was cold. I asked again if they had hot for bathing. He laughed and apologized for his English. We were happy having someone to talk with, perfect or not.

Bucket baths felt great. Mostopha put together a decent dinner. It was his first day on the job. He had only leftovers and dry foods available. He served a pasta dish with some strange vegetables and bread. "Sorry," he said, "we do not serve wine."

CAT TRAX Day 63, Rosso, Mauratania to Ross Bethio, Senegal, 42Ks Bike, 53Ks Taxi. Mostopha prepared a decent breakfast for our final day in Mauritania. Ready to roll, we asked to have a picture with him. He said, "Wait, I have called my friend Alex. He will guide you through the border." When Alex arrived, we got a picture of him and Mostopha.

Alex was nothing like Mostopha. He was a small guy with a small guy complex. He explained that police and luggage would cost fifty Euros. I complained, as we only had fifty. It was 100 Ks from the border to a village. We didn't want to be caught short of cash. I asked Alex if they would accept our Visa card. He responded, "Yes, of course," in French.

When we arrived at his tiny dirty office that smelled of sweat, I handed him our Visa card. He looked at it and asked, "What is this?" Apparently he thought I meant our Senegalese visas. We dug out 12,000 Os. He took them with our passports and disappeared. Back in thirty minutes, he gave me just 1000. As our hearts sank,

Mostopha came striding through the door. We explained our money problem and he spoke with Alex, then seemed to scold him. Alex left and returned shortly with a handful of CFA, Comunaute Financiere Africqine the currency used by several West African countries.

So, thanks to Mostopha we would start life in a new country with 13,500 CFA. We don't know what he said to Alex but we felt certain Alex had skimmed some off the top. With Alex and Mostopha leading, we made our way through the maze of military checkpoints and thick crowd. Border crossings were always a challenge. This was at least as difficult as most. How fortunate we were to have met Mostopha!

The border between Mauritania and Senegal runs through the

middle of the Senegal River. As we prepared to board the ancient old boat Mostopha put his hand on my shoulder and said, "Be very careful, Pat, there are bad animals and bad people over there." What a wonderful guy to be so concerned. I asked if he'd been there. "Oh, no, I wouldn't want to go there," he said with a shudder. Funny how often we'd heard terrible stories from locals about the land beyond, a place they'd never been.

We watched the desert sand and scrub brush fade into memory.

 As the boat struggled across we saw an amazing change to green jungle. On the far side of that muddy river lay danger adventure and intrigue.

CAT TRAX, Mauritania, 200 Ks (125 miles) on bikes, a plane, and 60 Ks in the van.

Chapter 8 Senegal, The North

NOW THIS WAS AFRICA

As the old tub hit midstream, oozing oil, we hugged in celebration of our arrival in Senegal and sub-Saharan Africa. Thanks to Mostapha, we had enough money to get into town. Alex led us through customs, then had us accompany him to a police shack. The border guard seemed to want money, but after a few words from Alex, he stamped our passports and, with a wave of his hand, dismissed us. Alex halfheartedly shook my hand and we were free to go. Pushing our loaded bikes along with the crowd, we struck up a conversation with a French couple, Eric and Sylvie, who lived in Dakar. She gave us their phone number and invited us to visit.

A wiry little guy sidled up and said "Passport."

I shook my head "No." He began to insist on receiving 1,000 Ouguiya. I shook my head again and under my breath said, "Scammer!" He continued to trail along. As we passed the French couple I asked for help.

Eric spoke with him then retorted, "Oui, ees scam!" Mr. Wiry whined. Eric said to us, "Go. You go!" We went.

The change was wonderful-no more sand dunes, just sugar cane fields, jungle, and grassland. Even some swampy places, with lily pads and floating flowers. We both felt queasy and at the same time relieved at having endured the border crossing into the "Real Africa." It was 100 Ks to the only small town between there and St. Louis (pronounced San Louie).

The road was straight and flat. Unlike the dry heat of Mauritania the air was humid, sticky, and balmy. Cat began to weaken, her pace slowed, and she became shaky and emotional. We decided we'd have to catch a ride. The first guy along was on a motorcycle. I waved and he pulled up. We asked how far to Ross Bethio, he told us, 5 Ks. Cat said, "We can do that, I can make it. We'll just need to get food before we continue."

The motorcyclist said, "Stop at Shell Station for food." We were envisioning a station like those in Spain, but the Shell in Ross Bethio was not air conditioned or clean and they didn't have food. The attendant sent us next door to a squalid hut he called Le Marche. The kid there had two cold Coca Colas. We sat on a dirty step in the shade, savoring the cool beverage. There was a Total Service Station across the street that looked nicer. We pushed across, only to find they had no food, only soft drinks.

It was obvious we couldn't continue riding. Diarrhea and lack of food had left Cat completely depleted. It had taken half an hour to ride the 5Ks into town. I asked about a ride. The guy in the station just shrugged. I pointed to a small pickup truck in the driveway, indicating we put the bikes in it and go to St. Louis. He shrugged and said, "No, no working." We sat in the shade, sipped Coke and discussed our plight. Just as I concluded we were doomed, the station attendant whistled and a taxi pulled into the driveway.

Abdellayah Douf the driver listened, then had me follow him across the street to the Shell Station. A guy there tried to speak English, but the process was futile. I pulled out my pen and note pad and then wrote CFA—St. Louis? They huddled, then Abdellayah wrote 10,000 on the page. I wanted assurance that was the total fare, as it was most of what we had. They huddled again then agreed that it was.

We had a ride into town and enough to pay for it.

Abdellayah loaded our bags in the back seat. He jammed the bikes into the trunk and we were ready to roll. Then he took out his prayer rug and got on his knees in the shade. It was hot, and a flock of kids hovered around us. Prayers finished, he stood at the trunk and spoke with the station manager. Then he took the pad and wrote 5000 CFA for bags. I was pissed-I grabbed the pad and scribbled out the 5000. He was dumbfounded. I acted like I was ready to take the bikes out of the trunk. He caved, and we were off to St. Louis.

The road was full of potholes. He swerved and swayed avoiding the worst of them. The rear seat had long ago given out, and I was sitting on a metal bar under the cushion. My back hurt, but knowing we were going to find money and a place to stay eased the pain. Our Guide Book suggested Hotel de la Poste. Hoping they would take a credit card, we directed Abdellayah there. He balked, said "Too far." Then we were negotiating again. I yelled, "Take us there, we'll work it out." The streets were littered, dusty, and jammed with people. He turned across a bridge and we were there, in front of the hotel.

Cat ran in to make sure they had a room and took credit cards. I stood arguing with Abdellayah. He began to complain about waiting. Cat reappeared, "They have a room, but don't take credit cards. The clerk says there's an ATM just around the corner." I was so happy that after Abdellayah helped get our things into the hotel I gave him three hundred more CFA. He looked at the last remaining bill in my wallet, smiled and said, "Boisson pour moi?" (A drink for me?) What a gutsy guy. I didn't give in yet admired his persistence. He was out of our lives and we were into an air-conditioned room. Life was good.

We savored our first pork (forbidden in Islamic countries) in almost two months, ham and cheese sandwiches. I signed the tab to our room. The bartender said, "Bar separate from hotel." Mr. Fall, the very nice desk clerk said, "It's okay, you pay when you get money." We walked to the ATM. An armed guard at the door wanted to see our credit card. I showed him our American Express and he said, "No." I whipped out our Visa Card and he nodded approval. The Visa Card seemed to want to work but required a three digit pin code? The bank was closed and we had no pin number, so we were lucky to have a hotel with a restaurant.

CAT TRAX Day 64, St Louis. We walked across the bridge to a service station/bank. Inserting our card, we were ecstatic to hear cash come clicking down. Yikes, the exchange rate Euros to CFA was 640 to 1, but only 500 CFA for one dollar. What had happened to the United States' *strong dollar policy*? We whimpered, then split 300,000 CFA between our wallets. It felt like Monopoly money. It took a lot, to get a little. The only good news, 500 to $1.00 made it easy to know what we were spending.

The beach was littered, but beautiful. Goats grazing on trash outnumbered people on the beach. There were lots of fishing boats pulled up on the sand, and fisherwomen were sorting their catch. They'd just come in on pirogues. A gal walking toward us had a pan of fish balanced on her head. She said, "Photo?" I said, "I take your picture?" She held out her hand, "1,000 CFA.

I smiled and we walked on. Another moment lost to the unreality of exchange rates, 1000 CFA was only $2.00 US. I should have offered half, we'd missed a terrific photo for pennies.

Great to have the money problem off our backs. Twice we had been stuck thousands of miles from home and penniless. Cat was a veritable "what if" machine in those types of situations. She had already started counting the days we'd be in Senegal, and figuring whether we'd need funds wired from home, again.

CAT TRAX Day 65, St Louis, Sick Day for Cat! Tough night for Cat. She'd spent most of it in the sand box, if you know what I mean. Even soiled the sheets. There's no worse feeling than losing total control.

We delayed our plan to taxi to Ross Bethio, then cycle back. *Après* breakfast we walked to a doctor's office. The waiting room was full of other sick folks. Not a very healthy place to hang around but Cat needed something to stem the flow. Prescription in hand, we walked to the pharmacy, where she got pills to be taken twice daily and charcoal powder to take before each meal.

This Hotel de la Poste was a special place. The pilots we'd met at Tan Tan Beach had suggested it. St. Louis was the southern terminus of the old mail plane route from Toulouse, France, to St. Louis. We talked with a gal whose grandparents had built the hotel in 1926. The bar had mounted animal heads on the walls. Politically correct back then.

At La Signare restaurant, we met the manager, Jack, a Frenchman and his beautiful African wife, Gilberte. He told us, "La Signare, were the good looking African women who marry rich French men." He smiled and continued, "I no rich, Just one of the lucky ones!"

CAT TRAX Day 66. Ross Bethio, St. Louis 53 Ks. At 7:00 a.m., plagued by queasy stomachs we asked the kitchen to cook rice. Cat had lost a lot of fluid. One of the owners spoke English and was very helpful. She brought the rice and a cup of tea for Cat. Breakfast of only rice, not bad. As for the taxi to Ross Bethio and cycle back we decided we'd play that by ear. If we were feeling stronger we'd give it a shot later. If not, we'd defer until the next day.

The thought of another day in St. Louis had Cat climbing the walls. By 11:00 the walls got the best of her. She wanted to ride. We would travel light, just handlebar bags and a bag of leftover rice. The crowd was thick and curious as we pushed the bikes into the bright sunlight. A pushy guy out front got the point we wanted a taxi to Ross Bethio. He grabbed the first passing cab and talked to the driver.

Turning to me and said, "This is my friend, he drive you, Ross Bethio." I asked the price and he said, "It be 40,000 CFA!" I laughed then told him we'd pay 10,000. He said "No, no, at least 30,000."

I stepped into the street to hail another taxi. The driver yelled, "10,000, okay, *entre*." The hang-around guy had tried to squeeze a few thousand from unsuspecting tourists. We hoped he'd been cut out of the deal. Who needed help like that?

Bikes in the trunk, we set off across the prairie. The only difference we saw in Ross Bethio was a different attendant at the Total Station. The new guy stared in disbelief as we pulled the bikes out of the trunk, adjusted the seats and pedaled out the driveway.

Our ride was fast, thanks to a very brisk tail wind. We stopped in the shade of a tree for a bite of rice. African cattle crossed the road a short distance from us. A dog followed, then the herdsman. When he saw us he stared in disbelief, then disappeared into the bushes behind the cattle. Soon the cattle came crashing through the brush, crossing close to where we were sitting. The dog had them on the run. The herdsman came

to the shoulder of the road ten or twelve feet from us, then squatted and stared. The tail wind wafted his strong odor directly up our noses. It didn't add flavor to our rice. We packed, bid him *adieu* and rolled.

We were back in St. Louis in record time. We went directly to the ATM. Temperamental, it didn't want to give big cash. Cat went inside the bank and a nice guy came out to help. He decided there was a problem in Dakar and went back in to call. When he returned he said, "The machine now out of order, you go to other bank."

The blazing afternoon sun was so hot that I began to fade. The streets were crowded with locals buying and selling. The other bank's machine wouldn't recognize our card. Cat went inside and fell into line. I was burning up, so I leaned the bikes and went inside for air conditioning. She struck pay dirt. The clerk couldn't take our ATM Card but advanced cash on our Visa Card.

Dinner in at our hotel restaurant, the Flamingo. The food was as good as the wine was expensive. We toasted to ourselves and the victory of the day's ride. A six-piece band played soft jazz. Four young people took the stage and began singing African songs. A girl began dancing. She wore western clothing, but her moves were authentic African!

CAT TRAX Day 67, St. Louis to Louga, 77 Ks. We were struck by a feeling of melancholy leaving St. Louis. Almost like leaving a new home away from home. By 4:00 p.m. we rolled into Louga. Signs led us to Hotel Casa Italia. We checked in, then took a seat in the restaurant near a Japanese girl and European guy. Hisako and Alain struck up a conversation. They worked with different NGOs assisting Senegalese schools. Small world-they knew Eric and

Sylvia, the couple that helped us through the border crossing. They suggested we all get together in Dakar.

 A young African guy with a t-shirt that said, "After the Bomb we'll all be EQUAL," led me to the back of the building and said, "We keep bicycle there, I sleeps on the floor there." I didn't like that, so I went back and pressed until the front desk allowed them into our room. Abdellaya the "After the Bomb Guy," helped drag them up the stairs. As we struggled, he said, "I have bicycle but it no work, you fix?" Later, he led me around the building. There, rusted and neglected was his dilapidated old bike. I tried to pump the tires. The old tubes were rotted. I dug out two spare tubes. A lot of sweat, a little cursing and he could actually ride the old clunker. He was extremely happy, which made me happy, too.

CAT TRAX Day 68, 102 Ks, Louga to Tivaouana. Alain joined us at continental breakfast. He assured us it was 125 Ks to Theis, then added, "I'm sure there is a hotel in Tivaouane about 100 Ks." That buoyed Cat's spirit a bit-beside feeling weak and tired, her bike was running poorly. The rear wheel was wobbling, no broken spokes, just out of true. I loosened the rear brake to keep it from dragging and we rode. All we had to do was make it two more days. There were new wheels waiting in Dakar.

More savannah landscape, more of the distinctive-looking Baobab trees, with branches that look like a root system. The locals say a displeased God plucked them from the ground then thrust them back upside down. We loved the look and size of those savanna giants. Baobabs are revered here, thought to have magical powers. They catch rainwater in their leaves and produce a fruit called "Monkey Bread," which locals eat or distill into a slightly alcoholic drink.

Road kill, too, was unique. A large fruit bat lay on its back, eyes open, grinning up at us. Other unfortunates that I dubbed "Bluebirds of Unhappiness" were scattered along the highway. Beautiful feathers in gorgeous shades from pale to royal blue.

At a shade and soft drink stop, several young boys we called the "Tin can Brigade" began to gather around. We'd heard they were orphaned or their families couldn't afford to keep them, so they'd turned them over to the local Imam, who sent them out begging with red coffee cans. All ask for a gift, a sweet, or money. One, with not a hair on his head, had an infectious smile. I took his picture. The others laughed. When I let him see it, the others crowded around, admiring him and the photo. Then

they lined up and asked for a group photo.

By afternoon, the road was thick with traffic and lined with people selling fruits and craft items. Cat was fading fast. We rolled in to Tivaouane at 4:00 p.m. and I asked a group of police for directions to the hotel. They pointed down the road and one said, "Theis, 20 Ks." That was *not* what Cat wanted to hear.

Cat stopped a woman and, in her best French, asked if there was a hotel or guesthouse, or even a private home, where we could stay or erect our tent. The woman listened intently as though she was thinking about the problem. When Cat stopped talking, the woman extended her hand and said, "Cadeau?" She'd missed everything Cat had said but was patient enough to let her finish before asking for a gift.

As we sat discussing our fate, a woman in purple sarong selling fried cakes did her pitch.

I said, "No, *merci*."

She responded, "Chaud? Hot?" She led us around the station to a water faucet. What a treat. She poured cold water over our heads, soaking our shirts.

The other women chided her as I raised the camera, but the woman in purple posed and seemed proud to be asked. One of the women lying on the ground started hollering, probably telling me not to take her picture. I showed the photo to the lady in purple then pressed a 500 CFA note into her hand. She seemed shocked. She told the others about her picture but kept the money to herself. I watched her go into a sort of trance as she sat back down. We hoped she was dreaming of the nice things she could buy with her dollar-500 CFA was a lot of money for her and a well-spent dollar for us.

Robert (pronounced *Ro-bear*) owner of the station, began to understand our dilemma. He took a telephone out of a locked wooden box and called someone, then indicated we should follow. He walked with us to a hotel the police didn't know existed. Robert was a minority there, wearing his religion on his chest in the form of a huge pewter cross.

He introduced us to the girl at the front desk. When we thanked him, he pulled the big cross to the end of the silver chain as if to say it was the Christian thing to do. Regardless of religion, for us he will always be a guardian angel. Another of our "friends in need" friends, indeed.

Hotel Aldjantou was an old colonial-era house. The girl at the desk said, "We all family, my two sista and four brotha. Our aunt and uncle own hotel." Our room had a rickety little AC unit that worked and a stinky shower. The smell of rotten eggs told us it had been used infrequently.

Dinner was Chicken Yassa, a Senegalese dish with sweet and spicy onion gravy and French fries. We salted them down, enjoying the treat after a hot day's ride.

Mosquitoes and bedbugs meant bites and Deet. Despite those inconveniences, we were thankful the hotel was there and we were in it.

CART TRAX Day 69, 94 Ks, Tivaouana to Dakar. The road

into Dakar was total bedlam. Trucks and cars forced us onto the dirt shoulder. All too often one of the crazies swerved around us, passing on our right, leaving us in a cloud of dust.

We found soft drinks, then Cat went searching for food. The kids began to gather as I guarded the bikes and sipped a Coke. When Cat and I had talked about Africa, she pictured natives in loincloths with spears. I was more realistic, guessing most would wear t-shirts and shorts. As the kids stood silently staring I took note of one. He wore a faded, tattered New York Yankees shirt. He was sullen. As the others asked for a gift his eyes looked  hollow, a haunting stare. I wondered what he was thinking, was he angry or curious? When I had a couple of gulps of Coke left, I handed the bottle to him. He continued to stare but passed it off to one of his friends.

There were dozens of colorfully-painted horse-drawn taxis on the street. Bells jingling, they wound their way through the trucks and cars. A merging of the past and present. The roadside was lined with peddler's lean-tos. Traffic thickened and an enormous truck clinging to the edge of the pavement hit my arm. We'd never cycled in more treacherous traffic!

At another stop, we were surrounded by girls selling bananas. Each had a full basket balanced on their heads. They were all persistent and pushy until I raised the camera for a shot. In unison they called out, "No, no photo," and fled, shielding their faces. So, they *did* know the meaning of no.

Rufisque, twenty-five kilometers from Dakar, was a terrible-looking industrial area. The road was crowded, full of honking horns and clouds of dust. At a huge roundabout, we veered left then circled and found ourselves on a divided highway. More space, a wide shoulder and fewer cars. When it became a freeway we pressed onward, despite the blaring horns of passing cars and trucks; we were forced back into surface street traffic at the edge of the city.

A service station attendant drew a map, to help us skirt the maze of one-way streets, but we were soon lost. Standing studying the map, a guy offered to lead us to the Hotel Ganale a place we'd selected from the pages of our guidebook. He flashed his ID card and told us he worked with the police department. He led us to the door of Hotel Ganale, then held out his hand. Damn, doesn't anyone do anything out of the kindness of their hearts? I asked whether he earned money working with the police. He responded, "It is not enough to feed my eight children." I thought about giving him my sermon on "Population Pollution" but gave up and gave him 1000 CFA.

When we asked the desk clerk for a three-day stay he said, "We not have room for trois, have only two day." The price was higher than our book advertised but they did have AC and CNN. After considerable negotiation, he conceded a three-day vacancy. We carried our necessary bags up three flights. A couple of cockroaches heralded our arrival. The shower was a strange hose with a shower head dangling at knee level. However, the water was warm and the room cool.

After dinner, we asked if there was a nearby internet café. Now semi-friendly, the clerk replied, "I can't allow you to walk there in darkness." We got pushy and decided to go anyway. He said, "You wait, I have man, go with you." A burly guy with a 45 pistol in a shoulder holster appeared. He chaperoned us, then stood at parade rest by the door. The street was pretty scary, with people sleeping on the sidewalk. Some held fingerless hands out toward us in the dim light. Dakar was going to be more than just a tough bike ride.

CAT TRAX Day 70, Day of Well-needed Rest in Dakar! After refreshing showers, we walked to a patisserie. On the way, we were overtaken by a guy who asked, "Remember me, I work at the Hotel?" We didn't, but didn't want to be rude. He tagged along, "I take you to good place for coffee." Cat told him we had already chosen a place. He stuck with us for a while then veered off saying, "I see you later."

Patisserie La Gondole was a strange standup bar. They had a wonderful icy manqué juice. Standing at the window proved to be too tough for us. Half a dozen guys sat outside looking at us hungrily. Several had no fingers, most likely from leprosy. Shifting around, we stared at a wall while observing the affluent crowd come and go. This place felt like San Francisco-well-dressed people stepping over the homeless, sick, and lame. As we recall, in SF there was room on the sidewalks to go around the unfortunates. In Dakar there were many more and they appeared to be much poorer.

Exiting, a gangly guy sidled up and said, "Remember me, I met you at the hotel, last night?" That sounded familiar so I asked which hotel. He replied, "The Al Baraka." I smiled and said "You must be mistaken, we're not staying at the Al Baraka." Slightly befuddled, he asked where we were staying, so I fibbed, "with friends," then we walked away. He stood dumbfounded. We had foiled an attempt-we were getting better at handling Dakar deception.

Another guy walked up and said, "I have a gift for you." We objected, telling him we didn't need a gift. He insisted, "My wife has had a baby boy, our firstborn. I must give a gift to a person of different skin color," he said, grasping my arm, pointing out the difference. I told him we weren't buying anything. He handed me a necklace, then helped Cat put one on. Once we had his gift, he turned to me and said, "Do you have a gift, for the baby?" Damn, a slick scam. I told him that we didn't but he continued to insist, "It will be terrible luck, if you don't give something for the baby."

I dug out a US dollar bill telling him it was a special gift. I made a joke that if the baby held onto it a few years, it might be worthless. That went over his head. He wasn't satisfied and asked if we had Senegalese money. I weakened and gave him 1000 CFA. He wasn't happy with that, either. I told him not to look a gift horse in the mouth. That was over his head, too. He mulled it over as we walked away. Not a bad deal, a learning experience for him and two interesting necklaces for us, for only $2.00 US.

At lunch, I began to feel the return of the dreaded African Guff-Guff. I tightened my cheeks and sprinted to the room. *Whoosh* and a new twist: it was blood red. Good news, at the second calling there was no red. Probably caused by that great-tasting bright red manqué juice.

Alain, the guy we'd met in Louga called, inviting us to share dinner at Eric and Sylvie's home the next evening. He, his wife and Hisako would also be there. Wonderful to have friends in far-flung and exotic places.

CAT TRAX Day 71, A Hectic Business Day in Dakar! So far, so good, no more diarrhea and a good night's sleep. We stopped at the internet cafe to send a message to Mr. Moctar, a man Abdallah (our friend Abdallah in Morocco) had urged us to contact. Cat called FedEx, and found that the wheels sent from our bicycle company were being held by Senegalese customs. They wanted to collect what the FedEx guy called, "A big import tax." We were hoping Mr. Moctar, whoever he was, would respond to the e-mail, and come to our rescue.

Avenue Pompidou was crawling with strolling hucksters. Each tried to get their merchandise into our faces. A guy began walking at my left shoulder asking if I was Italian. At the next corner, another guy moved in from my right. He leaned down and touched the leg of my shorts. As he did I felt movement from behind, a third guy had his hand in my pocket. I grabbed his wrist, he tried to wrest away. I twisted his arm behind his back. He yelped, jerked loose and ran.

The incident was over in moments-the adrenalin rush lasted several minutes. A guy standing nearby tried to hand me a 1000 CFA note. I pushed him aside, not knowing what his scam was. Later, I felt terrible. I'd placed three 1000 CFA notes in that pocket for small needs. He was trying to me give one of my own 1000s back. So there were good people, even in the midst of that evil-feeling place.

The US Embassy was typical, lots of concrete barriers on a street blocked to traffic. Once inside the bunker, we walked through the metal detector. They confiscated our camera and Swiss Army knife. The office was full of folks waiting to be seen and heard. One American asked about getting a visa for his Senegalese girlfriend. He told the woman at the window, "We have a baby, I want my mother to see him." The woman behind the glass quipped sarcastically that he should marry his girlfriend. He walked away.

Rita was a great find. Originally from Liberia, she told us that Liberia was a beautiful country before all the war and gruesome crime. She continued, saying "I now call Columbus, Ohio, home." She took our questions and needs to heart. Cat was concerned about the Casamance, the southern Senegalese region. Our book said it had been calm for several years. Rita recommended against travel there, but confessed she'd never been. She gave us contact info for the Embassy Warden. She said, "He's a nice guy, really knows the area." That bolstered Cat's confidence a bit.

Back at the hotel, Alain called to remind us we were having dinner later at their place. He also had the address of a good bike shop. Best news of all, he volunteered to drive us to the airport and help straighten out the "import tax" issue.

Hungry, we walked back down Ave. Pompidou, daring pickpockets to try it again. A guy did grab my hand. As I shook him loose, he got testy, shouting. "This is Senegal, not Iraq-you are my friend." I said, "Thanks, friend," as we ducked into a fast food place, leaving him spluttering.

Citi, our ATM card bank, had a branch on the Place de Independence. We hoped to find a fee-free ATM. No such luck. They were all closed. A guy at the door opened it a crack and said, "You take card to CBAO bank, just down the street."

A skinny-legged young guy sat on the sidewalk near the door of CBAO Bank. He walked on all fours, the thongs on his hands and feet protecting them from the hot concrete. He looked up as we passed and asked, "Can you spare a little help, sir?"

Amazed, I said, "You speak English."

"Yes sir, I'm from Ghana, sir." I had to tell him we didn't have money, we were going to the bank.

Concerned with our problems trying to shift money from home and being caught up in the Patriot Act, the cash we got was all large bills. They allowed only 200,000 CFA, a little over $400 US. Money was going to be a problem. We hated to carry that much, but we'd heard ATMs and banks accepting credit cards would be few and far between in most of Senegal.

Moving back up the street we ran headlong into the skinny-legged guy and his friend. Again he held out a hand and asked. Again I had to say, "Sorry, we only have big bills."

Once again his broadly smiling face shone as he said, "Okay, then, don't forget me next time you're by, sir."

Oh, man, I thought, there won't be a next time. Three steps

beyond, I spun around and pulled Cat back toward the bank. We got change and this time as we approached I had a 500 CFU note in hand. He was very happy and reminded us that his friend needed money, too. Another donation, another huge smile, and they posed for a picture. What had wreaked this havoc upon them? We'd heard it was a dose of bad luck, a bad Polio vaccine. There's little else they could do. Jobs were few, even for those lucky enough to be fully functional.

The sidewalk was littered with poor souls, most just down and out. A woman with three kids was living on a street corner. Cooking on a camp stove while potty-training her youngest. A couple of lepers held out fingerless hands. It all tugged at the heartstrings. So many needy, so little money.

Alain, his wife Martine, and Hisako picked us up and drove to Eric and Sylvia's. Their beautifully furnished home had a guard out front, as did all the houses on the street. What a fantastic evening-an incredible meal with constantly flowing French wine. It was like a night with old friends. As the evening ended, we made promises to meet again in France, Japan, or California. A round of hugs and cheek kisses, then a ride back to Ganale.

CAT TRAX Day 72, Another Business Day in Dakar. Alain drove to the airport through awful traffic. There, a bureaucratic nightmare had us going from building to building, desk to desk. Passed from civilians to military, we finally met the colonel. He listened to Alain tell the story he'd already told a dozen times, then

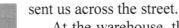

sent us across the street.

At the warehouse, they found our packages and demanded 5000 CFA. We didn't argue over $10. Then, they shuffled us back across the street and reversed the chain of command. Back in the colonel's office, we shook hands. He wished us luck and waived all other fees. A friend indeed, Alain wouldn't even let us buy lunch. He kissed our cheeks, then hurried off to work.

We carried the wheels and rode the bikes to Alain's favorite bike shop. The guys did a great job. They gave the bikes a thorough check up, repaired Cat's broken low-rider rack, then installed the new wheels and tires. All for about $45 US. We were road-worthy again. We cycled back to the hotel, ducking and dodging the crazy traffic. As we rounded the corner near Hotel Ganale, a woman driver hit Cat's back wheel. No damage, but a pretty good scare. When I shook my finger at her, she shook hers back. Pedestrians and cyclists were definitely second-class citizens in Dakar.

CAT TRAX Day 73, More Dakar and Mr. Moctar. The usual swarm of young boys selling things hovered around a couple seated on a high curbstone. One of the boys pressed us for a sale, then said, "They are America, too." I asked and, sure enough, they were African Americans from Detroit. Most of our conversation centered on the aggressive young sellers. She said, "What is it about no they don't understand?" The boys continued pressing until I tried the camera trick. Amazing, they not only knew what no meant they all begin saying, "No photo" and backed away.

Mr. Moctar returned our e-mail with a phone call leaving a message at the hotel. After several attempts I connected. The voice at the other end said, "I will send a car for you, now." We were almost ready to give up when he pulled up. The driver explained, "Sorry so late, bad traffic." The car had air-conditioning, what a treat. Mr. Moctar was Director General of his company Centre of Suivi Ecologique. His firm began as an NGO. He transitioned to private ownership, providing satellite imaging that charted rivers and erosion for the government and farmers. Interestingly, his satellite connection was located in South Dakota, USA.

Mr. Moctar asked, "How can I help you?" I told him we'd like to hire a van or truck to take us out of Dakar, rather than risk cycling on the dangerous roads. He introduced his driver Mr. Mamadou, and said, "He will pick you up in two days, for the drive out of town."

Meanwhile, Base Camp Charlie had warned us we were running out of money. One *big* promise I'd made to Cat was that we would not sell our house. We sat that night, sipped wine and discussed alternatives. It boiled down to stop cycling and go back home or sell the house. Cat took a big sip and said, "Sell the house, we can't stop now!"

With total confidence in his ability and trust in his integrity we signed the listing agreement and Power of Attorney that Charlie had faxed. He had the whole world (of our finances) in his hands. He quickly found a buyer and closed a timely escrow.

At CitiBank we attempted to set up new accounts insured by the FDIC up to $100,000. Our friend Ron who had a banking background informed us that the new "Patriot Act" didn't allow Americans outside the US to open new accounts. With Ron's help Charlie was able to use existing accounts. We felt safe knowing our money was insured!

At dusk, as I returned from the Internet Cafe, a guy called out to me, "Hey Pat, how are you? I recognize you-do you remember me? I meet you in California!" When I looked at him, he invited me into better light. I didn't remember meeting him. He started naming names of people, mutual friends we knew, using only first names like, "Jack, you know Jack, he is married to my sister." I suggested he give me his e-mail address or telephone number since I was late for dinner. He began to stall then finally the hook. He asked, "Pat, please can you help with some money for petrol, my car is out of fuel." I told him I had no money then invited him to stop at the hotel. He thanked me but said, "I must get back to Mother." Then asked "You do remember my dear old mother?" I had almost been had, again! We assumed he had gotten one of our WR2 cards.

CAT TRAX Day 74, Slavery and a Search for Roots. The Ile de Goree, where Senegalese were held before being shipped out as slaves, was a must-see according to several we'd talked with. After a short boat ride to the isle, the old rock fort confirms the sense of evil that once flourished there. The main feature was a hallway that led to the "Door of No Return." Men and women were herded onto boats, shipped to the new world then chained to slave blocks and sold like animals. The dark stone walls of La Maison des Esclaves, the House of Slaves, seemed to ooze sorrow and pain. What fear and uncertainty they must have felt, packed together in those tiny rooms. Did they have a sense of destination-of life continuing thereafter? Were their tears and fears solely based on their current predicament? Were they lamenting being separated forever from their families? Or, perhaps they already knew the life of harsh servitude that lay ahead.

We met Teddy, a doctor from Louisiana, on the boat ride. He told us his group from LSU came to study medical facilities and suggest training programs, but "We were immediately drafted into service at the hospital, and they've kept us busy from sun up to sun  down. Not much time for exploring Dakar but we all feel good helping the overburdened health services."

While at lunch we met Milton, another guy from LSU. He was there assisting in business growth and development. He confided, "I'm also on a personal quest, seeking my roots. My last name is Senegal. I believe my ancestors  departed through the "Door of No Return." Milton agreed, "Most Africans Americans are better off than the families they left behind. However it took generations as slaves and the slow ongoing process of equality to get to where we are today."

My poor forefathers from Ireland came on their own volition looking for opportunity. They had the ability to move around and seek a better life. His were stuck in dead-end wage-less obedience. And though the Irish, like most other immigrants, felt the sting of prejudice, it faded as they blended. There may be some remaining pockets of prejudice toward my ancestors but nothing compared to the bias against people of color.

CAT TRAX Say 75, 20 Ks out of Dakar in truck, 23 Ks to Saly-Portugal. Six days in Dakar, six days at Hotel Granale. It had been a long time since we'd stayed anywhere for that length of time.

Mamadou, pulled up in the Centre de Suivi Ecologique 4WD

pickup at 8:45 a.m.. We lay the bikes in, one atop the other, then filled in around them with bags.

Mr. Moctar was involved with a group building an African nature preserve that included big game animals. Since it was along the way, he insisted we visit. He was hopeful it would bring tourists. We were very happy being in Mamadou's truck rather on the road.

Mr. Moctar had said "Mamadou will stand by and watch your bikes and bags while you tour Bandia Preserve." At the gate Mamadou spoke with the Rangers. Because Mamadou was allowed to drive we saved 35,000 CFA almost $70.00. We were off to visit African animals.

First stop a herd of giraffe. What strange beautiful animals. Gangly, long-necked slow-moving and wearing patchwork coats. Samba, our guide, assured Cat they weren't dangerous. When a couple of them began to fight Samba laughed and said, "They not fight, want to make a baby." Oh, boy, the male was aggressive, ready for *love*! As I shot a photo, Samba chuckled and said, "Paparazzi, if you get good picture, you sell for million dollars." We decided to give them their privacy.

Mamadou wound his way through the ruts and bumps while Samba sat out the window spotting animals. He said, "Most dangerous animal, is buffalo. They charge at moment's notice and are deadly." The buffs pinned their ears back and flared their nostrils as we drove past.

Ousame, a young guy who'd lived in Atlanta, Georgia, took over as guide after lunch. The really big thrill was seeing rhinos. Two of the prehistoric-looking beasts were lying under a tree. We stopped and I shot a pic from the window. Then Ousame said, "Come quietly, Pat." We got out and I followed around toward them. Lying in the bushes, I could only see their heads. I asked if we dared get closer. Ousame smiled, waved his hand to follow, and we moved in a half circle. There they were, lying directly in front of us. Ousame grasped the branch of a tree and bent it until it snapped. The ears of the nearest rhino wiggled. *Snap*, he did it again, and the rhino rose up on its front legs. *Snap*, one last twig, and the beast was standing, looking directly at my lens. Ousame urged me to back slowly away. He didn't have to tell me twice.

At the gate Mamadou quickly helped offload the bikes, shook our hands and left us there in a cloud of dust. We loaded the bikes and rode down the lonesome highway! Saly was two kilometers off the road. The gate guard indicated they had rooms. It was a resort hotel similar to Club Med. Good news, they accepted our Visa card. Nice grounds, French guests, French wine and food. Our room was a spacious cottage.

CAT TRAX Day 77, Long Boat, up the Big River, Ndangane to Foundiougne. Our guidebook suggested we'd pay 25,000 CFA (About $50.00) for a boat trip to Foundiougne. We walked into the village and found Jimmy the boat broker. He quoted a price of 100,000 CFA ($200). We began making alternate plans to cycle back to the crossroads. It would be a two-day ride to Foundiougne. The thought of losing a deal prompted him to cut the price to 75,000. We had decided to ride, if we couldn't make a deal at 50,000. As we turned to go Jimmy conceded. We justified the $100 by figuring the savings from two additional days travel. The trip was mangroves, birds, and other pirogues, through channels and along the shores of islands. The ride was grueling and hot! We were soon overheated and bored. We finally sighted Foundiougne, but it took an hour to get there.

We helped lift the bikes out. Mohamed, our boat pilot, and his helper waded in and carried them ashore. Cat went into the nearby Spaghetti Café. The owner, a guy from Italy, kept saying "Eet ees catastrophic, eet ees catastrophic." We had a tough time understanding, but finally got his point that there was no water in the village. Also there were no hotels in the next village. The spaghetti with mussels was okay. The Italian said, "Ees un place for stay, un hotel and encampment."

We pedaled to L' Indiana Club, the place Alain in Dakar had recommended. Small, simple, and affordable thatched-roof cottages. We moved in, started to shower and found no water, same problem as the cafe. The owner, a relaxed-looking guy with a pony tail, laughed and said, "Plenty water, in swim pool. The Chateau d' Eau (water company) ees broke, no water in town. We can't know when eet will be feex." We took his advice and dove in for a cool, refreshing swim.

Paul, the ponytailed guy, and Martine, his wife, were the

Patrons'. Ex-pats from Switzerland, Paul said, "Thees my secondi life. I hated beesiness, and life in Switzerland. We see ad come to ere, see thees place, and buy." They spent most of their time at the end of the bar, sipping wine and chatting with guests.

CAT TRAX Day 78, African Guff-Guff! CAT TRAX Day 79, 70 Ks, Foundiougne to Toubacouta. Off down the bumpy dirt road and into the next step in this great adventure. Potholes and dust to Passy, the village that had no hotel. Then a sort-of paved road, by Senegal standards. The cars and vans swerved avoiding the divots, often driving on the dirt shoulders. They raised clouds of red dust that covered us and choked the foliage.

The word for the day was "Toubab." Kids called it out as we passed. Being slightly cynical we assumed it meant, "Give me money." It resonated from behind bushes, even from the mouths of some adults.

Cash was running low. Cat read about a hotel twenty Ks ahead in Toubacouta that accepted Visa cards. We had to find it and they had to take the card or we were in trouble. The sign for Hotel Les Paletuviers took us down a dirt lane.

"Watch it," Cat sang out, "Dogs ahead." As we drew closer a couple of the "dogs" loped across the road. Their posture-low in front, high in the rear-and long tails made it clear they were wild monkeys.

Picha, a gal from Belgium managed the hotel. She and her husband Piet had toured on cycles. She was excited to have us there. Piet was napping, she knew he would come find us when he awoke.

Good news, they took Visa cards, bad news they only offered full board. The cost for room dinner and breakfast, $140. We gulped when she told us but had no other choice.

The room was large and almost too cold, but too cold felt *good*. I'd just found the AC controls when we heard a knock on the door. Piet was very excited to meet us. He and Picha had traveled in Central America on bikes. He'd also toured much of Africa. I told him we had a wheel problem. He said, "Tomorrow, we fix it in morning."

Picha said, "Don't worry about the room, we will sponsor you. You buy food, but room will not cost." Amazing, they understood our need to be thrifty and related to our lifestyle. We asked about the "Toubab" thing. He said, "It is not a slam, or meant to embarrass, it just means "white stranger." He offered a word to call back that meant black person. We decided not to go there.

Piet was the epitome of rough-out bicycle touring. "All that is behind me now," he sort of whimpered, "We have two kids, Viktor and Charlotte. I still dream of big bike tour, but for now it is only work, and raise family."

Walking across the open space toward the office we were confronted by a huge lizard, I mean the two feet long kind of huge. As we sidled around it, Piet said, "Yea, that's one of babies, you should see Mama!" I told him about our monkey sighting. He said "We have many family of monkey, also a couple small baboon living nearby."

CAT TRAX Day 80, 45 Ks, Toubacouta to Banjul, Gambia. Piet had a complete mechanical shop to deal with problems from truck to refrigeration repairs. He pulled the wheel apart, greased the bearings and pondered the problem. For some reason, the plastic shifter pulley had slid onto the low gear. Puzzled, he tried to make a washer to place between the two but the idea failed. Giving up, we put the wheel back together. One of the downsides of the auto-shifters.

Piet kept saying, "Forget leaving, you're staying the day here." He was enjoying reliving his cycling days and wanted to hold onto us for as long as he possible. What he didn't know was The Cat and

I were beyond ready to get into The Gambia. Find money, comfort, and satellite TV at a rate closer to our budget.

Cat was loaded and ready to roll. We jammed my bags back on then pushed into the parking lot. Piet took a turn around the hotel driveway on Cat's bike. Picha said, "Oh no, now he'll want to take off, again!"

Piet told a story of cycling across the Algerian Sahara, "I survived 760 Ks, across desert. How I carry water enough? I carry water in Condoms." He roared with laughter then added, "This was true, I swears!"

It was noon by the time we finally pulled ourselves away from Piet and Paletuviers. Although hungry we chose not to eat there. We knew how easily we could fall into the trap of another day. The soft life with Piet and Picha was very tempting.

We found a Cuban Pub/Bar. Mamadou served Cuban style

chicken. He told us his wife, Malvine owned the restaurant, he sells only art. A likable couple, she was Catholic and he, Muslim. I took a picture of them with a Che' Guevara Pub ad and a Catholic poster. The food was tasty, the couple delightful.

On the road, we saw several guys on bikes headed to market, loaded with their catch of fish. Others had boxes filled with a variety of goods on rear racks. Some had drugstore items, one had tools and electrical connections. They were like small mobile stores.

It was a slow ride around potholes that, like landmines, could explode our wheels. Small villages clung to the terrible roadway. The remaining twenty kilometer ride took more than two hours to complete.

Chapter 9, The Gambia

THE GAMBIA, Just a Sliver on the River

The Gambia is a republic surrounded by Senegal. The smallest country on mainland Africa, it lies along both banks of the Gambia River. Slave trade was the reason the Brits occupied the "Sliver by the River," but in 1965, The Gambia gained independence from the United Kingdom. The country's capital is Banjul.

Karang was a little, crowded, dirty village on the border of The Gambia. I went inside the immigration office shack. Surprise, the people were friendly, they didn't ask for money. They just smiled and welcomed us, in English. Nothing like the horror stories we'd heard.

The next challenge was the Gambian military. A young guy in an olive drab t-shirt and beret held his hand up. When we stopped, he looked at my bike as though staring at a naked woman. He reached out and caressed the handlebars. He liked it. That and his AK47 made us nervous. Our bikes weren't expensive, however, their value in The Gambia amounted to six months' wages. Cat faced the military check-in, as I fended off the lusting young soldier. He kept saying "Nice bicycle, expensive?" A lovely sound: The Queen's English with an African accent.

Cat told me when she showed our passports another young soldier fondled the taillight on her helmet. They really liked our equipment. Officially checked in, we moved on. Small villages clung to the terrible roadway. The twenty kilometers to the Gambia River took us two hours.

It was chaos, as a line of trucks and cars waited impatiently for the two ferries plying back and forth across the river. We cycled past the lineup, up to the ticket office. The crowd crushed in as we tried to park. One young guy wearing an Australia t-shirt attached himself to us. "I can help, I can get tickets, I have connections." We doubted his ability, but loved the gutsy approach. Seeing us pull our bikes onto the walkway, a guard bellowed. "You cannot park there, you are blocking the walk!"

"Sir", I replied. "all but very fat people can pass." He became pushy, then one of the other uniformed guys burst out, spewing forth the local language. The only word we recognized was "American." Suddenly, everyone became friendly. One of the uniforms said, "Follow please, I will help with tickets." He took us inside a fenced area, helped us buy tickets, then had us sit in the shade away from the madding crowd.

Fearful we'd miss the 5:00 p.m. ferry, we kept asking. The guard tried to calm us. When the passengers started coming down the ramp from the ferry, we jumped up. Once again, he indicated we should relax. We couldn't! Finally he shook my hand, opened the gate and we pushed upstream into departing passengers. We were the first to board. Cars and trucks were packed aboard. The most unbelievable thing, guys unloading cargo from freight canoes tied up adjacent to the ferry. They put huge bags of rice or boxes of freight on their heads then waded to the dock and set them ashore, high and dry.

Dusk was closing in as the overloaded old tub of a boat pushed off into the swift-moving river. It drifted downstream then powered back up to the dock at Banjul. During the ride we befriended a young boy wearing a t-shirt that said, "Success Comes Through Hard Work." As I talked with him, three young Senegalese toughs squeezed in between us. One said something to him and he clammed up. I turned to the little tough but he hid behind his French language. As  we sat, I felt his hand moving into my pocket. I grabbed it and twisted his arm. He complained as I put my hand in his pocket and threatened to take his wallet. He was pissed, but didn't let it show, and kept a distance for the rest of the crossing.

We found a service station where a fellow was filling gas into barrels on a donkey cart. We asked for a hotel, he just pointed ahead. At a huge gate towering above the street a guard shouted. We were trying to get around a chain blocking the way. He yelled, "Only President Yahya Jammeh, is allowed to  cross there." Don't you love that name, Yahya? It had us singing, "Sittin' in my Lala waitin' for my Yahya, unhuh, unhuh!" the old song from the sixties.

The guard directed us down the street, around the corner, and through the gate of the hotel. Nice guy, yes he wanted a tip, sorry we had no money. We could tell by the look on his face as we shook his hand that he hadn't believed us.

Being off the dark, dirty streets was a relief, but the Atlantic Hotel was a bonus. It was a tourist haven for sun-seeking Brits and we needed a haven. They accepted Visa, so we knew we'd be there until we found enough money to move on.

We went directly to the restaurant. They shooed us out, no shorts allowed. The waiter said, "You may be served on the patio, they have pizza and ice cream." Pizza sounded great. The haughty waiter there said, "You have come too late, we are now closed, the oven is off." We complained, the waiter ignored. I got vocal, and as he argued, Chef Henri waded in scolding the waiter. He arranged a truly enjoyable meal. The joy interrupted only by the relentless bites of mosquitoes on our bare legs. "Aren't you glad, we're taking the Chloriquine," Cat chided.

CAT TRAX Day 81 and 82, R & R in Banjul. Our objective: get to a bank, free up cash, pay up, and move on. At the gate, we walked through a cluster of guys in yellow t-shirts wearing official-looking plastic badges. One attached himself to us and said, "You must have a guide, it is Ramadan, too dangerous out there."

"I thought Ramadan was a religious holiday, why would it be dangerous for us?" I asked.

"Oh, those boys out there, they'll be in your face, they'll try to sell you shirts and things," he responded in a somber British/African accent.

When I told him we'd walked Ave. Pompidou in Dakar, he said, "You will probably be okay out there, then." He shrugged and went back to trolling for more naive foreigners.

Standard Chartered was the only bank with an ATM that also accepted Visa cards. The machine wasn't user-friendly. After a couple of tries, we went inside and waited in a long, slow-moving line. Impatience set in. Cat went to a window without a line and ask who we should be talking with. The friendly gal told her we could use the machine. After hearing we'd already failed there, she said, "The machine isn't working, you should go to our other branch. It's in a nearby city, fifteen kilometers from here." We asked her to call and confirm their machine was working.

When her call went through, she acted surprised to hear that their ATM was out of service, too. We asked her to advance us cash on our Visa card. She hemmed and hawed, then confessed, "We have discontinued our relationship with Visa, due to lack of use by locals. However, the other bank in town might accept Visa." She pointed us in the right direction. The other bank not only didn't accept Visa, but indicated they probably never would. It was beginning to look like we'd be calling Base Camp Charlie for funds via Western Union.

Since the Hotel Atlantic accepted Visa, we decided to ask for a cash advance. There we were, stuck in a hotel again, living off our credit card, unable to eat or drink anywhere else. It wasn't all that bad, in fact the Atlantic was a marvelous place to be marooned, if you must be marooned.

Mrs. Job, the hotel accountant, said she'd have to get the general manager's approval to advance cash. Assuming the best, we asked for a $200 dollar advance, half in local Dalasi currency half in CFA. She said, "We only use Dalasi, you'd have to exchange that at the bank." An indication she'd be able to do a deal? Within an hour she called our room, they would help.

Quite a few women around the pool sunbathed topless. We didn't hear French spoken so assumed the usually staid Brits were letting it all hang out. Their pasty pallor was a hint they were Brits. Some looked as though their boobs had never seen the sun. Others looked as though they'd look better discreetly covered.

Each time we walked out the front gate, Bindo, a security guard, cheered, clapped, and chanted "Pat and Cat, Pat and Cat." Perhaps he was inspired by our crazy bike ride or, more likely, going for a tip.

We wore long pants to the buffet dinner to conform—and to ward off the skeeters. A dance show offered after-dinner entertainment. The dancers were from Guinea and their drums sounded great. They invited audience members to dance with them. Of course, Cat accepted the challenge and shook it like an African. The audience cheered. We enjoyed the show and after the finale the group invited us backstage, then hit us up for money. We might have given a tip but were concerned about getting to Senegal's Casamance with what little money we had.

CAT TRAX Day 83, 45 Ks, Banjul to Bikama. Damn, a flat tire-our first since Morocco. A long, thin nail had penetrated the Kevlar belted tire and thorn-proof tube. *God, how I hate to fix flats.* It was after 11:00 a.m. by the time I had it patched and back together.

Our benefactor, Mrs. Job, had the desk clerk check for hotels in Bikama. One option was Motel Dormor Dima. She thought it wasn't very nice. The desk clerk agreed. He called and spoke with someone then said, "Go to West African Mission, ask for Mr. Lee, there is hotel close by."

We pushed over to the nearby Shell station to air the tires. A tall bushy-haired guy walked along with us, trying the old line, "Remember me, we met at the encampment?" I wasn't in a great mood so I waved him off, telling him he was wrong, we'd never been to the encampment. He said, "It was a guy that looked just like you." I began not liking him.

At the Shell they didn't have or wouldn't provide air. The irritating guy I'd begun calling Mr. Bushy Hair said, "Come to my shop, just across the street." Another lie: guys like him always tell you they own the shop, lead you there, and expect money from the owner.

We tried to shake him, but he stuck with us as we crossed to a tire shop. The guy there was fixing a truck tire but stopped and pumped ours. Then Bushy Hair said, "You pay him for the air, 150 Dalasi." I got in his face and said, "That's Bullshit, I could buy a new tube for 150 Dalasi." I took out 25 Ds then knelt down and put it in the mechanic's pocket. He was Senegalese and spoke only French. When I stood back up, I told Mr. Bushy Hair I wasn't paying him anything and I thought he was a bad guy. Several others had gathered round and watched. One older guy in a robe gave us a smile and thumbs up. A young guy said, "You don't give him money, good." Mr. Bushy Hair just stood and stared as we mounted up and rode away. It doesn't pay to mess with me after I've fixed a flat tire.

The road was wide, the surface good. We crossed a bridge and came to a police checkpoint. The policeman acted as though he was drunk. He insisted we come to his station, about 100 meters through soft dirt. There, he said, "It is Ramadan, there are many dangers for you." We told him we weren't afraid and that people were good people. Then he asked for money. Damn, everyone there was on the take!

The crossroad was confusing, we chose the Beach Route. The smell of rotting flesh singed our nostrils. The sound of competing vultures filled the air as they fought over a carcass. Bikama was a teeming town, a cross-section of humanity, trucks, and cars. We pulled into the Shell station for directions. The attendant asked, "Why you people always ask me this questions?" I told him it was because he was the Shell Man and he knew everything. He smiled and said, "Go to the next left turn, then out the highway for one kilometer, there you will see the Mission, on the right." Then he said, "You should make donation for the Children's Community Garden." We gave 50 Ds, about $1.60. He confirmed, "Ask for Mr. Lee."

A group of kids surrounded us. One said, "Mr. Lee's wife is beautiful," A boy speaking very good English said, "I need money, fifty Dalasi to buy shoes for school." Cat pointed to his feet and said, "You have shoes."

"They won't let me wear these sandals and I want to go to school," he replied.

Kids swarmed us as we rode. We cranked up to lose them. A teenage boy on a bicycle caught us and tried to talk. Wary, we shunned him, until he held out our bottle of chain lube and one of our wrenches. The little beggars had unzipped my under-seat bag, taking everything. We turned around and followed him back. In the dusty street, an older boy held one of the kids by his arm. He hit the little boy and gave us more of our missing tools.

The Mission guard said, "Pastor Lee has been gone for four years." Guess the folks around there didn't keep up with the comings and goings at the Mission. The not-so-new Pastor Kim was away, but would return later. We sat for an hour, then decided to ride back into town and find Motel Domor Dima.

The motel was very basic but Cat said, "It'll be okay for one night." The room was too tiny to handle the bikes. The motel staff wanted us to leave them in front of the restaurant and promised they'd move them in when they closed in the wee small hours (due to Ramadan). Not a good option. We headed back to the Western African Mission.

Lamm, the boy who wanted new shoes followed us around like a puppy dog. His t-shirt said 'Children Against AIDS'. He was bright and knew a lot about the area. I enjoyed his company. "I am only son of my mother," he said with pride. "But my father, he haves three wife, and 11 childrens." We were sure he lived in extreme poverty.

Using the Mission phone, my call to Pastor Kim surprised him. He said, "I return to Mission in one hour." We sat talking to the shoeless boy and two of his friends. One was proud to tell us he was the only son of his mother, too. Then he said. "My father have die, but had two wives and the other wife have seven sons." Two more examples of population pollution!

Pastor Kim and his wife were gracious, they invited us to eat Gambian food with their group. Fearing diarrhea, we politely declined. They showed us to one of several bedrooms in what they called their guesthouse.

Cat cooked on their stove while Mrs. Kim told her about their life. "I no happy with this assignment. Life very difficult, health dangerous for our children. We been robbed when first came, house broken open, many of personal things taken. Church get guard for protect."

CAT TRAX Day 84, 112 Ks, Bikama to Bignona. Damn, another flat tire. Yesterday's nasty nail had punched a second slow leak in the "impenetrable" tube. I made a fast fix-my skills were improving.

We got a picture of the Kims and staff then were out the gate and down the road. Lamm, the boy who'd asked for money to buy shoes began trotting along with us. I stopped and told Cat I had to give him the 50 Dalasi about $1.65. I was remembering a time in 3rd grade when my Mom came to parents day at school, and when the other moms bought their kids a hot dog and coke for a dime, my Mom said, "I can't buy them, I don't have a dime."

Maybe Lamm was scamming us but I'd been there, I knew the feeling. As I put the bill in his hand, he stared in disbelief. I shook his hand, then helped him stuff it into his pocket before one of the bigger kids could take it away. We'll never know whether he got his shoes, but I'll never forget the feeling I had and the lump in my throat as I looked back at him in my mirror.

Potholes began outnumbering the patches of asphalt in the road. A huge old truck tailed us, then, in a powerful spurt, moved past. It spewed black smoke each time the driver accelerated. The road was so bad, he couldn't pull away from us, so we were trapped in his exhaust and choked by the dust. We pulled our shirts up over our mouths. The roadside tropical scenery was beautiful except the first twenty feet, that was covered in red dust.

The military checkpoint on the Gambian border was a rope barrier with rags tied to it. The uniformed guards were seated on the porch of the outpost shack. The guy pulling on the rope relaxed it as they waved us through. This time, Cat would stay with the bikes. I took our passports and faced the system. Inside, a short crass guy looked at our passports then got in my face. He asked, "Have you read this?" I looked at the visa page and told him I had.

"You must stay for thirty days," he snarled.

"Oh, no, look, it says we may leave anytime during thirty days."

"Yes, but you cannot come back," he said, as though it was a penalty.

"That is not a problem," I answered, "We don't want to come back."

He faded, his fishing expedition for a little money had failed. A small win but one that felt good. He flaunted his authority, insisting he personally stamp my passport. The other soldiers all enjoyed the scene. Some smiled and nodded as he stamped and signed.

"Who is that woman?" he asked in a friendlier tone.

I told him Cat was my wife and he said, "You bring her here!"

"I will go watch our bikes, she'll come in," I said confidently— getting a little cocky, but why not? He was a sweetheart with Cat, in minutes we were ready to get out of The Gambia into Senegal's Casamance, and onto another adventure.

As we started to mount up, a guy came out asking if we wanted to change money. I thought it was a good idea, but Cat wanted to hold out for a bank. I traded my Dalasi for CFA at a rate of 27.50 to 1. Cat felt we should have gotten 30. I feared we might be left with a pocket full of souvenirs if we didn't get rid of the Gambian money then and there.

Between The Gambia and Senegal's Casamance lay a 2 K strip called The Frontier, a "No Man's Land." Funny, there were houses, farms, and people living daily lives in that "No Man's Land?"

Chapter 10 Senegal, the Casamance

The largest city in the Casamance is Ziguinchor. The Casamance was subject to both French and Portuguese colonial rule before a border was negotiated in 1888 between the French colony of Senegal and Guinea Bissau to the south.

Leaving The Gambia, the guard on the Senegalese side looked

at our passports and waved us through without question or fanfare. The road upgraded from terrible to great as we crossed the border. A military vehicle passed, brimming with heavily armed soldiers. They stared at us as though we were aliens. We hoped they were the good guys.

Diouloulou was little more than a crossroads. Spotting a Teleboutique, we decided to call Dennis the area Warden that Rita at US Embassy had introduced us to. He suggested we stop and say hello to the people at the Catholic Mission. He was a very open friendly-sounding guy.

The Mission was just two one-story buildings. Father Jean Bernard greeted us and insisted we join the others on the back patio. Dennis had said, "They'll offer you a beer." Their offer was a shot of rum. They laughed and joked, saying Father Jean Bernard was called J. B. like the whiskey. We ruled out rum but accepted Coca-Cola. We spent an enjoyable hour talking, listening, and enjoying a respite from the hot sun.

The next twenty Ks was flat, fast, and hot, we were ready to get off the seats. Bignona was another crossroads. The Hotel le Palmier was an forlorn-looking old building. Desiree, the manager, sat out front reading his mail. Desiree was also the bartender. Cold beers never tasted better.

Desiree informed us. "We only cook if we know in advance,

that a guest wants food." Luckily they had pots and pans and allowed us to cook. Jessica, a cute teenager working there, spoke great English. She helped fan the fire and cook our dinner. Squatting next to the cook stove, fanning the flame she was a living picture of ancient Africa. The spell was broken by a familiar sound. She said, "Excuse me, my boyfriend is calling my cell phone. He's at the internet cafe." Wow, a collision of cultures and eras giving way to today's youth.

The ceiling fan was covered with clusters of black bugs. Turning the fan on dislodged them and they flew down on us. I felt one hit the back of my neck and fall inside my t-shirt. I tried to catch it but gave up. Then came a burning pain in my groin area that made me jump and dig for the culprit. I dug him out, but too late, the damage had been done-I'd been bitten in a most sensitive spot.

CAT TRAX Day 85, 30 Ks, Bignona to Ziguinchor. The British influence of The Gambia gave way to French in the Casamance. While talking on the phone with Dennis, Cat brought up the issue of a recent rebellion among locals. That thought had increased her fear of being kidnapped. Our new benefactor Warden Dennis said, "Stay on the main road, you'll have no problems!"

We stopped to watch a guy roadside tinkering with bikes and selling parts. He suddenly pointed to our camera and asked, "Take photo?" I took his picture, then when he and a younger man seated nearby saw it on the camera the boy insisted on a photo with me. Knowing that we couldn't give them a copy didn't seem to matter. We think they just wanted to be remembered, perhaps their idea of immortality.

The ride to Ziguinchor was tropical, the scenery inspiring. The Casamance River was wide, with large cargo passenger boats and pirogues plying her waters. An oversized roundabout held signs pointing to Centre Ville.

Hotel Flamboyant was as unique as the name sounded. A three-story building with a pool that took up most of the front courtyard. Not pretentious, it was named for the Flamboyant tree found on the grounds. We called Warden Dennis to let him know we'd arrived. He insisted on coming right over and taking us to lunch.

Cat spotted the Guinea-Bissau Consulate across the street and decided to check on a visa as we waited for Dennis. Good thing she did, the guy was preparing to close for four days for Ramadan. She rushed back, we gathered up money and passports. When Warden Dennis drove up, I saw him and called out. He joined us at the Consulate and helped us with language difficulties. Within minutes we had our visas to ride through Guinea-Bissau.

Still in our stinking cycling clothes we jumped into Dennis' SUV. For lunch, he chose Hotel Kadiandoumagne. Dennis knew everybody, passers by all stopped at the table to say hello.

CAT TRAX Day 86, Day off in Zig. Surprise, Patrick, the young guy from Germany we'd met at L'Auberge Anacardiers in Ndangane was there. Dennis came in and we did the intros. He extended an invitation for Patrick to join us on a tour of Zig. Dennis was a volunteer with the Catholic Church. He pulled into a small village and introduced us to two priests, Fr. Nestor and Fr. Charles. We chatted as best as language allowed. Dennis was not only fluent in French, but as Patrick put it, "He speaks French with the same accent as local Casamance people."

We visited a farm house in the jungle and met the mother of a young priest stationed in South America. Dennis had received a letter from him and wanted to let her know he was okay. The area was thick with trees. Dennis said, "They call the forest a warehouse because it stores so many usable things.

They brew a tea of sorts from the leaves. Oil of the palms is fermented into palm wine and the fronds are used to make fences and roofs."

As we bumped along a dirt road on the way back, we encountered a line of women returning to the village after a day of harvesting. They had baskets full of rice on their heads. Gathering was women's work, the men do the heavy lifting-turning the soil with their unique shovels called *kadiandoumagne* (the name of the hotel where we had lunch). It was as if Dennis had transported us back to a simpler Africa!

He said, "I have helped set up a shop where locals work carpentry and wrought iron. My first project was the re-building of an old mission. It had been used as a hotel was run down and they were going to close it. We saved it! I think I'll spend the rest of my days volunteering."

CAT TRAX Day 87, Another day in Zig with the Barber of Zig. "As in the world, we have here both groups of Muslims, Sunni and Shia." explained Dennis."They're sort of like the Baptists and the Pentecostals, if one says the moon is white the other feels compelled to say it is blue. At any rate the town gets two different holidays out of the deal."

I'd wanted a short haircut like Dennis wore. I asked about his barber and he said, "I cut hair. If you like it, I'll give you my famous Dennis Short Cut." We laughed and I began calling him "The Barber of Zig."

It was not quite a shave, he set the shears at about an eighth of an inch. I told him "When I was a kid we kicked off our shoes and got 'Baldy' cuts on the first day of summer vacation every year."

He laughed and said, "My brothers and I did the same thing in Iowa." I felt the electric shears cut a swath down the middle of my head, too late to turn back. The look would take some getting used to, but I did like the idea of low-maintenance.

Cat asked Dennis how he ended up in Ziguinchor. "Funny story," he said. "Out of college I took a summer job, but was completely bored. I saw an ad for US AID and applied. I was hired, trained and my first assignment was right here, in Ziguinchor. I spent a year learning the ropes then was transferred out. My career lasted twenty-nine years and I was posted in all corners of the world. When I retired, my brother convinced me to come home to Iowa. He even found a job for me at the plant where he'd worked all those years. I didn't last very long-like any first love, I couldn't get Zig out of my mind. I told my family goodbye, bought a ticket, and here I am."

That night we began to ponder our own fate after this four-year journey. How would we adjust to normal life. What is "normal life"? Would we miss the road? Would we be able to simply live, work, and enjoy our family again?

Cat Trax   Day 88, 25 Ks, Ziguinchor to Sao Domingo. Thanksgiving Day, and we had a lot to be thankful for. Most of all our health and the health of all our family. We had been living on the outer edge for more than a year and a half. We'd faced lots of difficulties, some fearful moments, and survived without serious illness or injury. We'd also met some wonderful people and stored up lots of memories.

A short way out of Zig, my bike began to wobble. Damn, another flat tire. We fixed it and then made a quick stop at the Shell station for a blast of air, taking the tire up to 4 BAR, 60 pounds. It was 3:30 p.m. by the time we got back to the main highway. Our plan was to cycle twenty-five Ks and stay in Sao Domingo, then take the daily boat to Cacheu. It was all iffy, as no one seemed to know whether the boat still ran, or, if it did, whether they'd allow bikes on board.

Leaving Senegal was fairly simple. A guy in fatigues standing under a tree motioned us over. When we pulled up, he pointed toward a second guy seated under the tree. That guy took our passports leafed through the pages then asked, "Where is your Customs Declaration?" Oh, boy, we figured here it comes. He continued to demand a form we didn't have. Our defense was ignorance, we kept telling him we only spoke English. He became annoyed and seemed to be stalling, trying to figure out how to communicate. Frustrated, he waved us on into another No Man's Land. Whew!

Chapter 11 Guinea Bissau

The Republic of Guinea-Bissau, once part of the kingdom of Gabu, existed until it was colonized as Portuguese Guinea. The Bissauans declared independence in 1973. The following year, the name of its capital, Bissau, was added to the country's name to prevent confusion with Guinea (formerly French Guinea). Guinea-Bissau has had a history of political instability since independence. At the time we were there no elected president had successfully served a full term.

We'd heard so many horror stories about the border guards of Guinea-Bissau that we were a bit fearful. As we pulled up to the rope with dangling rags the control guy dropped it and the soldier motioned us over. Continuing our plan of feigning ignorance, Cat went inside with our passports. She was back in just a few minutes. They had stamped our passports without question or request for money. The guys outside were very friendly, asking as best they could about our trip. We were pleasantly surprised, all our paranoia was for naught!

The road condition improved and we sailed into Sao Domingo by 5:30 p.m. Then more frustration, trying to find Hotel Constantine. Bissauan's spoke a combination of languages, Criollo and Portuguese. A well-dressed guy said in broken English, "You go around corner, down dirt road." There were no signs and nothing that looked like a hotel. Back to the asphalt and to the crowded street market. Another ask, another direction back to the same dirt road. A guy on the corner holding a cardboard box called me over. Hoping he had information, I stopped. He lifted the flap on the box exposing a huge centipede. When I told Cat she expressed joy in not having seen it.

Back on the dirt road, a fellow pointed to a house. No sign, but when I walked into the hallway the numbers on the doors were a giveaway. We'd found Hotel Constantino, the only game in town. The price, 5000  CFA ($10.00), so we signed in for the night.

Joao Constantino, the proprietor, looked like he might be in his sixties but how could we tell? Men's' life spans in Guinea Bissau were the shortest in West Africa. His office and the place he held court was a metal table on the back patio. The toilet in the hallway was basic. Joao pointed at two fifty-gallon barrels full of what looked like clean water and said, "For bath."

Joao led us to our room. Cat saw a huge spider on the wall. Joao took a small broom, smacked it then slid the broom down the wall. He furled his brow searching the floor. Cat said, "Where did it go? I think he missed it." Her confidence was sinking. Spiders are one of her worst fears. The screens on the windows had holes large enough for the big spider or any flying bug to get through. We decided to wait until dark and set the tent as a mosquito net.

 The hotel had five rooms, no other guests and the family lived in the rear. Taking advantage of the water barrels-we stripped and washed each other's backs. The cool water felt heavenly as it rinsed off the day's road dust and sweat.

With no restaurants in town, it was another "cook in" evening. Joao set up a typical charcoal barbecue. Cat prepared our on-board soup and pasta. We cagily poured a bottle of wine into our water bottles. As the pasta boiled, a party next door began to pulsate. Joao told us they were celebrating the end of Ramadan. So we would have entertainment with our meal. As darkness set in a young boy began to gyrate on the other end of the patio. Five young girls soon joined him though they paid him no attention. They all looked about twelve. Some of the girls had the moves down pretty well. They even taught each other how to slow dance, as the boy watched and gyrated alone. Dinner, music, and a floor show.

The music continued to throb as a noisy crowd milled about in the street. We likened it to a reverse Mardi Gras. Instead of jamming sin and gluttony into the day before Ash Wednesday they were living it up after a month of deprivation.

We took the mattresses off the two beds, placed them on the floor, and set our tent on them. It was so hot inside the tent that we worried about heat stroke. Crawling out, we sat on the bedsprings near the window. The air hung hot and thick, not a whisper of a breeze. After several real or imagined bug bites we slipped back into the sauna tent. We lay there sweating, worrying about spiders, and wishing the rowdy revelers would tire and go home. We were doomed to a fitful night of sleep.

CAT TRAX Day 89, 20 Ks by Kanoa, 4 Ks via Bicycle, Sao Domingo to Cacheu. For breakfast Joao boiled coffee water. Cat found bread and butter at a nearby store, so we had continental breakfast on the porch. The consensus between Joao, his brother and friends was the boat downriver to Cacheu

would leave at 12:00 noon. At the store, the clerk had told Cat it would go at about 2:00 p.m. on the tide. George, a Greek guy trying to develop a shrimp business, was positive it wouldn't depart until 3:30 or 4:00.

The owner of the small store was from Portugal and spoke English. He said, "I not sure what time boat will go, they must come to me, buy fuel, before." After a few minutes, he told us, "I go home now, I tell me clerk, help you, when arrives boat."

The boat tied up at the dock. Arriving passengers walked up the dirt path. We were preparing to go when the clerk called out, "No get excite, one hour before leave." At 2:30 we pushed down the littered sandy path to the ramshackled dock. There was no shade, and the sun bore down with a vengeance. A bunch of local kids were swimming and diving off the rickety dock. The cool water looked inviting. Our guidebook warned us to avoid swimming, no matter how alluring. There were bacteria and viruses that could cause severe sickness. Sweat trickling down our backs, we heeded the advice.

I handed the heavy bikes down to the deck hands. They lowered them into the hull and we crawled aboard. A young guy pulled up on a moped and they lifted it aboard too. At last at 3:30 we were underway down the Cacheu River. The sun was unbearable. The small shaded area on board had filled quickly with prudent locals. The river, part of the Parque Natural Dos Tarrafes Rio Cacheu, was vast and lined with mangroves, shrubs that grow in the water. The hippos and crocodiles we'd hoped to see remained hidden. Just a few large birds were the extent of visible wildlife.

Getting ashore was a chore. I had to climb into the hull and lift out the bikes. None of the crew offered to help. When I finally muscled my bike up, a young guy stepped forward and pulled it onto the bulkhead. He did the same with Cat's bike. Once ashore, I expected him to hold out his hand. Instead he spun around, waved and trotted off down the pathway.

We'd been required to buy four tickets, two for the bikes. As they hoisted the young man's moped ashore, an argument broke out. The crew grabbed his handlebars, demanding money for a second ticket. He resisted, so they started to confiscate the motorbike. He squealed, but paid.

Stymied at a crossroad, Moped Boy stopped and offered advice as we looked at our map. He'd seemed sort of confrontational on the boat and his motorbike had an Osama Bin Laden sticker on the fender. Now he seemed anxious to help. Lesson learned: never judge a person by their bumper sticker.

Moped Boy told us we'd find the Parque across from the radio tower, but it had no hotel. Our guidebook said they rented bungalows. He and the book were both correct. Numo, the Head Ranger greeted us then showed us one of the bungalows. Surprise: a thatch-roofed three-room cottage with full bath and shower. We had running water but, alas, it was cold.

We needed food. Numo offered a ride to the store on his motorcycle. Pretty funny, he had me don an old jet pilot's helmet and off we went on Mr. Numo's wild ride.

The store was just a little shed but they had cold beers, bread, soft drinks, and canned milk. Another real find was a powdered mango drink. I wanted bananas, Numo drove down the street to a girl with a full basket. I felt they were related. He took four bananas and spoke with her then said, "You no pay!" I didn't feel good about that so I gave her a handful of change.

Back at the bungalow, Cat was organizing. Numo fired up the generator and we had power. He showed us how to turn on a couple of solar lights. Our showers were cold and brief but it felt good to be clean and the cool wasn't all bad after our day in the sun.

Numo lit a fire in his barbeque. Cat cooked pasta again. Watching Cat's progress Numo said, "I likes my job, but they no pays much. Also, no funds for running of park." We took the pasta to our bungalow and dined by candlelight.

CAT TRAX Day 90, 100 Ks, Cacheu to Bissau. We rode through several tunnels of trees, their branches intertwined with those on the other side of the road. We learned the ten-foot-tall mud towers along the road that looked like drip castles we used to make on the beach, were termite mounds. They appear in places where trees have been cut, perhaps thriving on the rotting roots.

In order to straighten Cat's wobbly rear wheel, I propped her bike against mine. As I lifted hers, they both fell on me. The bikes were undamaged, but Albere's cheap sunglasses were a total loss.

On a downhill run through a small village, we saw a boy holding a monkey by the neck. It was dead, gutted and ready to eat. He held it out toward passing cars hoping for a buyer. The poor monkey's haunting eyes stared at us. They seemed to ask, "What happened? Why am I swinging from this boy's hand instead of a branch?"

Entering Bissau, we passed a rusting Russian tank. The street, teeming with pedestrians and cars, was lined with little booths offering lots or little of nothing. A guy decked out in cool clothes and sunglasses called out in English, "Where are you going?" I stopped to ask directions to the hotel. He pointed to a rundown-looking building. Then, I had a tough time getting away from him. I gave him our card and said goodbye leaving him in mid-sentence. He kept yelling, "Pat, come back, I have something to show you, please, come back!"

The shabby look of the hotel extended into the lobby. Cat went in to check availability and price. She returned with the price: $89 US per night. It was too late to go shopping for a room, so I pushed the bikes inside as Cat checked out rooms. Looking from room to room she found some problem with each. The clerk finally threw up his hands, gave in, and gave us a suite.

CAT TRAX Day 91 and 92, Days Off in Bissau. Hotel Bissau, formerly the Sheraton, was three Ks from downtown Bissau. We took a taxi in, the city looked like a war zone with potholes in the streets large enough to be shell holes. A shopping trip to the supermarket was disappointing, no meat or cheese. We did find essentials like water, wine, mango juice, and cookies. Outside, a young man with leprosy held his fingerless hand out, begging. You'd think we'd be used to the sight. Teddy, the doctor we'd met on Goree Island said the victim's fingers and toes get numb, then painful as they shrivel. There are drugs that slow or stop progression, but no one in that impoverished place could afford them. That boy clearly hadn't been treated, his fingers were small and twisted.

The Guinea Conakry Embassy was a drab little building, the office dark and dingy. The clerk motioned us into his office then worked on another person's visa while we sat. Suddenly, he rose and left, without a word. As we waited, Cat looked out the window and saw him working on a car. I tapped on the window. He came back and said, "These visa cost 30,000 CFA, for each." Cat told him our guidebook said they would cost 20,000. He sort of clucked then said something curt in a native language and again left the room.

When he returned, he was friendlier. He accepted 20,000 for each and said, "Visas, be ready noon today."

Searching for the tourist office we came across a UNCHR (United Nations Commission on Human Rights) truck like those we'd seen in Ziguinchor. What a pleasant surprised, Lucien, a man we'd met in Zig, stepped through the door. He was amazed to see us. We told him about our idea to find a boat across the Gabu River and down coast to Kamsar in Guinea Conakry. It would save us 300 Ks cycling up, then around the river. Lucien listened then asked his co-worker Alisau to help. He pulled down a map on the wall but it wasn't helpful.

UNCHR's mission was attending to the needs of the thousands of refugees from Sierra Leone who'd fled to Bissau. Abrahim was one of them. He said, "I flee when my parents are killed. I live here, Bissau, now eight years." He added, "Sierra Leone is so beautiful, you must cycle  there." When we asked why he hadn't returned, he said, "Oh no, they would kill me!" That helped confirm our decision to take a flight over Sierra Leone.

Godfrey, the Director of Planning for UNCHR said, "Most of the boat lines indicated on our maps are no longer available. Also, cycling could be unsafe as there has been recent unrest on that highway. You might take the boat to Bolama Island, then find another boat to go around the peninsula. You will find several Americans live on the island."

We walked to the Mavegro Market, a disappointment of empty shelves, and grabbed a clunky taxi back to the hotel. The power in our room went out about 5:00 p.m. We sat in the dim light, enjoying sipping wine and discussing a plan, but without AC, it soon became hot and sticky. Cat noticed that the fan in the bathroom continued to run. She looked into the hallway and found the lights were shining brightly. I flipped the main switch and lo, we had lights and air.

We ran into Chase, a young guy we'd met in Ziguinchor. He joined us at dinner and said, "I was successful getting funds through

Western Union." He added that his trip on the ferry to Bolama, "Was on a slow rusty old tub I dubbed the Death Boat." That made Cat shudder.

Maria, originally from Hungary, was manager of food service for the hotel. She and her husband Attila joined us. They'd been in Africa fifteen years. They were tired of the hardships and were planning to move back to Hungary. Attila was frustrated by things that didn't work. He'd been chief engineer for the hotel but had given up. Management wouldn't budget for proper maintenance. We met a French guy working with the World Bank and the Guinean Ministry of Finance. Cat was shocked to hear he'd been living in the hotel for six months. She asked why he didn't get a house. He said, "Simple, they have constant edible food here, constant power and water, and good security." Cat conceded Hotel Bissau was undoubtedly our best choice, we wouldn't move.

Chapter 12 Five Days in the Jungle

CAT TRAX Day 93, A Best Laid Plan in Guinea Bissau. Our indecision continued, what to do? Attila, Maria, and their son Thomas hovered over a map of Guinea-Conakry, suggesting new itineraries. Cat told them, "We're getting low on money. Counting on Western Union is costly and takes time. Cycling up and around the Atlantic Inlet would take six or seven days."

Searching the guidebook, Cat found info on Gahlinas Island. Futre, a friend of Thomas' said, "I have boat, we sail to Kamsar, Guinea Conakry. My boat, fiberglass, seven meter, very fast, we be there, one day." Then the bad news. Without hesitation he said, "You pay 300,000 CFA." ($600 US). We didn't have that kind of money.

"Even if we cycle, we'll be short of cash," Cat whispered. She was right, in a week our money would run out somewhere in the backcountry. Attila interjected in his thick Hungarian accent, "You vould luf zis yungle track I propose, vee hunt der often. Ees beauutifool place und people are nice." I hid my concern but thought, "Sure, people are nice and it's safe, when you're in an SUV and carrying rifles."

As a last-ditch effort we walked into town and found Banco da Africa Occidental, the only bank in Bissau. There was a crowd of people at the door. "What do you think's going on?" Cat queried. "Are they making a run on the bank, trying to get their money out?" I asked and several people tried to explain in Criollo. Then a guy with some English said, "We government workers, no be get pay, six week. We want pay!"

That wasn't a big surprise. Attila had told us Hotel Bissau was owned by the Gambian government. (Guinea Bissau had purchased a fleet of 4WD vehicles from The Gambia; when they defaulted, Gambia took over the hotel.) Attila said, "Dees country, Guinea Bissau, are bankrupt!"

The bank doors were locked and chained. We were doomed to wait for money from Base Camp Charlie. Back at Hotel Bissau, another friend of Thomas', Gabor, greeted us "I have try to find boat, not possible. I think you must to do, what Attila say, you must to ride bicycle."

CAT TRAX Day 94, 57 Ks, Bissau to Mansao. So the die was cast. We spent the morning with Attila, planning the route. "Zee main highway, she go 300 Ks inland," he said. "Zee Yungle Track way is short much, by 150 Ks, und more interest."

At noon we rolled out the driveway with a hand-drawn map and Atilla's notes. Passing cars and trucks honked and waved. "Being on the road again feels great!" Cat yelled, above the din. Mansoa, our first stop, was a tiny village with a rundown motel. After fitful sleep, splintered by night sounds of the jungle and a drunken neighbor, we set off early the next morning.

CAT TRAX Day 95, 124 Ks, Mansao to Saltinho. The road surface was good and our spirits high. As we rolled through a valley, the pavement stopped at a gaping hole where there'd once been a bridge. Water cascaded over the old footings. People walked across on a concrete wall.

"We'll never be able to push the bikes across," Cat muttered.

The crowd surged around us, pushing, shoving, and offering advice. A guy who spoke a little English said, "You ride my pirogue, 1,500 CFA."

Cat tried to bargain, I believed it was a bargain at less than $3.00 US. She accepted, and we thought they'd take us across one at a time. He motioned for me to bring my bike down the steep embankment. He and his buddies lifted it aboard. He signaled that I should get Cat's bike.

With both bikes in the hollowed log he gestured for us to get in. Cat said, "They're going to dump us in the river." I felt confident that the guy knew what he was doing. The boat rocked and pitched, but didn't take water. Once on dry land, the boss held out his hand and said, "3,000 CFA." As we argued, another English speaker said, "He charges 1,500 for *each bike*." Okay, the lesson, "If you want to be terrific, be specific." The curious, thickening crowd convinced me we should pay. A second lesson learned the hard way, always carry small bills. When I handed him a 10,000 CFA note, all hell broke loose.

"Can you help us?" I asked a policeman. He took the note, held it up to the sun, decided it wasn't counterfeit then spoke to the crowd. A tall, thin guy pulled out an even thinner wallet and exchanged the bill for two well-worn 5,000 CFA notes. The crowd pressed in. Greedy eyes seemed to ponder how much more I had in my fat wallet. I quickly handed the boatman one of 5,000s. Cat, the ever-mindful budgeter objected. "Let's go," I said, swinging my leg over the seat. "We need to get out of this crowd right now, the extra couple of bucks is a bargain."

The sun was beginning to set as fatigue hit. Between riding seventy Ks and the adrenaline rush of the river crossing, we were fading fast. A guy along the highway indicated there was a motel twenty-two Ks ahead in Saltinho. Fear of free-camping in the jungle breathed new life into our weary legs. It was worth the extra effort, as they had a room with indoor plumbing, even a shower. Cat let the water run until it was steaming, stepped in, then started screaming. A huge spider had fallen from the wall and was swimming around her feet. I hated to kill the creature, but this was a crisis. Showers, food, and fatigue left us sleeping like jungle babies.

CAT TRAX Day 96, 29 Ks, Saltinho to Quebo. Argh, broken

spokes. A young guy, Suleimani, led me down a path to his village and into bygone times. A fellow there had parts and tools. Sitting in front of his mud hut, the guru of bicycles applied his talent. Soon we were back on the road.

Adding to the National Geographic-style scenery, we began seeing topless women. After a couple of pictures, the sight was so ordinary it became the norm. A strange paradox: we'd just heard that a woman breastfeeding her baby in a California mall had been arrested.

Quebo was just another small village. When I asked about a room, a young man led us to a mud hut bar. The place was dark and dank, two men sat sipping beers. The adjacent room and filthy bed looked fit only for a paid quickie, a work shop for hookers. I dared not show it to the Cat.

Pushing along in a gathering crowd, a man in traditional Arab robes began urging us to follow. "My name Saido," he said in French, "You follow." He took us to his home. I tried to ask how much. He just shook his head back and forth. Price at that point seemed irrelevant, it was getting dark. He took us to a messy bedroom. His wife Adema began clearing the clutter. They were giving us their bedroom. Once again we were hosted by Muslims. For us it was more than just a room, we had a new family for the night.

We sat on the porch as neighbors paraded past, staring at us. It was evident Saido and Adema enjoyed being the center of attention. They were affluent by local standards. He owned a truck and hauled freight. She ran a small grocery store attached to the side of their house. Obviously an ordinary hard-working family.

CAT TRAX Day 97, 66 Ks, Quebo to Kandiafara 6 paved, 40 dirt, 20 in jungle. A short distance out from the village, we feared we were lost. Stopping drew the usual crowd. After we asked directions an older man said, "You go dot vay." He pointed with a wrinkled finger toward a dirt road. We'd hit Attila's jungle track. Let the adventure begin.

At 10:30 a.m. we encountered a "frontier" (border) roadblock. The guards were cordial but tried to charge for a visa. When he saw the visa in my passport he clucked, probably a lost opportunity to pocket some cash. He and the others swarmed around as we took out our map. After a boisterous argument they agreed it was shorter to go to Kandiafara. "You tak dees roat," one said, pointing toward two ruts leading off into the jungle. Just when we thought the road couldn't't get worse, it did. The jungle thickened, and ruts full of loose dirt and rocks slowed us to a crawl.

Each downhill led to a creek. At every creek crossing, we removed our shoes, pushed, and waded. Then put our wet feet quickly back into soggy socks. The water was cool and the jungle trees kept the hot sun off our backs. Some of the uphills were so steep we had to double team. It took all the strength we could muster to push the bikes up one at a time. The path deteriorated further. The strain from exertion and heat began to take its toll.

Bare-breasted women and girls were the routine. We felt guilt, as though invading their privacy. At one crossing several women were scrubbing and pounding their laundry. As I pushed Cat's bike through the water I yelled to her, "Grab the camera, get a picture."

She was nervous, "What if they don't want their picture taken?"

"Just raise the camera, say 'photo,' if they object they'll make a sign, for no."

When Cat said, "Photo," one woman yelled and they all ran toward her. As she prepared to take flight, they stopped and lined up smiling and chattering as if posing for posterity.

At the next crossing we encountered a natural Nubian beauty slowly tending her wash accompanied by her younger siblings. She was a vision of simple splendor. A commonplace occurrence in an ancient setting.

The narrowest bridge of our challenging day was simply a series of twelve-inch-wide boards four feet above the water. I took the bikes across one at a time. With each step my legs became more and more shaky. I imagined myself falling into the water and being pressed into the mud by the weight of our bike and bags.

Residents in a cluster of mud huts were amazed to see us. Cat asked, "Kandiafara?" In unison, they spoke words completely foreign to us and pointed out a single rut pathway. A woman offered us bananas. Cat dug out a few Guinea Bissau coins and handed them to her. Puzzled she and her children rolled them around in their hands. A local boy, cycled up and said in English, "I am Sadio. Do you need help?" When he explained the value of the coins the woman offered her entire basket of bananas. Sadio took us under his wing, became our guide. We were painfully slow, he was patently patient.

Chapter 13 Guinea Conakry

The border of Guinea Bissau was little more than a handful of thatched-roof mud huts. Several soldiers in faded fatigues, carrying worn-looking AK 47s, stood gawking. Sadio waved to us then rode on down the hill, apparently not wanting to be involved. The man in charge barked through a slit window in French for us to come inside. We played dumb and spoke English but were soon busted. One of the soldiers said in English, "He is boss, he is Douane, Customs Officer. He say, you remove all item from bags."

Instinctively I resisted, "Why, we weren't asked to remove things for the border guards?"

The Douane gruffly yelled through the slit, "Passports!"

I handed him mine and he thumbed through the pages. After staring at my picture then at me several times he shouted, "1939?"

When I confirmed "Oui", he barked and a young soldier lit out on the run. Cat whispered, "I think we're in trouble."

The words had barely left her mouth when the soldier came dragging an old man back. The English speaker said, "This man 1939, oldest man in village!" The anger and squabble vanished and the Douane came out of his hut. Suddenly we were all best friends. The village elder shook my hand, then we hugged. The Douane took both our hands and spoke to Cat in French. In a halting discussion he told her the average man there lived only 49 years. He called the Commissair d' Militaire over and they spoke. With a wave of the Commissair's hand we were off the hot seat and back on our bike seats.

So, age had its privileges. More than just retirement and Social Security, aging could also be a ticket to international friendship and an unrestricted border crossing.

Sadio had been hovering near the shore of the river. He explained, "They have motorized ferry but pirogue cost three time less." Having already experienced riding in a dugout, we chose the ferry. The operator paddled his pirogue across to get the ferry. We thanked Sadio for all his help. Plastic bottles seemed to have value to locals. We offered him one. He was thrilled. He shook our hands excitedly then rushed away to show off his new treasure.

Kandiafara, a short way from the river, was only slightly larger than the cluster of huts on the Bissau border. Sadio had suggested we should stay there for the night. Several women sat roadside selling junk and little else. They chuckled when Cat asked in French for a grocery store. It was 4:00 p.m. and the sun there, so near the Equator, sets promptly at 6:00. Cat summoned up her best French and spoke with Jean Pierre, chief of the gendarmerie. He stamped our passports then waved, setting us free to travel in Conakry. However he also indicated it was thirty-five Ks of jungle track to Dabiss, the city.

Cat asked about a place to sleep, he resisted. After asking three times and getting three no's she commented on his Britney Spears T-shirt. He softened and told her we could sleep inside the gendarmerie.

The room was vacant, save a small table and bench, oh, and big spiders on the walls. Our food supply was down to the dregs. I set the tent while Cat searched for food. She came back empty-handed, no food in Kandiafara. Jean Pierre was holding court with his cronies out front.

Cat, carrying our pan like a neighbor borrowing sugar, asked if he had rice we could buy. He scowled then went inside. Emerging, he upturned a raggedy bag and poured the last grains of rice from it into our pan. Cat asked, "How much should we pay?" Jean Pierre dismissed her with wave of his hand and a smile. So this hard on the exterior guy had a soft spot inside.

As we cooked the rice, a group of gendarme's children gathered in our room, chattering and staring. We ate, then shooed them away as we prepared for sleep.

CAT TRAX Day 98, 69 Ks, Kandiafara to Boke. Daylight, like dusk, comes at the hour of 6:00. The sun streamed through cracks as babies next door began to cry for milk.

With an early start, we were soon cycling into civilization. Lots of people walking to and from Dabiss carrying plastic bottles. Imagine a four-hour walk to get water, food, or cooking oil. Once there, we found a village similar to Kandiafara. A small grocery stand, sans electricity, sold warm American colas that tasted fine. We sipped and worried about Africanized bees as a swarm buzzed around us, looking for a sip of the sugary drinks.

Hallelujah, we finally rolled onto an honest to goodness dirt road. The jungle bush opened to grassland and trees. A tower of smoke we'd been watching was revealed to be a raging forest fire. I didn't see any option other than pressing through the heat and smoke. Cat was on the verge of tears, but pedaling fast, with burning branches and embers falling on and around us, we were able to take the heat.

It was dark when we finally arrived in Boke. You recall my vision of Immortality? This was the car driver we'd commissioned at road marker 26, the one with the flat tire, took us to Boke's only hotel, Le Chalet. They had no vacancy. I whined a bit and they offered to move an employee and let us have her room but for only one night. Having no other option, we took the deal. Our newfound driving friends took our CFAs, shook hands, and we exchanged goodbyes. We'd built a camaraderie. They seemed to sense they were part of our adventure of a lifetime.

We were covered in red mud and road dust. Our sweaty clothes were reeking. However, first things first, we headed for the bar. It was dark inside, the electricity was out, but the beer was cold. The bartender sent out for fried chicken and salad. The electricity flickered then failed twice. The beer and our joy at having survived the jungle turned the evening into a celebration of life and good fortune by candlelight.

Life is not a journey to the grave with the intention of arriving safely in a pretty, well-preserved body, we plan to skid in broadside, thoroughly used-up, totally worn-out, and loudly proclaiming "Wow, what a ride!"

CAT TRAX Day 99, 7 Ks, Moving day in Boke.

An annoying squeaking kept us awake. Drifting in and out, we finally decided it was an insect. I turned the lights on and found the culprit on my shoe: a baby mouse crying for its mother. Using a piece of paper, I set it out onto the walkway. I dared not tell Cat that, if there was a baby there was probably a mother and almost certainly other siblings living in the room. Also she needn't be reminded that based upon the laws of nature and the jungle the helpless little squeaker would become part of the "circle of life" within moments.

We slept soundly, despite the heat and odor of a smoldering mosquito-ring, and awoke still covered in red dust and stinking of sweat. The bikes had been limping along on broken spokes. We needed another night's stay to get back into traveling condition.

However, the hotel remained over-booked. They wouldn't let us stay, even in the employee's room. They suggested another place that had no telephone.

I met Doctor Adama-Marie from the Conakry Minister of Health in the courtyard. She was there for the conference

124

that had filled the hotel. She spoke a little English and wanted to help. I asked about breakfast and she invited us to come with her to a small café. We devoured an omelet and washed it down with Fanta orange drink.

Dr. Adama-Marie paid for breakfast as we had no Guinea Francs. She instructed her driver to take us to a moneychanger. The money merchant in a tiny stall exchanged our CFA for a huge pile of Guinea Francs. Asking about a hotel we were told to take a taxi van. An already-overloaded compact van pulled up and we crammed in. The old clunker had a hard time getting rolling. Passengers near the door jumped out and pushed.

Hotel Le Filaou was seven Ks outside town and away from the highway on a dirt road. We booked a room then taxied back to Hotel Le Chalet. Mohamed, the reception clerk at Le Chalet had hosed off the bikes. We gave him a tip then mounted up and rode to our new home.

True joy, a warm shower and cool A C. Amara, the desk clerk at Le Filaou took our dirty laundry. I asked about a bicycle mechanic and they called a young boy over to look at the bikes. He knew a lot about bikes but couldn't repair the wheels. Baba the waiter insisted on accompanying me and our wheels into town. He found a group of young kids working on bikes. One, a preteen named Amadou Korka took charge. He and the others had never seen the wrench I had to remove the cluster gears from the axel. They changed out the broken spokes. Baba explained they had no way to true the wheel. Amadou returned with us to the hotel.

Back at Le Filaou, Amadou installed the wheels on our upturned bikes spun and tweaked the spokes back to trued form. I bought three Cokes, treating him and Baba. I had a feeling that was the first time Amadou had tasted Coca-Cola.

He asked for 5,000 Guinea Franc for his work. (About $2.50 US) I gave him 10,000. He stuffed it into his greasy pocket like it was a treasure. Cat and I felt sure it was the most he had ever earned in such short time. As he turned to leave, I called him back and gave him cab fare. He was astonished.

A strange-looking animal roamed the courtyard. A poster in the office identified it as a Celephalophe. We'd never heard of or seen an animal like that. About the size of a Greyhound dog, it ate leaves on bushes and walked up to us without fear. Only in Africa.

CAT TRAX Day 100, 126 Ks, Boke to Buffo. It was 10:00 a.m. by the time we bumped down the dirt road and out to the highway. There were two buses and several vans full of chanting singing people. It was election time, and they were a group of President Conte's supporters.

The day was all ups and downs, one small hill after another. Hot, we poured water on our heads and down our backs. It was especially cooling when trucks and cars swooshed past. The hills and heat took their toll. The late start and slow going had us a long way from Boffa as the sun began to set. We mounted the lights on our helmets to caution cars and trucks. It was after 7:00 p.m. and dark as we entered the village. A guy directed us to the Hotel Niara Bely.

The dining room had two ceiling fans. We enjoyed the breeze, several beers, and a pretty good meal. Later, sitting out front, Cat conversed with a few young guys. They were amazed that we'd cycled all that way in one day. We were pretty amazed ourselves.

The young guys, Aly, Ousmane, Amara, Youssouf, and Al Hassan gathered around Cat asking English translation of words like head, neck, and shoulder by pointing at them. They wrote each down then pronounced them with her. They loved it, she did, too. A young

guy came in who spoke very good English. Mohamed told us about his school and invited us to visit the next morning. We wanted to go but told him we would be cycling more than 100 Ks again and would need to start early. He confided. "I want to come to America, work and be rich."

CAT TRAX Day 101, 60 Ks, Boffa to Gamesiah. It was a short ride to the banks of the Fatala River. There was a scramble for position as the ferry pulled in to shore. The people arriving ran to avoid being run over by the cars and trucks. Pedestrians and bicycles rushed to get aboard, dodging through the departing vehicles. The ramp was slick with oil. Cat lost her balance and almost went down. As she struggled, two guys held her upright and helped her aboard.

The boat was old and grimy, but soldiers on board warned us not to take pictures. The mouth of the river was wide, the current strong, and the boat felt unsafe. Getting off was the same insane scramble in reverse. Once off without incident, we felt like kissing the ground.

Another late start, another hilly ride, another hot humid day. Feeling puny, we stopped for soft drinks at every store we passed. At a small stand we asked for water to pour on our heads. The banana lady said, "No" then walked across the road and filled a pitcher. She poured the cool water over our heads and down our backs. Refreshed, we bought her bananas.

At 3:30 we reached Hotel Relais de Campos. Just a few thatched roof huts surrounding a bar it looked better to us than the prospect of another forty kilometers. The brothers who owned it were real characters. They had no power or running water.

Christopher, the elder brother, ran the show. Toure, the middle son, looked and acted like he was out of it. He danced around singing along with tapes of African music. Harvey (pronounced Ar

Vay) the youngest, tallest, and thinnest of the brothers also seemed not quite together. We settled in at a table and drank a warm beer.

Toure uncovered an old pedal sewing machine and patched Cat's raggedy cycling shorts, falling apart from wear and washings. Harvey brought a bucket of water for bathing. It was cold and felt great. The toilet was also the bath, we flushed with the bucket.

127

Christopher said, "We have no food, you may use kitchen for cooking." As we pulled out a package of pasta, Christopher's wife came from their house with a big metal pot on her head. Christopher waved for us to join them. He dished out plates of white rice with red sauce topped  with dried fish. We sat on small chairs, the boys crouched down and ate with their hands. They gave us lessons rolling the rice into an oblong ball then popping it into our mouths.

Toure wandered in, squatted, took a couple of bites, then straggled off, still singing to himself. We washed the rice and red fish down with another warm beer by the light of a kerosene lantern. A marvelous dining experience.

Returning to our thatched hut by lantern, we sat out front enjoying a jungle symphony. Bugs and birds called out to each other in the darkness. After bathing we'd sprayed with Deet. The hungry mosquitoes ignored it and began to attack. Retreating inside, Cat felt claustrophobic and hot. We lay atop the sheet sweating and inhaling smoke from the mosquito spiral.

CAT TRAX Day 102, 84 Ks, Gamesiah to Conakry. Early to bed, early to rise. We were anxious to get on the road. Damn, three broken spokes. Breakfast was bananas and two orange drinks. A terrible diet to begin a difficult day. A couple guys on bikes sold baguettes. Two loaves and we set off looking for a quiet spot in the shade. Neighborhood kids gathered and offered green oranges. We asked how much, a boy about six said, "Two hundred."

I admired his spunk and handed him 200 GF. The boy's father insisted he return the money. I shook hands with Papa and got the point across that we wanted the boys to have the money. I had tried to peel one of the green oranges. The crowd laughed, then Papa cut the top off one he'd peeled and sucked out the juice. In moments we were all sucking and slurping.

128

Onward, through lush tropics into coastal mountains. Unfortunately, it was slow going for our wounded machines. Cat had a broken spoke too. By 1:00 p.m. we rolled into Dubreka. That forty Ks would have been impossible in the dark of night. The main

street was dirt, dusty, and littered. The food in the little shacks smelled good. Cat would say "It looks great." I'd respond, "Looks like diarrhea to me!"

With thirty-three Ks to go, the road joined the east-west highway and turned dangerous. The traffic thickened to a steady stream, all of them in a hurry. We felt like two ants stuck in a herd of elephants.

Our guidebook recommended Hotel Le Riviera in Conakry. We began the ask, ask, ask program as we worked our way off the main highway. At a Shell station, a group of young guys surrounded us, chattering among themselves. After consensus, one drew a map that turned out to be accurate, but it didn't reflect the distances so we ended up asking again and again. It was getting late, and we worried we'd be stuck on the street after dark. A scary thought in those crowds and traffic.

At last, Le Riviera. Through the gate and into a different world. The restaurant was deserted. We heard a guy call out to the waitress, "Hey, I'm over here." Wow, American English. He was sitting alone. We sat near, then opened conversation. Tim was in construction, building the new US Embassy. He said, "I'll be here two years. Originally a Philadelphian, my wife and I worked, and traveled the world together. I lost her to ovarian cancer two years ago." Despite the loss, he remained upbeat saying "I intend to continue working, traveling, and learning about the world and her peoples."

Our bed was king sized, the AC efficient. We tumbled in and slept.

CAT TRAX Day 102, Day of rest, Conakry. After enjoying the best sleep we'd had in weeks, our task was to get to the Ghanaian

Embassy for visas. The Le Riviera gate guard waved and a taxi pulled over. Our friendly guard made a deal and we were off. A jolly fellow at the Embassy gate asked, "What you are wanting?" When we said "Visas," he smiled and said, "You want visit my country?" He ushered us inside, then we sat. Cat became impatient, opened the door, and asked if anyone was working. A huffy gal flounced out and reluctantly handed us forms to complete. That took a few minutes, then we sat until Cat asked again. When the woman reappeared she seemed disgusted, "Don't you know you need three copies of the application and you pay $20 US?" We had no US cash. The jolly gate guy said, "No problem, just go to hotel, get money and make copies."

Tim told us the most generous currency-exchange in town was three guys with handheld calculators sitting on a corner. They had wads of every kind of money we could imagine. With unfamiliar-looking US cash and the copies we hustled back to the embassy. The laissez faire lady smiled, almost smirked then said, "You come back after weekend." Then she slipped our forms under a stack of others.

The jolly guard gave advice, "Go now, get airline tickets, lots of peoples travels at holidays." Our driver honked and swerved through dreadful traffic to Ghana Airlines. The clerk was friendly, he should have been at $332.50 US per ticket plus $162 for excess luggage. Damn, they too, took only US Dollars or Guinea Francs, no credit cards.

Another challenge: where to get more cash. We tried two banks and struck out. Then, tired, hot, and hungry we went back to our hotel to ask for help. They were great and advanced 900€ on our Visa card then exchanged it to Guinea Francs. Amazing, who would think it could cost more than 1.3 million to fly two hours to Ghana.

Le Riviera was a tiny island of luxury in a sea of dust, exhaust fumes, and trashy streets. Tim invited us to attend a party at Marine House. A contingent of US Marines guard the Embassy. We met him at 7:00 p.m. and walked around the corner. Wow, a security

fence then an iron door with a little window like a prohibition-era speakeasy. Tim knocked and the little window opened. We showed our passport and suddenly we were back in the good ol' US of A. The party was to honor the new gunnery sergeant, a woman. We met the outgoing G. S., Kurt a very gung ho guy. He gave us a commemorative coin, "Marine Security Guard Detachment, Conakry, Guinea." He and the new G.S. were shooting a game of pool. Most of the rest of the detachment were watching a current movie.

An interesting aside, about half the marines were African American. They stood apart, drank and told stories amongst themselves. Though the Corps takes pride in its integration and equal opportunity policies, it seemed there was still a color line among the troops.

CAT TRAX Day 103, Another Day in Conakry. Cat pulled the cash, our wad of bills, out of the hotel safe. They gave us a big envelope for the bundle. We felt conspicuous, we were packing almost one and one half million GFs. The airline clerk issued tickets and provided an in-flight magazine with a map of Accra.

At dinner English with a slight British accent popped up at an adjacent table. George, born in Hong Kong, now lived in Seattle, Washington. His told us his best Guinea story: he and a local friend were out driving in the countryside. They parked, had a soft drink and when he started the car they ran over something. A goat had crawled under but was only slightly injured. A crowd gathered, muttering about how bad it was. They wanted his friend to pay for the damaged goat. The owner appeared, lamenting his loss even though the goat was up and walking. Negotiations began, his friend suggested they should offer 25,000 Guinea Francs. The owner wailed saying "60,000 would be more realistic." The reaction of the crowd was mixed, he could see some felt 60,000 was rich for the slight injury.

They offered to give a little GF to each person in the crowd. Once that was done, things calmed down. The owner confessed he didn't own the goat, he was just watching and fattening it for a friend in the next village. The actual owner's name came up and it was a guy related to George's friend. The crowd laughed. No clansman could possibly take advantage of another. The matter was settled for the original offer of 25,000. George said, "The experience was worth a million, US!"

CAT TRAX Day 105, Another lazy day in Conakry. Back to the Ghanaian Embassy for our passports and visas. The ride was slow due to a political demonstrations for President Conte. Trucks loaded with people carrying signs adorned with Conte's photo blocked the lanes.

The Embassy had told us our visas would be ready but, you guessed it, they weren't. The gal mumbled about visitors and meetings then said, "You come back at 2:00 p.m."

At exactly 2:00 we pulled into the embassy. Our jolly pal laughed and said, "She got em' all fix for you." With fresh visas and receipts in hand we headed back to Le Riviera.

A park near the hotel sat fenced and unused. In the middle a huge obelisk with a soldier, a woman, and a boy atop. It commemorated Portugal's unsuccessful attempt to invade the country. The win created opportunity for dictator Sekou Toure to take the reins and begin a reign of terror that lasted for the rest of his life. He died in 1984. His death brought President Conte into power, perhaps also for life.

CAT TRAX Day 107, Another Boring Day in Conakry. The bike boxes were ready. It was the 100th anniversary of the Wright brothers flight. Imagine the changes our world had seen since Orville and Wilbur flew that short flight into the history books. The brothers owned a bicycle repair shop. We felt it a good omen. Once off the ground, we'd have Orville, Wilber, and Ghana Air to thank. Rumor had it that if we didn't fly the next day President Conte would close the airport Sunday during the election. OMG, we'd be stuck until the following week.

Chapter 14 Ghana, Togo and Benin

We were reminded of being kids playing Hop, Skip and Jump. We hopped over Sierra Leone then skipped Liberia and The Ivory Coast to avoid West Africa's "hot spots." Sierra Leone was controlled by UN Peacekeepers; the President of Liberia had just been exiled; the Ivory Coast was in an uprising and might explode at any time. The jump was to Ghana, Togo, and Benin.

CAT TRAX Day 108, the flight to Ghana. We met a group of Peace Corps volunteers in the airport waiting area. They were on vacation and excited to explore Ghana. Take off was delayed, and the captain apologized, saying "We're waiting for a passenger." A man in a suit ran up the stairway onto the plane. Once on the ground in Ghana, the captain had us remain seated. The late passenger was the Prime Minister of Ghana. He de-planed at a different terminal than we commoners. There was a red carpet and TV cameras awaiting his arrival.

Smooth landing and a smooth passage through immigration. Cat changed a little of our CFA for Cedis, the local currency, to pay the taxi. We snagged a station wagon taxi to handle the bikes and bags. The driver quoted $30 US to the hotel.

Cat howled, "It's only 4 kilometers."

"Who says that," he asked? (They speak English in Ghana.)

Cat told him "our guidebook."

He chuckled, and reduced the price to $20.

Hotel Niagara Plus was basic. At dinner, we heard two black women seated nearby speaking US English. They were a mom and daughter from Santa Rosa, California. Phyllis, the mom, was a go getter. Her projects were designed to make a difference in people's lives. Her business card read, "Visit Ghana – Philanthropy Host Family Services." Her business in Santa Rosa was Diasporan Boutique, specializing in African drums, clothing, and Shea butter. Her daughter hung on her every word like an apprentice, clearly anxious to learn and grow into Mom's shoes.

Phyllis was proud of their Jembe drums, built by a student in Ghana. She ships them home, sells them, and the profit becomes a college fund for the student. Also Shea butter is a local product used in body oils, creams, and lotions produced by a women's co-op. The women manufacturing the products earn a living and build self esteem.

CAT TRAX Day 109, A Day in Accra, the Capital of Ghana.

The sun flooded through our window at 6:00 a.m. Ready to bathe, we had no hot water. We called the front desk, they had us wait forty-five minutes, then provided a bucket of warm water. Boat baths for us, then we washed the clothes we'd worn for three days in the same bucket.

As I assembled bikes, Cat called the Togo and Benin Embassies. Good news: if we got to the Togo Embassy before noon they would have our visas back by 2:00. And the Benin Embassy was open in the afternoon. We decided the first priority was "cash." We needed Cedis to pay a taxi and embassies always wanted money to process visas.

The taxi driver quoted 20,000 Cedis. Cat wanted to argue, but I took the deal. It was easy to lose track of values. If he'd reduced his fee to 15,000, which he said he wouldn't, we would save 60 cents.

Barclay's Bank rejected our Visa credit card. We wouldn't make the Togo Embassy, but no reason to go without money. The American Express office was in a small travel office called Afro Wings Ltd. "Yes," the girl said, "You can get money but only our manager can help and we don't know when he will return." We waited for a while, then gave up in frustration.

Back at Barclays, they declined our Visa card due to security hold. We bought pay telephone units then spent a frustrating twenty minutes trying to get a call out on a broken phone. Back again to Barclays, Cat stood in line and I went looking for a functioning phone. Damn, the nearby phone wouldn't work with the type of card we'd purchased. A long walk, a long line, then at 3:30 I finally got through to Visa. Their security prompts burned up half the phone card units, then I was cut off by the Visa operator. Frustrated, and with time running out, I got Visa back but as the woman started to transfer me to security, I screamed. The crowd waiting for a phone stared. Finally, the woman at Visa said, "We have released the hold."

The bank was closed. If Cat hadn't scored, we'd be penniless for the weekend. She was standing inside the locked door, next to a guard with an AK 47. She did a thumbs down sign, then convinced the guard to allow me in. We ran up the stairs and the teller tried the call again. After a long, nerve-wracking delay, we were approved.

Wow, $500 US bought 4,240,912 Cedis. Five bundles and a handful of loose bills. They put it all in a black trash bag. We felt conspicuous. Surely everyone on the street knew what the bag held.

CAT TRAX Day 110, Searching for Our New Bike Wheels. Lots of bike parts, but no wheels. Back at the hotel we had a message. The bike company had sent new wheels. They'd soon arrive in Accra via FedEx.

CAT TRAX Day 112, A Business Day in Accra. The passport photographer Cat found would take twenty photos of each of us for 160,000. (A little less than $20.00) We went to his shop under the sign, "Instant Passport Photos." He shot our photos then said, "You come back in one hour." Instant had a different meaning in Ghana.

At the Togo Embassy we met three guys: Bastian, half German, half Brazilian; Markus, half Thai, half German; and Ben, 100% Ghanaian. Markus had been volunteering in Ben's birth village. Bastian had flown in to visit. The three of them were going to Togo and Benin.

Luckily, they adopted us. Ben bargained for the taxi to the Benin Embassy. He spoke not only English, but French and Twi, the language of Ghana. We had a great time waiting, joking and laughing. He convinced the staff to expedite the visas. They charged extra but would have them for us by that afternoon. Another couple came in. The woman worked with a refugee group in The Ivory

Coast and confirmed the place was on the verge of full-fledged war.

For lunch, the guys invited us along for genuine fu-fu. Ben led us through a row of tumble-down shacks. At one, a gal was pounding fu-fu, casaba root pulverized to paste by a wooden pestle in a mortar. We watched Ben eat with his right hand and copied the technique. He pulled the dough apart, swished it around in the sauce, then popped it into his mouth. Fu-fu was the same, or similar to the rice we rolled into balls with Christopher and Harvey.

The Togo Embassy had our passports and visas ready. At the Benin Embassy, Bastion argued with the guy in charge. We'd paid extra for express service. He felt they were making us wait for no reason. Ben took over and finessed the staff. Soon we were all hovering around the desk signing and receiving our visas. What a fun day we'd had, we truly hated to say goodbye.

Other than traffic, we felt safe as we walked to dinner in the dark. Tiny stalls lined the road, tables stacked high with goods. People crowded around blazing barbecues, enjoying fish, rice, grilled platanos (large green bananas) and fu-fu. Everyone smiled and said hello.

CAT TRAX Day 113, Just Another Day in Accra. As we were walking, a boy sprinted past. A man jumped out of his car and tripped the kid. A group of vigilantes caught and began beating him. He had stolen a wallet, or at least was accused of stealing one. The frenzied crowd fed on the violence. As they surged past, I wanted to yell, "Let ye without sin cast blows upon this boy." Everyone in Ghana seemed religious however this display of rage was driven not by virtue but by vile hatred and a wish to inflict pain. We felt sorry for the boy. As he passed, taking blows to the head, he started to run again. Where were the police? Was the crowd going to kill him? We'll never know.

Good news: FedEx had one of our packages. Bad news: they didn't know where our wheels were. Their computer was down, so they asked us to call back. Our call back was disappointing, still no news. Cat was crawling the walls. We WorldRiders needed to get back on the road.

CAT TRAX Day 114, Christmas Eve in Accra CNN broadcast bad news. A Lebanese plane taking off from Cotonou, Benin, had crashed at the end of the runway. Lots of people trying to get home for Christmas were killed. We would be departing on that same runway in a week.

Another visit with the friendly lady at Barclay's Bank. We tried our Visa card. It worked, but was limited to 80,000 Cedis. (About $100 US) We wanted another 2,500,000, Cs ($ 295 US). Enough to pay the hotel, and survive cycling three days in Ghana. I was in line when an uproar broke out at the cash windows. A guy yelled, "Oh my, they've run out of money." I saw Cat and warned her of the fracas. Easy to see how tempers would flare if you couldn't get your cash on Christmas Eve.

FedEx had our package and were working hard, tracking the wheels. They gave us a phone number for their warehouse guy, Charles. We struck pay dirt when we reached Charles. He had the wheels. We grabbed a cab and rushed to the freight area at the Airport. Charles was a great guy, he greeted us then had us take a seat. The plane had just arrived, they hadn't sorted the packages. A very jolly guy, Nicholas, joked with us. We started calling him St. Nick but he didn't get it. Cat explained, "You're Papa Noel." His infectious laugh sounded like Santa Claus.

We tried to give Charles a Christmas gift 15,000 Cedis. He refused, ducked away and yelled "Merry Christmas." Charles and the bike company had made our Christmas *bright.*

Opening the boxes felt like Christmas. They'd sent four new wheels. I installed them as Cat packed. By 11:00 p.m. we snuggled in bed, while visions of cycling danced in our heads.

CAT TRAX Day 115, 52 Ks, Accra, Ghana to Tome, Togo. It was 9:30 when we pushed out the driveway. The security guard walked to the middle of the road and held out his little red flag to stop traffic. There was none, it was the thought that counted. We quickly realized the bikes needed adjusting. Gears clattered and brakes were dragging. So it became ride, adjust, then ride again, stop, and adjust again. Pat's repairs by trial and error.

The main road led to Ring Road East. Accra's suburbs were larger than we'd thought. The 'Burbs' were clean and affluent-looking. Although we'll never forget the frequent signs stenciled on walls and fences, "Do Not Urinate Here!"

Seeking food, we rode directly to the harbor. Lunch at "Chicken Lickin." A Christmas feast of fried chicken legs, French fries, and soft drinks.

Entering Tome, we asked about a hotel. One fellow said, "Friends Hotel, just ahead on right." What about others? He shrugged and said, "No others." Friends Hotel was a motel with an outside bar and tables under copula roofs. We checked in, then swigged a couple of cold beers. It was 3:30 p.m. and hotter than Hades.

Christmas dinner as good as lunch, again fried chicken and chips (French Fries). The wine we had onboard heightened our holiday spirits. The blades of a Casablanca fan wafted warm air down. Not even close to a white Christmas.

CAT TRAX Day 116, 96 Ks, Tome to Ada. We'd lost our left gloves at the laundry in Conakry. Voila, a golf course. Golf gloves are an alternative to cycling gloves. We bought left hand only in the Pro Shack. The staff stared in disbelief. We guessed not many gloveless gringos stop by.

Cat bought soft drinks as I took a picture of a breast-feeding mom. She objected, until she saw the photo, then called excitedly for everyone to see. They became unruly, demanding more pictures. A young boy naked from the waist down let loose a stream of pee. His mother spanked his bare butt. I guess peeing on your own doorstep wasn't tolerated.

It was 5:00 p.m., decision time. Locals agreed the next hotel was 20 Ks down the road. The final four Ks were on loose dirt, covering our clothes with red dust. We looked like a couple of bums. The staff stared as if to say, "Can you afford to stay here?" The place was aptly named Manet Paradise Hotel. The room was spacious, cool, and pleasant. Also a buffet dinner with French wine. Depleted, Cat ate two desserts but was embarrassed to ask for a third.

CAT TRAX Day 117, 10 Ks by boat, 85 Ks cycled, Ada, Ghana to Lome, Togo. Searching for bananas, we walked to the nearby village. It was a world apart from Paradise. We met Thomas and Catherine, doctors from Germany, at the pool. They worked with a non-profit, trying to turn the tide on HIV/AIDS and Malaria. They told us ten percent of people there were infected.

Seek and ye shall receive. James the desk clerk thought we might find a boat to cross the river. We felt crossing the Volta River Delta would be an interesting boat ride, and hoped the road on the other side would be better. James made a call and two guys quickly showed up.

He said, "This is boat captain, he can take you."

The price was right $33 US. We made a deal, and I asked his name.

When he said, "Joshua," I sang out "Joshua fit the battle of Jericho."

Captain 'J' quickly responded, "And the walls came tumbling down!"

We pushed the bikes to the dock. Joshua helped lift them aboard. He was an excellent riverboat captain. He knew the shallows, sand bars, and the interesting sights. Ditza was a very picturesque village. Pirogues and huts lined the shore. Life there moved slowly, as it had for centuries.

Landing was another treat. The concrete dock was loaded with

firewood for heating and smoking fish. The guys on shore helped lift the bikes ashore. We took some photos, including one of a guy who had a huge dead snake wrapped around his shoulders. We called him Monte and his Python. Cat said, "The only good snakes are dead snakes!"

We mounted up and cycled for 2½ hours, then stopped for soft drinks. The shop owner was twisted terribly with scoliosis, but his attitude was straight up positive. He posed for a photo with his two beautiful children. He asked for our help to get him a visa for America then for copies of the pictures. We could give neither.

At 2:00 we saw a sign, "Hotel with GOOD food." The Chef served chicken again, this time with slaw and yam chips. They were hot, but tasteless. As we sat on the patio, praying for breeze Le Chef told us, "The road ahead is under construction." This struck fear in our hearts. Then he said, "It also has paved surface, not yet officially open. You will be mostly to yourselves." He was mostly right. Little traffic, but the surface vacillated between paved and loose gravel. The new road was replacing one washed away by the sea. The look reminded us of the Great Salt Flats in Utah. The sand was white and went as far as the eye could see.

Kids at a bus stop looked too foreign to be locals. We enjoyed a few minutes chatting with a terrific group of Peace Corps volunteers. They give so much and get so little, yet they love what they do. The trade-off will come later in life, like our friend Dennis in Ziguinchor. So  many have had their lives shaped in places like that.

Stopping for directions, a lady pointed toward a large party walking on the road. She told us someone had died. Cat had read about the Ewe people whose funerals lasted for days. They play drums and dance to chase away evil. They also believed the soul of

the departed would reappear in the next child born into the clan. As we cycled through the crowd which parted courteously but apprehensively, then swarmed back together and partied on.

Villages lining the broad and sandy beach lay off to our right.

To the left, another broad river delta. This was the tropics, the Africa we'd anticipated. Aflao was a typical border town. Quickly through the Ghana exit and suddenly we were entering Togo. Several guys gathered round, each offering help with Togo formalities. We resisted all, except one very personable fellow. He helped by taking Cat to Togo immigration then finding a moneychanger. We traded our few remaining Cedis for CFA, gave him a tip, and pedaled onward into gathering nightfall.

Lome was only half a kilometer from the border. Cat had chosen Hotel du Benin but the first place we saw, Ibis, looked like home. Ibis Hotels had hosted us in many European cities. They had plenty of rooms. The hotel had just opened two weeks earlier. It felt and smelled like Europe.

CAT TRAX Day 118, Day off in Lome. Drums and cowbells  pounded and rang in our heads. We threw back the drapes, wondering whether a revolution had begun. How very western, a 10K run and event on Main Street in front of the hotel.

The phone rang, it was Femi a guy we'd met last evening. Cat whose Guff-Guff had returned couldn't risk leaving the toilet. I met him and his wonderful family in the lobby. The mom, Bunmi, was a pharmacist with Pfizer, in Ghana interviewing pharmaceutical reps. Femi was an architect, and a proud father. The family had come along for a short vacation. When I told them we'd decided not to visit Nigeria, Femi was indignant.

"But you must come, you stay with us!" He said. They lived in the Capital, Lagos.

Bunmi spoke up, "Femi, remember they are riding bicycles."

He took a deep breath, then said, "You must not come to our country. Labor strife, kidnappings, and other problems make it too dangerous for you, on bicycles."

After exploring Tome we returned to our Ibis haven and napped. Wow, did that feel good. We were both completely fatigued or as they say in French, "Fatigay."

Out at 3:00, we got caught up in a huge beach party. Wanting to catch the action, I stood atop a block wall. Two police officers pulled at my legs, they wanted me down. The party was loud, throbbing. We learned that the run that morning and the party were regular Sunday events.

CAT TRAX Day 119, 84 Ks, Lome, Togo to Popo, Benin. The dangers of that day were second only to Dakar. The road was rough and narrow, traffic as thick as the haze in the air. On a narrow bridge, Cat took a lane. Very gutsy and smart on her part. Drivers slowed and waited impatiently.

Small truck farms lined the roadway. Fresh vegetables and greens were hand-watered and harvested. A boy stood guard over a stack of sacks filled with fresh-picked carrots. The air smelled fresh but there were ominous-looking clouds of smoke ahead.

We thought they were burning sugar cane. Several times we rode in smoke so thick we could barely see the lines on the road. So many fields were ablaze we were rarely out of the cloud.

A stop for Lion Killer, a lemon-flavored frozen drink that hit the spot. I needed a toilet so the girl led me across the alleyway into a fenced area behind a bamboo hut. There were two cement block stalls with holes in the concrete. The wall was five feet high, so my head was above it as I stood and peed. Several passersby looked me in the eye during the process. Cat needed the facility for a squat. I told her about the filthy floor and gave her our toilet paper. Returning, she said, "I left an African Guff-Guff deposit, but my head was below the spectator's stare."

We rolled forty Ks to the Togo/Benin border. The Togo checkpoint was hectic; I stood guard while Cat stepped into a shack to have our passports stamped. Inside, she met an American, Sarah from Spokane, Washington (Pat's childhood hometown). When Sarah finished checking in her pile of passports she came out and

we talked. She was driving a huge Mercedes truck, on an adventure tour of Africa. She'd been driving Africa and South America with Dragoman Tours for more than five years. We posed illegally between borders, in front of her truck. The guard came running yelling, "No photo, no photo." Sarah charmed him.

The Benin border was boring after the tumult in Togo. The checkpoint had seating and took each person in order. The road was cleaner, traffic lighter. We were checked in and rolling on in just moments.

Grand Popo was twenty Ks from the border. We'd heard of a resort called L' Auberge de Grand Popo. It sounded great, so we hoped for a two day stay. Oops, the best laid plans...L' Auberge wasn't on the highway, we had to bump down a long cobblestone roadway. More disappointment, the clerk stared over his book and without emotion said, "We are fully booked." We couldn't believe it, so we retreated and talked it over.

"No room at the inn" meant back to a place called L' Etoile de Mer. Riding in, we met Matte and Tuula from Finland. They were having a gin and tonic, so we joined them and ordered beers. Cat went to look at a room and returned, another disappointment. The rooms were awful, the price high. Tulle said, "We looked at a room out of curiosity, but didn't ask the price. We are staying at L' Auberge. Our room costs less and it's better than these." She added, "These drinks are the most expensive we've had in Africa." Matti was a writer of Finnish history and culture. The museum, Villa Karo, adjacent to L' Auberge, was a Finnish-African Cultural Center. They were shocked to hear we'd cycled all the way south from Vaasa, Finland, in the past seven months.

As the sun began to sink, we walked to the beach. It was a beautiful, undeveloped place. Fishermen mending nets, others working on their boats. Some, like us, simply enjoying the sunset. I took a short swim in the warm tropical waters of the Gulf of

Guinea.

The room was even worse than it looked. The AC had only one speed, hurricane force. The temp filled the room with a chill. No hot water, however the cold was lukewarm. Cat got the last word, "It's only for one night!"

CAT TRAX Day 120, 82 Ks, Cotonou, Benin. I wanted to see Ouidah, the Port City in Benin where thousands of Benin and East Togo natives had been shipped out as slaves to the US, Brazil, and Haiti. It was also a Voodoo center.

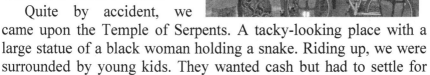

Quite by accident, we came upon the Temple of Serpents. A tacky-looking place with a large statue of a black woman holding a snake. Riding up, we were surrounded by young kids. They wanted cash but had to settle for

friendship. The attendant was shocked that we wouldn't leave the bikes and tour the Temple. Our book said they only had a few sleepy snakes. That was enough to keep Cat away!

A local restaurant drew us in. Two ragtag boys had run with us all the way from the

Temple. The waitress shooed them away and tried to explain her menu. Failing, she invited me into her lean-to dirt-floor kitchen with single gas burner. The menu was just as simple, rice with oily meat sauce.

As she served, the two boys drifted back in. They stirred up memories of my brother and me. I told Cat that we'd never eaten in a restaurant until my family moved to California. My first was at a truck stop, as a freshman in high school. I bought Cokes for the boys. They rolled their eyes at the waitress and took a table. Now customers, they savored the service, the moment, and the Coke. I liked watching them as much as they liked the colas.

Tall poles with fluttering white flags identified the homes and clinics where Voodoo was practiced. There were a lot of local believers. They worship and make contact with dead ancestors. Rumor was you could have them cast spells on your enemies.

Traffic funneled down to two lanes as we neared Cotonou's Pont Ancien (Old Bridge). Cat thought we should push across on the sidewalk since traffic was inching along. I yelled, "Use your take-a-lane technique." She took the curb lane and rode into the fray at their slow pace.

Hotel du Lac was visible from the bridge and we were glad to see it. The security guard challenged us, telling me to park away from the building. I was in no mood to be pushed. We compromised and I leaned the bikes off to one side. The place was decent, Cat took a room with river view.

A couple there, David and Barbara, were from Stinson Beach, California but currently lived in New York. He was a Professor at Oswego University. Like others we'd met, he began his interest in Africa as a Peace Corps Volunteer. After his tour, he returned home to study African History. He'd had articles published, and had lectured on Mali, Burkina Faso, and Benin. Barbara had owned a clothing store in Santa Barbara for several years. We became instant friends and sat talking into the wee hours. Well, we made it until 11:00 p.m. then gave in to exhaustion. They were jet-lagged, we bike-lagged.

CAT TRAX Day 121, New Years Eve in Cotonou, Benin. We arranged for a car to take us to AAT, Agence Africaine de Tourist. The driver got onto the bridge and into a huge traffic jam. He muttered something about an accident. Persisting for a few minutes in the slow-moving mess he suddenly made a U-turn. Dumping us back at the hotel, he said, "You take Moto Taxis." But, there was no way we'd ride behind a driver on those squirrelly little things in that traffic.

David and Barbara were in the lobby, waiting for a car they had hired to take them to Ouidah. Turned out, our driver was the driver they'd contracted. What the hell? He'd tried to slip us in and make a quick 2000 CFA, then return in time to pick up David and Barbara. They were upset too, and demanded he take us to AAT on their way out of town. We loved that, more time to talk. I was telling David about our times with our band Acadiana and mentioned our fiddle player Phil Salazar. Barbara and Cat were talking, but she overheard and asked, "You mean Phil Salazar was with your band? I know him! Phil and my best friend played weddings together." It really is a small world after all, isn't it?

The best part of our Odyssey was awakening daily in a new place. Seeing the wonders that lay just over the next hill. The worst was saying goodbye almost daily to new friends. And so it was with David and Barbara. Hugs and a few tears mixed with promises to meet again in California. Barbara begged us to come with them to Ouidah. We hated to say no to an opportunity to learn about Voodoo with a guide like David. They honked, waved, and drove away into the dust and haze. We scurried across the street, dodging motor scooters.

Our package from DHL arrived. Amazing on a holiday eve. Two Armadillo tires, two thorn-proof tubes, a new guidebook and Michelin map of East Africa. Still awake at the stroke of midnight, I nudged Cat. She sleepily wished me a Happy New Year then it was lights out. What adventures we'd experienced. Imagine, we had cycled away from home and had been on the road more than a year and a half. Incredible journey, to have cycled so much of the world in such a short time.

CAT TRAX day 122, New Years Day in Cotonou. A typical New Year's Day except no Rose Parade or Bowl games. At dinner we heard a family speaking English. Dad Craig and mom Debbie were there with daughter Lindsey and son Erik. They were from Springfield, Missouri, visiting Matt their eldest son/brother, serving in the Peace Corps.

Nadine, the Chief Agent at AAT, had spent a lot of time exploring possibilities and prices. We wanted to visit the Giant Silverback Gorillas in Uganda. Air fares ranged from $1,100 to $1,250. Cat began reading our new East Africa Guidebook and studying the map. She had highlighted areas she called "Must see!" Seeing the gorillas meant another flight, and more money: $1,000 in park fees and $1,000 for the cheapest safari. And that didn't guarantee we'd see any gorillas. Also, BBC reported the Ugandan government was arming civilians in Northern Uganda to resist Joseph Kony and his Lords of Resistance Army.

So, a new plan. Fly to Nairobi then cycle through the Maasai Mara Reserve, the Serengeti National Park, Ngorongoro Crater, and climb Mt. Kilimanjaro. A huge savings in time and money. We hated missing the Silverbacks. However, we agreed it gave us a reason to return.

 *CAT TRAX Day 124, last Day in Cotonou?* Matt was fascinated with our trip, he wanted to travel on bicycle when he'd finished his Peace Corps tour. He and a couple of Peace Corps buddies helped get our bikes ready to fly. Cat headed for the travel agency to get the tickets. My bicycle tech group worked and talked of things African. Things they'd experienced like Amoebic Dysentery. They laughed when Matt said, "Normal table talk here includes daily discussions of stomach issues and bowel movements."

With a little help from my friends, the bikes were quickly ready to travel. In the process, I replaced our tubes and installed the new tires. I gave the old tires and tubes to Matt. He had a bike and also knew locals in his village who could use a tire or tube. What a terrific young guy!

Cat returned with bad news. We'd thought the flight would depart at 2:15 p.m.. Nadine told her it departed after midnight. Yikes, we'd have to stay up most of the night then wait in the airport in Douala, Cameroon, from 6:00 a.m. the next day until midnight for the flight to Kenya.

At the airport, our Hotel du Lac driver Tiarou helped get the bikes out of his van. A porter pushed a cart toward us. I told him we'd need two carts and started to pull his cart across to load the bikes. I wanted him to get another cart to take the bags while I took the bikes. As I tried to take the cart he ripped it from my grip. We were both getting pretty upset. I called for a policeman but there were none close by. Tiarou came to the rescue. He pulled our things back into his van and drove to the other end of the terminal. He helped carry the bags and bikes inside. I gave him a tip. Smiling, he said, "If you need me, call."

Cat had gone inside, looking for the freight counter. Bad news, the flight was delayed, we'd be stuck in the airport for twelve hours and it was uncomfortably hot. I gave up and called Tiarou. He was back shortly, just as cordial as ever, and drove us back to the hotel.

We spent the remainder of the evening sitting in the lobby. Tiarou wheeled in a little after midnight and we went through the loading process again. At the airport, we got our things out and met Porter 23, who was the exact opposite of the jerk we'd met earlier. I took one bike, he managed all the bags. As we checked in, word that the flight wouldn't come in rippled through the passengers. It wasn't a very happy time. Several of us confronted the Cameroon Airlines employees, yelling and complaining. Cam Air staff told us to return the next day at noon. We were disappointed, but it meant we could get some sleep.

It was Tiarou to the rescue, again. By the time we got checked back in at the hotel and into bed it was 2:30 a.m.. We were dog tired.

CAT TRAX Day 125. Another Last Day, in Cotonou! Tiarou rolled in, we loaded and once again headed off to the airport. Everyone was upbeat, the check in lines moved quickly. We were last on and happy to be. It meant our bikes and bags would be on top of the pile and first off.

Daniel, a guy from France, watched as we set the bags and bikes on the belt to be weighed. When the agent figured the cost of excess baggage Daniel went to bat for us in French. We caught

148

the word "cadeaux," gift, as he rattled off reasons we were upset: Two trips to the airport and the cost of another night at the hotel. The gateman turned to us, waved his hand in the air and said, "Okay, no cost for excess!" Daniel was a new friend, in deed!

After waiting two hours, we were all herded into the restaurant and Cameroon Air bought lunch. Pretty good rice and beef. We sat and talked with Daniel. Just as everything seemed a go, they announced the flight had been cancelled. Angry passengers milled around the terminal. Daniel made more noise in his beautiful French then we took our carry-on bags, left the bikes and big bags and took a cab back to Hotel du Lac. Home again, home again, jiggety jog!

The best of it, as we arrived so did David and Barbara. They were as surprised to see us as we were to be back. Cat and I took our wine onto the pool deck and chatted with Barbara as David swam laps. The three of us met for dinner. Daniel was across the room so we invited him to join. David spoke French, and Daniel's English improved quickly. We had a great dinner, what lessons we learned about Ouidah, Voodoo, and Benin.

CAT TRAX Day 126, Finally, a Flight to Cameroon. We loafed around a bit, thinking that we would leave for the airport at noon when the desk called. "Be prepare to leave by 11:00." The tireless Tiarou dropped us at Cam Air, took my hand, and said, "This time it will fly!" He was such a nice guy, he'd made the airport run with us four times.

Airport security wouldn't allow us in. We sat in the arrival area, sweating and longing for the little wafts of air that occasionally drifted down from a fan. We learned the delay was because there were no Cam Air employees. A woman said, "Cameroon open 12:00, then you go."

At noon, we were allowed in, then shepherded to the restaurant. Worrier that I am, I climbed the stairs and tried to see our things. The bags were there but no bikes. What good was a bike ride around the world sans bikes? I went to the baggage area asking over and over until they tired of the game. They sent a guy with me to look. They were hidden behind luggage.

Once checked in, Daniel led us to the end of the counter. A Cam Air representative took Daniel's receipt then handed him CFAs. He signaled to us and Cat asked the guy to pay for our first night. He instantly said, "No!" Daniel questioned him in French. The rep reluctantly counted out CFA to Cat. He even paid for breakfast. Yes, it was the fault of the airline and in the States that was how it would work. However, at Cameroon Air in Benin, it was a pleasant surprise. Without Daniel we knew they wouldn't have covered the costs.

Chapter 15 Marooned in Cameroon

CAT TRAX Day 127, Into the Heart of Africa. What a strange flight. We all craned our necks, trying to see the remains of the Lebanese plane that had crashed a week earlier. We didn't see it and were comfortable with that. Neither of us are fond of flying. Seeing burned-out remains would only have heightened our anxiety The flight had another strange aspect. We lifted off only to land in Lagos, Nigeria twenty minutes later. Cat asked if they could allow us off there to get a flight to Kenya. The attendant was courteous and anxious to help. He came back later explaining that without visas it wouldn't work. So we were off to Cameroon, like it or not!

Flying in cramped quarters was tiring. We were glad to feel the wheels bump on the runway.

We asked for information about connecting flights. A young guy named Achu appeared and asked us in English to follow. The station manager told us there was no connecting flight for two days. We had a problem, we didn't have visas for Cameroon and had no place to stay. "We will solve the problem with a 48-hour temporary visa and we pay for one night."

It looked like we were doomed to have to pay for one unwanted night. I gave him our WorldRiders2 card and told him Cameroon would be our 26th country visited and we'd never had such an experience. I asked for his card but he hemmed and hawed then said, "I am out of cards." I asked for his name he wrote down "Philippe" and a phone number. When I asked for his last name he said, "You call me, you ask for Philippe." In the hallway as we were leaving, I told him I would write about our experience with Cameroon Airlines. He sent Achu into another office to get vouchers then turned to me and said, "We give you 2 nights, 2 breakfast and five meals." He had changed his mind. A tender-hearted tough business man.

Achu led us to the temporary visa counter and got that going. As we rounded a corner near the baggage claim, a young guy threw three quick punches to my arm. I spun around, taking a defensive stance. He waved his arms, shadow-boxing. It was obvious he'd been drinking. I continued to hold my fists up, signaling for him to bring it on. He backed off. I started clapping. Several bystanders joined in. He chose to move on. I was too old to take a punch or have my face rubbed on the floor. However, I was ready. My mother always taught me that even when the other guy is bigger or stronger, "You should at least get a sandwich while they're getting a meal."

Bjorn, a guy we'd said hello to, was standing near the bikes. He said, "These two guys have been waiting to help you and keeping your bikes safe."

Of course, they would be our porters. As we struggled down the driveway, another aggressive young guy grabbed one of the bike wheels. The porter shouted, but the guy continued to press. I grabbed his arm and told him to keep his hands off.

He fought back and shouted, "You keep your hands off me!" I ignored him, but he kept yelling and following.

I bellowed back, "Don't yell at me!" I thought I was going to have to go for a sandwich, thank goodness he turned and walked away.

He and a couple of others watched as we loaded our bikes into the hotel van then started giving me a hard time again. As I gave our two porters a 1000 CFA tip, the crass young guy shouted "Where do you come from? Why do you give them worthless money?" The porters smiled and thanked us. I ignored him. He milled about as we climbed into the van, then went hunting for an easier victim.

The van was waiting for two more guys. Hendrik walked across the parking lot, surrounded by the loudmouth and three of his cohorts. As I prepared for confrontation, Hendrik paid them. Next, Bjorn, surrounded again by the same cast of characters. He too, gave a little change. One of them thrust his hand in the window and jogged along as the van pulled away. Man, those guys were aggressive, more so than even the boys in Mauritania.

Hotel Lewat was basic but the rent was right. What's not to like about "paid for?" The room was hot, the water was not, however the AC worked. Dinner with Bjorn from Germany and Hendrik, a Danish geologist. The conversation drifted to the airport hullabaloo. We told them we typically wouldn't give, especially to jerks. Bjorn said, "At the social center where I work, the locals are paid about $20 per month. Most don't have jobs but try to make a little by hustling, selling fruit or anything they can. I give to someone once a week but I think about who, before giving." What a thoughtful guy!

Cat let out a screech as she stepped into the bathroom. A huge cockroach lay on its back taking its last gasps. Its legs were moving but it was a goner. I threw the twitching remains into the trashcan. The bed sheets didn't fit, yet we slept soundly. Travel and hassles had taken a toll.

CAT TRAX Day 128, Marooned in Cameroon. Cold showers and only one towel. Cat said, "We can survive, it's only for a couple of days." Bjorn and Hendrik were in the lobby trying to hook a ride back to the airport. We sat and talked. There is a bonding amongst stranded travelers that is unique unto them.

Achu took our tickets back to Kenya Airlines. What a nice guy. He said, "I have sister in Boston, Massachusetts, and a brother in Los Angeles. I travels to see them, I fly free."

Cat went down the street to an internet cafe. By 5:00 p.m., I was getting nervous. She'd been gone three hours and darkness was approaching. She hadn't taken her wallet or identification. Gathering our wallets, I set off to find her.

The street was alive with small merchants, selling all manner of goods. The banana lady was pushy, she'd sold us a bunch earlier and wanted me to buy more. The air was thick with fumes from motorbikes. Worrying, I walked quickly. I spotted Cat coming up the street but she didn't see me until we were almost face-to-face. She was surprised, my concerns unfounded. She'd found a site, Tour d' Afrique, that Ben, our benefactor in Benin, had mentioned. A group leaving from Cairo, Egypt, would cycle to Cape Town. She'd sent an e-mail, asking for their route.

CAT TRAX Day 129, Preparing for a Flight to Kenya. Cat called Kenya Airlines and confirmed we were booked on the midnight flight. We had to vacate our room. The lounge with two small couches would be our home until departure. Achu called and verified we were booked and that he'd arrange transportation to the airport.

Our driver arrived at 9:15 but didn't help with our bags. We carried and the hotel bellman helped. Cat thought the driver had been drinking or doing drugs. He was completely silent, even nodded off to sleep a few times. Ah well, we made it. Our preparations for the onslaught of porters was for naught. Two guys helped us shuffle the bags and bikes into line at the Kenya Airways counter. As we entered Achu greeted us, assuring us all was set to go.

As I put our bags on the scale, the agent said, "You overweight!" I lifted the bikes onto the scale one at a time. They calculated excess of forty Kilos. The gal reduced that to twenty-six and told us it would cost 4800 CFA, $130! We gasped, complained,

and she said, "You must talk with boss." The terminal was hot. Effort and nerves had us sweating profusely.

Kenya Airways was somehow related to KLM, the Dutch Airline. Christophe, the boss, was young, tall, thin, and blonde. He looked up from his computer as we entered his office. We stood respectfully and explained our Around the World Bicycle Odyssey and the overweight problem. He sat quietly for a minute, studying the paper from the agents. When he looked up he said, "I like to ride bicycle, I give you the excess."

Ecstatic, we hustled back and handed the signed paper to the surprised clerks. They gave us baggage claim tickets, plus our boarding passes, and finally, we were on our way to Kenya.

Boarding began at 11:40 p.m.. Christophe was a great friend to have. He stood at the front of the pushing, jostling line and shouted, "Families and groups of two or more will board first." We edged around several guys who were trying to bypass him. He insisted that a lady with a baby board first. Then, with a wink and nod, he whispered, "Your bikes are on board, I saw them go up."

They fired up the engines and at midnight we pushed back into the darkness of Cameroon night.

Chapter 16 Nairobi and Masai Mara

CAT TRAX Day 130, The Long Night to Nairobi. Unlike Cam Air, our Kenya Airways seats had legroom. The plane was a newer Boeing 737 and felt much safer, but I can't ever relax in flight. Sleep came easily for Cat. At 4:00 a.m. we were beginning final approach. The Captain announced, "It is 6:30 a.m. local time here at Jomo Kenyatta International Airport, Nairobi, Kenya. Your crew and I wish you a safe and enjoyable visit." Our African adventure was back on track. We were heartened when we saw that the bikes and bags had made it.

The line at immigration inched slowly along to the window. The officer grabbed our passports stamped, looked, then said, "100 dollars, please." I started counting our CFA he said, "No, 100 US." We argued but he said "Only US Dollar, from US citizen. Currency exchange upstairs."

Bad news: the currency exchange clerk said "No one here accepts West African CFA." Back at Immigration, the guy was less than empathetic. He barked, "You go to bank, get US Dollars." I followed a guy from the booth to a Standard and Chartered Bank's kiosk. The teller took our Visa card but a cash advance was denied. I got nervous, then he suggested I try the ATM. I slipped the card in, and like a slot machine it spewed cash. Money made everyone friendlier. Passports and visas in hand, we picked up our things. No pushy porters. Cat pushed our bags, I pushed the bikes.

On the sidewalk we encountered a bit of a hustle. I asked, "Do you have a taxi large enough for our bikes?" The guy who seemed to be in charge said, "No problem 2000 Kenya Shillings." Wow, that was $25 US, three times more than a taxi should cost. As we discussed it, a guy walked up and said, "We have a van, we take you for 1,000 Shilling." I said, "May we see your van?" Suddenly, Mr. In Charge taxi guy said, "You can take our car," as he pointed toward an English taxi, "For 800 Shilling."

That pissed me off. The other van pulled up. It was shabby but looked like it would get us to the hotel. Mr. In Charge pressed us but I told him we'd made a deal. Of course, he tried to drop the price again. I told him, "Even if it's free, we won't take it." He turned to the driver of the van and started yelling, pointing his finger and saying "Don't do this bullshit, I'll get you for this, don't you do this bullshit."

I stepped between them, put my finger against his and said,

"Don't point that thing at him, it has a nail in it!" That might have set off WWIII, but, after a moment, everyone began to laugh. We jammed in and were off to Nairobi. Damn, they drove on the left side. I told Joseph the driver, "Those damn British came here and taught you how to drive on the wrong side of the road!"

The city was clean. It reminded us of San Francisco. Tall buildings with the typical hustle and bustle of a big city. It was 8:30 a.m. by the time we checked in to Hotel Oakwood.

The guys at Oakwood arranged a driver, and we set off for the US Embassy. The drill was the same as all US Embassies. A gate with thick bulletproof glass and a cranky local woman in control. Once we cleared the metal detector, she buzzed us in. The room for US citizens was empty. The gal there was great. We needed extra pages for our passports. She accommodated us quickly. Base Camp Charlie had sent papers for our signatures. We handed her the deed for the sale of our house that required a Notary. She said, "We will have this Notarized for you, later today."

Later on, we visited the Tanzanian Embassy for visas. Again, our driver waited as we got the applications. Darn, we'd left our passports back at the hotel. Cat dashed back, while I filled out the forms. I had them completed and paid the 8,000 K Shilling ($50 each) just as Cat returned.

The U.S. Embassy was crowded with Kenyans applying for visas to visit the USA. The cranky lady had the notarized deed. Finally, we were signed and sealed. The driver was glad to see us. He was on fixed price and wanted to get back to business. Of course we gave him extra.

CAT TRAX Day 131, Waiting and Planning in Nairobi. Nairobi felt sophisticated and scenic, but we had to constantly remind ourselves that traffic was British-style. Stepping off the curb was dangerous, as we habitually looked the wrong way. Easy to forget. We made a rule, always look both ways.

Masai Mara was a must see. We wanted to cycle there, then down the length of the Serengeti. We phoned a company called Bike Treks. The owner Nigel said, "This could be done, but not on bikes." We met in a shopping center food court. He sipped a coke while outlining why our plan wouldn't work. "You won't be allowed to cycle in the National Park. There are animals—lions, hyenas, cheetahs, all would love to eat you. Also the border between Kenya and Tanzania in the Park is closed to all traffic."

Nigel presented several ideas, most too expensive. The best for us, go by van to Masai Mara with bikes on board. Stay at a tented camp and visit "The Big Five" on  a game park tour. Above budget, but do-able.

CAT TRAX Day 132, A Shopping and Mechanical day in Nairobi. **_Lion Attacks Bicyclist?_** Africa's Sky News carried a story of a lion attack. Not in Kenya but in the foothills of Los Angeles. A cyclist had been attacked and killed by a mountain lion. Strange, many people back home warned us about Africa's wild animals, never thinking of a lion attack there.

Nigel came to the hotel, gave us vouchers, and collected his fee. Cat was ecstatic. We'd spend two nights in a tent camp on the Serengeti, with a full day safari in Masai Mara National Park.

Walking to dinner, we were surprised at the number of young kids on the street asking for food. A security guard told us, "Their parents drop them off, and expect them to make money." One little guy was especially compelling. He just kept walking beside us, saying, "You buy me food? I am hungry, you buy me food?" It was hard to say no. Another guard used his nightstick to threaten the group of waifs trailing us. We moved on, not wanting to see the stick fly.

CAT TRAX Day 133, Off we go, on Safari! Daniel, our driver, arrived at 8:30 a.m.. We threw our bags and bikes in, then he headed for the Park. He stopped on a cliff overlooking The Great Rift Valley. "The Valley is a geological fault system of Southwest Asia and East Africa," Daniel explained. "The valley is huge, the main section of the valley runs through Ethiopia,

Kenya, Tanzania in to Malawi and Mozambique, maybe more than 3,000 Kilometer."

Daniel pointed out a Maasai Warrior herding his cattle in the shadows of two giant satellite dishes. An African time warp. As we pulled back onto the road a family of baboons ran along beside the van. Daniel said, "If we stop, they would jump on the van, try to open the doors, looking for food."

We arrived at the tented camp by 4:30. Two Maasai warriors working at the camp, Dichi and Kinagner, posed for pictures. By day they were groundskeepers, at night, watchmen. Dichi said, "The night is full with dangers, hyena and leopard, must be kept away."

Settled into our tent, we sipped a glass of wine on the porch. A Swedish family moved in just before dusk. Dichi chopped tree branches and built a fire. The Swedish folks gathered around and sang. Ronni, who lived in Kenya, told us, "Good Swedes feel compelled to sing when gathered round a campfire." He was a professional hunter and a great source of information regarding the animals of Africa. The night was dark on the Serengeti. The stars thick like a sparkling net of diamonds in a coal-black sky.

CAT TRAX Day 134, On Safari in The Masai Mara. Wild

Animals. Wild Places. Anxious to get an early start, we'd worried about waking. No problem, at 3:00 a.m. we awoke to the screams of what we later learned were hyenas. Ronni told us they sometimes had leopards show up at the camp. There were no fences, the animals roamed freely. That made for light sleep.

157

We were all at the breakfast table and talking animals by 6:00.
Cat and I had a separate van. We
moved out in the glow of sunrise.
Dirt roads with tire tracks criss-
crossed the savannah. First
sighting: a herd of zebra. Next, a
family of elephants crossed the
roadway. We became part of the
herd. They moved slowly, swaying
around us along the tire tracks. The largest were the size of our van

and probably weighed more.

We encountered a huge variety of antelope. The grassy plains of
the Serengeti were awakening. A surprising flock of ostrich ran
along the track, we'd always associated ostrich with Australia.

Wildebeest were roaming near the Mara River. We'd seen
National Geographic film of the herd surging and struggling across
rivers during their annual migration. Approaching the water, the
Beests sense that some would be sacrificed as food for crocodiles.
And yet nature requires the survivors and their young take the same
chances year after year. An armed guard with an AK 47
chaperoned as we walked to river's edge. He told Cat, "We no kill

animals, gun is for scare them." A huge croc languished on the bank, waiting patiently for the next wildebeest feast.

The hippo pool was amazing. They wallow, float, yawn, and occasionally waddle onto shore. Hopes of seeing lion and cheetah were waning with the afternoon sun, then Daniel got a radio "heads-up" from another driver. He spun around, and headed for a clump of trees. There in the tall grass were two gorgeous cheetah. We observed them for half an hour as they stretched, groomed themselves, and lay about like house cats. He also found a pride of lion, all female. Hoping to see the King of Beasts, we had to settle for his brood.

Later in the afternoon at Keekorok, an upscale hotel, we witnessed monkeys mischievously trying to break into cars. A lone warthog named Pork Chop was nearly tame. He delighted in challenging and herding us about.

We spent a full twelve hours searching viewing and enjoying the animals of Masai Mara; it was dusk when we rolled through the gate of the tent camp. Tired, yes but still on an emotional high. I'd always felt that game parks were just large zoos, but this trip changed my attitude. The Park felt a bit less contrived, yet controlled. The animals are constantly watched, even cared for at times, yet they continue to live as they have for thousands of years, despite the recent invasion of motorized humankind.

Dinner was accompanied by jungle sounds. The campfire died down, the stars shone brightly and we lay back in the safety of our tent.

CAT TRAX Day 135, Pee in the Night, Maasai Warriors, back to Nairobi. Fearful of meeting a hyena or leopard on the path to the outhouse I cut the top off a plastic water bottle for night use. We had both peed in it when in a clumsy, drowsy moment I kicked it over. Yikes! The yellow stream quickly flowed across the tent's plastic floor onto the carpet between the beds. Instantly wide-awake, I began mopping. The worst, having to tell the camp manager the next morning. At first, he thought I was saying we'd been sick. When it sunk in that the towels and rug were soaked in piss he smiled and said, "Hacuna Matata," No problem. Embarrassed, I wondered whether this was a first in Phinius's career?

That morning, we cycled to a nearby Maasai village. As we rolled in, the tribe danced toward then around us, grunting and chanting. A moment we shall never forget. Cat knew how I hated the contrived films of tribes people cavorting for cameras. She had struggled, not  wanting to pay $40 for the visit. I saw it as a rare opportunity. The village was off the beaten path.

We spent more than an hour learning about their traditional lifestyle and the troubles of merging with modern life. Many Maasai live as their ancestors did for thousands of years. The men herd and guard the cattle, the women gather wood and water, and build the houses. Cat suggested to our young host that the women seemed to do all the work. The lead villager had studied law in England and tried to practice in Nairobi but couldn't adjust to city life. In perfect Queen's English he said, "We herdsmen are warriors. We risk our lives keeping the cattle safe from lion and other predators. Our family's wealth is measured by the size of our herd. Cattle are so valuable we don't kill or eat them, until they are very old."

Ronni had told us that the traditional Maasai diet consisted of milk and blood. They bleed the healthy animals though a hole in their necks. Curdled blood and milk are mixed and drank. Our friendly Maasai lawyer told us, "Young people now mix some vegetables into our diets. The elders' stomachs aren't able to digest them." He also explained, " All of the boys living in this village are my brothers or half brothers. Our father is very wealthy, he has many cattle. Accumulating cattle affords a man more wives. Our thirteen houses are home to my mother and Papa's twelve other wives, his many sons and daughters."

Speaking of old ways, the mud-like material they build their huts of is a mixture of elephant and cow urine and dung. Centuries back their ancestors learned that lion and hyena didn't like that smell and avoided their villages. We sat inside one of their homes, talking with the young man and listening to his sister's point of view as he translated. The brothers demonstrated spinning a branch on a piece of wood to start a fire. They didn't allow matches in the village as the huts were too flammable.

There were issues between nearby farming tribes, the Maasai and their foraging cattle. The government was involved, trying to settle the matter and our young lawyer friend was involved with the negotiations.

Leaving, we noted a few cement-block huts scattered outside the village. Times were changing, slowly. They'd recently installed a telephone in the village. No cell phones or computers yet, but those would come. Like it or not, they were on a track toward change and transition into the 21st century. They seemed happy to have us and we were happy to have been invited.

Daniel's van began to overheat as we left the village. He pulled over several times, adding water. Finally, he stopped a passing van and had us join their group. The new driver was running late, his office would be closing soon. At the Hillcrest Hotel, we asked him to wait while we made sure that they had a room. The clerk was apologetic-sorry, no vacancy. Back at the van, the driver was throwing our bikes and bags out into parking lot like a raging bull elephant. I was pretty pissed, he didn't care and drove away. We'd have to load up and cycle to the nearest hotel.

Cat went back to the front desk to ask directions to another hotel. As she approached, the clerk's phone rang. Call it the luck of the WorldRiders, a group of eight cancelled. We happily retrieved the bikes and bags and made our way to our room. From homeless to celebrants, we devoured a great dinner and toasted our success with an okay bottle of wine. We reminisced about our incredible moments shared with the Big Five beasts and tribesmen of the Serengeti.

Chapter 17 Nairobi, Kenya to Kilimanjaro

Cat Trax Day 137, 92 Ks, Nairobi to Kajiado. The staff at the Hillcrest had suggested we cycle from Nairobi toward Ngong Town. It was very hilly, so steep that we pushed at times. A guy going our way stepped in behind Cat and helped her push up one hill. At another spot, a Matatu van bus whipped in front of us and stopped to let off passengers. Cat yelled to me, "Don't stop, keep moving." As I started around, he took off. I grabbed the brakes, Cat hit me and toppled. The bike hit her leg and heel as it fell. Another Good Samaritan lifted it off.

We'd been urged to ride through Karen, a town named for its

most famous former resident, Karen Blixen. She'd written *Out of Africa*, a bestselling book that became an award-winning movie. She'd died a few years back and her home was a museum. No time for that today, we still had far to go. The area was lush and tropical.

At lunch in Ngong Town a couple of older guys, obviously lifelong friends, engaged us in conversation. When they heard we were going to Namanga, one said, "You must stay at River Hotel and meet the owner John. He is half Maasai and half European and looks as though he could be your brother."

The Ngong town was teeming with kids walking home from school. They loved to call out "How are you?" Then, before we could answer, they'd say "Fine." Probably the first two English phrases they'd learned.

Night was descending as we rolled into Kajiado. Hotel Empeut looked like a 1950s Motel. Priced right, it was 2000 KS about $22 US, and included breakfast.

CAT TRAX Day 138, 91 Ks, Kajiado to Namanga. Hotel Empeut was named for the area. Empeut meant "Wet place," a place with year-round water. Living up to its name, it rained during the night and was cloudy, cold, and windy as we pedaled away toward Namanga.

A tourist stop called "The Bull's Eye" drew us in. At the curio shop, we told the young boy there that we needed food. He said, "My mother will fix you lunch." Michael, nineteen, had just completed secondary school,was studying for college exams, and owed the opportunity to his aunt. She owned the Bull's Eye, he and his mother worked for her. Michaels father died when he was one year old. His aunt paid his mother to run the place and paid him 15,000 T Schilling per month, about $15. He worked almost every day to earn it.

Some age-old cures work regardless of modern medicine. A huge ant crawled near Cat's foot. She asked Michael if it would sting. He said "They bite, it is painful. We Maasai use mucous on bites and stings to ease pain and speed healing." He put a finger in his nose to make the point.

Michael wanted to study religion and become a pastor. He told us, "A neighbor went to the US and spent three months there with the church. When he returned, he started a church and became rich." So, religion and money do mix. He tried to convert us, convinced that prayer worked, "I prayed to go to college, now I will go." He said, "You are also a prayer answered, when I come to America, I will visit you!" What a nice young guy.

Lunch was ugali, a local food of beans and mutton. Ugali was ground maize or casaba flour. White and gooey, not to our taste, but we did enjoy the beans and meat. The best was meeting and talking with Michael. I advised him to learn about computers. He didn't think it was important as they had few there. I told him they would come and it would be important to understand them.

Just a few Ks down the road we came upon a big Mercedes truck loaded with Hare Krishna followers. Two Brits, a Scot, several African adults, and a group of orphaned African boys. They traveled around Kenya, performing rap music and raising money. It was interesting talking with them. One of the Brits, a woman, said, "I have followed Krishna for more than fifteen years," The Scottish guy was quiet but as we were leaving he held out a book, *The Path to Yoga* and said "Please accept this as a gift." We loved his accent and accepted the book.

Nearing Namanga, we ran into a herd of camel. We hadn't seen any of the gangly beasts since leaving Mauritania. A boy sauntered down the road toward us, the camel herder's son. I took his photo, and he called his father to see it. The father was amazed, so we took his, too. They were completely intrigued, perhaps it was the first time they'd seen a picture of themselves.

By 5:00 p.m. we rolled into Namanga. I asked for the River Hotel and a friendly guy pointed toward a dirt road. Running low on cash, we hoped they took Visa. The grounds were beautiful. Bad news, no credit cards. After counting our Kenya Shillings, we felt we could stay if they'd reduce the rate. The girl squirmed, then Cat pointed out the price list on the wall. Kenyan prices would be lower, so she relented.

John, the half-Maasai half-European man who owned the place wasn't there. Darn, we'd wanted to see my look-alike. A warm shower, a glass of wine, and we set off for dinner. There was a tent top on the lawn, a lounge for tent campers. The light had drawn a huge cloud of flying bugs. We moved inside and watched them swarm to the lit dining room window, virtually covering it. The waiter explained, "They are swarming termites. They fly from those mud stacks when it rains."

CAT TRAX Day 139, 61 Ks on Bikes, 45 on a Tire Truck,

Namanga to Arusha. At breakfast, we met John. He'd owned the River Hotel for thirty years, and been a member of the Kenyan Parliament for twenty-five years. We told him about the guys we met in Ngong Town who said I looked like his brother. That was good for a laugh, the only feature we shared was our receding hair lines. John's friend Chase was a third-generation African, a Sikh who'd never been in India.

The Tanzanian border was at the edge of town. The crossing took an hour. Stop, show passports, fill out Kenyan forms for immigration and customs. Then the same drill on the Tanzanian side. Most of our time was spent in line. The customs officials had stopped a truck pulling double trailers full of tires. They made them unload all the tires onto the ground.

It was downhill onto the Tanzanian savannah. At thirty Ks we entered the village of Longdido. I turned to avoid a speed bump, my wheel dug in, and I went down. I just lay there, feeling for injuries as a crowd gathered. I think they thought it was funny. And it was, once I felt sure nothing other than my ego had been bruised.

Fearing Longdido might be the last food we'd see, we ate early lunch of goat stew, beans and chapati. The flies buzzed round, and the locals swarmed around, checking out the strangers. They were a mix of Maasai and another local tribe, shorter and stockier built. I asked for lemonade, the woman held up Coke and orange drink. I chose Coke and she asked for 1000 Tanzanian

Shilling, about a dollar. I thought it was too high and tried to bargain. She gave me 200 T Shilling change, and opened both bottles. A communication issue lost in the value of foreign currency.

As we ate, a group of white faces came by. James from Seattle was there teaching English to the Maasai. A couple, Paul and Sally, stopped as we talked. They, too, were volunteers from England. Caring, giving people, making a difference in other people's lives and their own.

Peddling on, Cat felt pain in her knee and Achilles tendon. The pain increased with each turn of the crank, and she was soon in tears. We decided to catch a ride to Arusha. As a Land Cruiser passed, we waved our arms, indicating desperation, but were ignored.

A young Maasai boy with his dog began to jog along with us, signaling he wanted food. He looked about ten years old. He was carrying a big iron spear that had to weigh much as he. At the speed Cat's knee allowed, he easily stayed with us, begging and gesturing. I decided I'd speed up then turn back, and get a picture of him running beside Cat. I pedaled hard, he sped up and stayed with me. I pressed, he sprinted. I couldn't outrun him. We stopped and I asked to take a picture. He held his hand out and said, "Shilling." I held out 200 T Shilling. He shook his head, "No, 5,000." I put the camera away, smiled, and thanked him. He stood staring as we continued struggling up the hill.

The next vehicle along was the big tire truck we'd seen at the border. I stood on the edge of the road, waving my arms. They stopped and the driver asked, "What are you wanting?" When I explained Cat's leg pain, he said, "Yes, we can take you." Four young guys in the cab jumped out as the driver Joel pulled off the pavement. It took all five to lift the bikes up onto the load. Three of the guys crammed into an area behind the seats, another sat on a pillow  on the console. Cat and I shared the passenger seat; uncomfortable, but better than continuing our slow struggle. Rain came pouring down as the truck slowly bounced up the hill.

There was a sticker on the dashboard: "Ladies are like Matatus, (Taxi Vans) if you miss one, there'll be another by soon." The guys laughed as Cat read it. We passed two Maasai boys dressed in black. Cat asked about their blankets. The guys laughed an uneasy nervous laugh. One of them, Robinson, who spoke good English, said, "They have been circumcised, they must wear the black for about a month, until the scabs falls off."

We were going to the Impala Hotel, Joel knew the place. I said, "Go to your company, we'll cycle to the hotel." Robinson said, "We would turn here for the Trucking Company but Joel will take you to Impala." We rode high and dry through the streets of Arusha to the door of the hotel. What a spectacle as the guys handed down the bikes. We posed for a picture, then I asked Robinson how much we should pay Joel. He spoke with Joel then said, "He will not take money."

What terrific people, satisfied just to share our adventure. And a great way to get a painful leg off the road. Several guests stared as our double-trailer-truck-limousine drove away.

A couple, Joe and Deborah, watched our impressive entry. They had just returned from climbing Kilimanjaro and we were anxious to talk with them. She was full of energy, he said, "Kili kicked my butt." She suggested dinner at 7:30. He said, "I can't wait that long."

The hotel delivered ice and we packed it around Cat's sore knee, then sipped a little wine, which always helps. Deborah stopped by as we sat down for dinner. She answered Cat's questions and calmed her qualms about Kilimanjaro.

CAT TRAX Day 140, A Day Off in Arusha. Joe was a personal

trainer and exercise lecturer who'd written a book, *I know I should exercise, BUT...* He worked at a health resort where he'd met Deborah. Joe had also ridden his bike across the US, twice. Parting he said, "When you get to Tecate, Mexico, stop at Rancho La Puerta. I'll get a rooms comped, you can speak about your trip, to guests."

The taxi fare was 2000 Ts to the first bank, but Standard and Chartered Bank wouldn't advance cash on our Visa or ATM card. So, we turned to Barclay's. They accepted our ATM card and the machine spewed out 200,000 T Shilling. The taxi fee grew from 2000 to 8000, due to all our running around. Too late to negotiate, we thought the driver probably got us for a couple of bucks, but that's life. The best thing about Tanzanian Shillings, they were 1000 to $1.00, easy to calculate.

Chapter 18 Climbing Kilimanjaro, Tanzania

Picture a twelve-year-old kid sitting in the flickering light of a movie theatre. It was 1962 and Hemingway's "The Snows of Kilimanjaro" leapt off the silver screen in living color. That image was never to leave my mind and always to pose the question "How can there be a place in African where there is always snow?" I knew that one day I would go there, I had to go there.

CAT TRAX Day 141, The Climb Begins, Moshi, Tanzania. We learned we'd have to hire a guide and porters through a tour company.

We found a company and a great guy, Genesis. He took us to his boss's home to rent suitable climbing togs and equipment. Genesis spoke of his many climbs up Kilimanjaro. His stories of Kili excited us and increased our love for him. We asked, "Why don't you guide us to the top?" He replied, "I'm manager of the sales office, my boss doesn't allow me to climb." We begged, he nodded toward the Boss, and she broke down. "You may take them, if your work at the office is caught up." He seemed happy, we were ecstatic.

CAT TRAX Day 142, Marangu Gate to Mandera Hut. Our

bikes were stored safely at the hotel. Genesis helped load our bags into their SUV. We were seated in the first row. The porters, Salvo, Rafael, and Johnson were jammed into the back with our baggage and supplies. Genesis sat with us, our introduction to the pecking order. The aged Toyota struggled up to 6,534 feet, a steady sometimes steep, climb to the Gate of Marangu National Park. They arranged our gear and we checked in. The porters were also required to have a minimum of equipment and clothing. We watched each as they went through the check point, then walked down the fence and threw some of the clothing back over. The next porter to check in would take the same clothing to the gate to qualify. A real learning experience: our porters would be underdressed. Genesis matter-of-factly said, "They can't afford the required expensive, warm clothing."

It would be a five-day walk up Kili, with a day off to acclimate at 13,000 feet. Suiting up, my toes hit the ends of the rented boots. Genesis said, "Here, I fix for you." He removed the insoles. I found a little more toe room, and we were off.

The first days climb was 7.2 Ks the rise just 2,400 feet. A pleasant walk through a tropical rain forest. Genesis pointed out two breeds of monkeys swinging through the vines. He was very serious about sharing his knowledge. Rain spit down at times, thickening the already sultry air.

We stopped for sandwiches. As we ate Rafael fell ill and decided to turn back. Porters were only allowed to carry 25 kilos, about 55 pounds. Genesis shouldered his load. We'd gone just a short distance when Turo, our replacement porter, caught up. He must have jogged.

Genesis urged us to drink plenty of water, which necessitated pee stops in the bushes. Cat squatted, and later discovered she'd lost her sunglasses. Back to the area, we searched to no avail. All the bushes began to look the same. Genesis came to the rescue, digging out a funky-looking pair from his pack. Like a Boy Scout, he was always prepared. We noticed that the equipment worn by the porters was, like ours, all used. Probably lost or left behind by previous climbers.

The Mandara Huts were A-frame structures, designed and built by Norwegians. Each hut had four single bunks. The toilet was a short walk down a narrow pathway. Bad news for me, as I usually had to go three times during the night. After settling in, Genesis led us about 800 feet above camp to Maundi Crater, unfortunately the wonderful view was hidden in clouds. The crater we couldn't see had been created eons before by a huge volcano.

Dinner was potatoes and vegetables, cooked by Johnson, served by Salvo. It was tasty and filling. The clouds parted, treating us to a beautiful sunset. We were in our bunks ready for sleep by 8:30. A wonderful first day on the slopes of Kilimanjaro.

CAT TRAX Day 143, Marangu to Horombo Hut. Tired, we slept better than we'd expected. At 6:30 a.m., Salvo rapped on the door and left a basin of hot water. We had to drag ourselves out for breakfast by 7:30. Obviously we cyclists, thinking we were conditioned, were fooled by the climb. Different muscles and altitude. Cat rinsed off, I rinsed and shaved without a mirror. By 8:10 our boots hit the trail. Genesis set a slow pace and we were grateful.

Cat asked Genesis how he got his name. He responded with pride, "I am the first-born son, of my father's first wife. My father was a teacher and Christian, Genesis is first book of Bible. When his job took him away he married another woman. My Father couldn't afford or just didn't send money. It put a lot of pressure on me, the first-born." He bowed his head, then continued, "I took work at age fourteen, supporting my mother and siblings. Mother had a heart problem, by the time we'd saved enough money for treatment it was too late, she died."

When we asked how he began working as a guide he laughed and told us, "I had a good office job but wanted to experience Kili. I bribed a guide to take me along as a porter. I was fit, a tennis player and felt I could handle the trek. Hoisting the bag onto my head, I soon realized I couldn't carry fifty-five pounds all day. The guide allowed me to carry a big box of bread. It looked impressive but was light."

Continuing, he said, "That company specialized in German tourists. I didn't speak German but my English was better than their guide's. After that, I knew I wanted more of the mountain but didn't feel strong enough. I was astonished when the tour operator called and asked me to guide for his company. I later learned that first group had written letters, suggesting Genesis was very likeable, and his language skill made our climb a fantastic experience. I climbed Kili sixty-four more times, before taking my management position."

Genesis who was fifty years old had a dream, "I want to save money and buy a Land Rover. I will conduct freelance tours to Ngorongoro Crater, to visit the large animal populations. I think my strength lies in my knowledge of the plants and animals." For us it was his ability to relate to his clients. By then he was a good friend.

We met a Russian girl, Ludmila, on the trail and struck up a friendship. Her pace was similar to ours, except she often stopped to take pictures of plants and flowers. Genesis pulled a book out *The Plants and Animals of Kilimanjaro*. He drew the three of us into stories and photo sessions of flowers.

Genesis took Ludmila's guide aside, telling him, "I think she is not taking enough water, don't you fear she will be sick?" As if on cue, a strange-looking stretcher on a single bicycle wheel rounded a curve above us. The two porters stopped to catch their breaths. It shook our confidence, seeing the guy strapped in. He looked at me through glazed eyes. I asked, "Are you okay?" He gave a thumbs up, but couldn't speak. Altitude sickness was said to be awful and the only cure was getting back down the mountain. He rolled his eyes, then closed them tight.

Rain drizzled down as we ate our box lunches. Genesis was constantly saying, "Pole, pole." He explained, "This means slow, slow in Swahili." It was 4:45 as we walked in to Horombo. Looking forward to taking the next day off, we'd just begun to relax when Genesis said, "Tomorrow we hike up to Zebra Rock." A day off hike.

The dining hall was jammed with excited climbers. It was cold and the sun was setting. We were shocked to see a guy sitting near the door in short sleeves and flip flops. Even in heavy jackets, we were shivering. At our table, we were joined by Wayne, the underdressed guy. He was from Orlando, Florida. He apologized, "I'm not a good conversationalist, I just got back from the summit, I feel woozy." Then he shouted, "I'm going to be sick!" His vomit spewed across the table toward us, covering his legs, the table cloth, and bench.

We jumped up and went searching for Wayne's guide. Salvo joined the search, then moved our things to a different table. Poor Wayne just sat staring into space. I asked how he felt. He mustered the strength to say, "Bet you've never had dinner entertainment like that before!"

The clouds rolled in and out endlessly, we returned to our hut just as they parted, exposing the City of Moshi far below. Above us, the stars twinkled like brilliant gems. By 8:00 p.m. we were snuggled into our toasty sleeping bags.

CAT TRAX Day 144, Acclimatization at Horombo. An outhouse trip at 2:00 a.m. chilled us to the bone. The vastness of shining stars shone down like a neon light. We lay back and listened to the pounding of our hearts, the effect of being at 12,976 feet.

My usual 6:00 a.m. "wake up" toilet call was a brisk walk and early eye opener. Salvo brought a basin of hot water at 7:30. We both did PTAs. At Cat's request, I shaved. Walking toward the chow hall, Cat stopped a German guy coming into camp. She asked if he'd made summit. He said, "Is my first ever high altitude, first ever altitude sickness." He caught Cat's attention when he said, "It is vera dangerous, vera dangerous, but beeuutiful. I vas seeing sun rising und I vas puking and puking. It vas fantastic!"

Genesis led us up to 13,600 feet, a place he called Zebra Rocks. Breathing became more difficult as we adjusted to the thinning air. We rested beneath the striped rocks as Genesis spun his tale. "A fellow, once long ago, decided it would cost less, he'd save money, by hauling supplies on donkeys rather than using porters. Under heavy burdens, the zebras struggled to this spot then keeled over and died." The rocks were called zebra because they were striped. We didn't get the correlation between donkeys and zebras but loved the way Genesis told the story.

Genesis, Johnson, and Salvo joined us for lunch and a wonderful round-table discussion. They told of the terrain and how the final leg would be climbed at midnight. The idea, as we'd heard from the German guy, was to see the sun rise from Uhuru, the summit. Genesis decided to allow the porters to join us on the final assault. They'd never been at summit and wanted the experience. It would be a step in helping them move up to guiding. Johnson had already earned official Assistant Guide status. A German group coming down gave us their leftover Maxim a powdered drink similar to Gatorade. We mixed it with hot water. Cat and I liked it. After just a sip our team turned up their noses, turning back to their favored Lipton's Tea.

Camp began to bulge at the seams that afternoon. A group of fifty-three Brits and their entourage of guides and porters straggled in. They were tent camping. A descending group also set up tents. Matt, from San Diego, California, made the experience sound dreadful. "We camped at summit, all our water froze. I lay shivering, anticipating sunrise all night." He added "I'm tired and weak but thrilled, we made it!"

Sudden weather changes often occur at high altitude. Winds began to howl as the skies grew dark. Angry shards of lightening followed by rolling thunder accentuated Mother Nature's power and fury. It was cold, we spent the afternoon huddled in our sleeping bags. Cat suffered a brief bout of upset tummy and diarrhea.

That evening at dinner Genesis went over the game plan. Wake up as usual breakfast at 7:00 the hike to Kibo Hut would begin at 7:30. We were experiencing anxiety, not so much about the climb, but about getting through the hardships and back to our bikes.

We slept unbelievably well at 12, 976 feet, interrupted only by bites of what Cat felt were high-altitude bed bugs. We sprayed our bags with repellent and fell instantly back into dream land. Cat later admitted she'd suffered nightmares about the hazards of the summit.

CAT TRAX Day 145, POLE, POLE, UP, UP To KIBO HUT. We gathered at 7:30 and Genesis led the charge upward at Pole Pole speed. The terrain was changing again. We'd come through jungle semi arid and now desert like rocks and scrub brush. At a rest stop Genesis explained "The Porters, are weighed in each morning as they leave camp to check the weight they carry and to calculate the amount of trash that should be returning." Trails were free of litter although we did see lots of discarded blue strips from the caps of plastic water bottles. We picked up all we saw for disposal at the next camp.

Our greatest disappointment of the trek was learning how guides and porters were paid. It became *the* conversation between all trekkers, once tales of climbing and sickness had been told. Guides were paid 25,000 ($25 US) Tanzanian Shillings, porters 13,000 ($13 US) for the entire six days. We all agreed it was slave wages. They had to carry our baggage and supplies on their heads all day, set camp, cook, and serve our meals. With that in mind, conversations with other Kili climbers became, "how much will you tip?"

Ludmila, our Russian friend, came walking down toward us. She had skipped the day of acclimatization. Looking sickly and fatigued, she said in a quivering voice, "I climb half to summit, I sick, very sick, I turn back." As we tried to comfort her, she said, "I no unhappy, I glad to go down, go Zanzibar."

A young couple approached us and asked, "Are you the guys that are cycling around the world?" Sana and Mohammed were from Boston, Massachusetts. He was a doctor, she worked with a non-profit serving the homeless. We exchanged small talk, then they surged onward.

Wind chilled the air and temperatures plummeted. Approaching Kibo Hut at 15,500 feet the snows of Kilimanjaro appeared close

enough to touch. However, they were a long, tough night's climb above. The trail zig-zagged upward through green shale, as though daring us to accept the challenge. It was a mere 4 Ks from Kibo, than less than 3 miles, to the 19,300 foot summit. Genesis said. "It will take 7 hours to reach Uhuru, top of the ice." The thought of clawing our way up through loose rock in pitch-black night sent chills through us.

Kibo Hut was similar to many African hotels. The room was dorm style, we'd be sharing it with Mohammed and Sana. The four of us sat on the bunks, talking about adventures, life, and the summit. Missing several panes of glass, the windows allowed the wind to howl through. Cat began putting on layer after layer until she was wearing all her clothing. She crawled into her sleeping bag and shivered. I lay our Maasai blankets across her feet. She lay

shaking, purple lips quivering. My head began to throb.

Mohammed, a physician and general practitioner, was the most popular guy at there. Every one called him the Doc of Kibo. Everybody, whether ascending or descending, had maladies. One

Chinese guy was very upset, he wanted a pill to cure his friend. Mohammed told him the only cure was to go down. In broken English the guy said, "You docta, you help!" Mohammed shook his head, raised his voice and said, "He sick, you go down!"

We snuggled in our sleeping bags and watched daylight wane as the cold wind whistled through the hut. Johnson brought cold pasta and potatoes for dinner. Hot when he'd started, it cooled as he crossed from the galley. I ventured out for a thermos of hot water. Genesis and the porters cooked and slept in the warmth of the galley. With wind chill it was minus 12 degrees Celsius.

Genesis and I walked back in the cold and dark. He conducted a team meeting and pep talk. "We awaken you at 11:00 this night and begin climb to Uhuru, at midnight. You will be fine, no worries, we will be there for you." Then we stacked hands and he led a sort of sing-song cheer, "We go, we go, pole, pole, to the Uhuru."

Within ten minutes of his taking leave, Cat felt woozy and her heart rate accelerated. I tried to calm her, knowing she was worried about having another heart attack (she'd suffered one in October, 2000). At the same time, my head felt like it was being crushed by a steel band. Then my old nemesis, atrial fibrillation, what I call flippy-floppy heart, began to hammer in my chest. Irregular heartbeats feel terrible. No way to describe it, if you haven't had the experience. My doctor had said, "It won't kill you, unless it continues for more than three days, then it could cause blood clots to form." I wondered what affect altitude would have. We were a mess. Mohammed and Sana were sleeping.

At 10:00 p.m. we both needed the toilet. Knowing the wind would whistle through and awaken our roommates, we had done our best to hold off, but nature's call finally won out. As we struggled, putting on our boots, Sana stirred, then asked if she could join us. Mohammed was awake too, but chose to stay and bolt the door after us to keep the frigid airstream at bay. We three walked together, following the beams of our cycling headlights. It was bone-chilling. I felt sorry for the girls having to pull their pants down in order to squat above the "long drop."

Back inside Kibo Hut, Cat sought medical advice from Dr. Mohammed. After hearing her story about the heart attack he said, "As a doctor, I must advise you not to go higher, however as an adventurer I feel you could go onward if you carry medications, especially your Nitro Glycerin. Also, ask if the staff has oxygen they could carry for you." They had neither oxygen nor meds.

Cold air rushed in as Genesis burst through the door. He shook us out of our sleeping bags, putting on his cheeriest face as he told us it was time to go. I halfheartedly asked about oxygen he just shook his head, no. Cat and I held hands, squeezed hands, then I told Genesis we would not, could not go. He was visibly disappointed, but nodded his understanding. Sana and Mohammed, kneeling on their prayer rugs, arose shook our hands and disappeared with Genesis into the cold and dark. We wished them luck, then bolted the door.

We snuggled in our sleeping bags but there'd be little sleep that night. A line was written on the bunk slat above me, "I stink, therefore, I am." I read it aloud and we filled the hut with our laughter. It had been six days since our last real bath.

At 4:00 a.m. came a knock on the door, barely heard above the howl of the wind. It was Sana. She said, "I began hallucinating, seeing angels flying above the lights shining up from the toilets. Soon I was dizzy and throwing up. Mohammed insisted I return, with one of our porters."

At 7:00 a.m. Salvo brought cold toast and a thermos of hot water for coffee. Mohammed came back as we were eating. He said, "I had to abandon my dream. We waited below Uhuru, but the wind never let up. Nobody made the summit, due to high winds and icy conditions." Then he admitted, "I too, had been sick, throwing up. Once we turned back, as I hurried down to check on Sana, I began to feel better."

Sorry for Mohammed, we were happy that we hadn't tried, only to fail. We told ourselves "we're cyclists not mountain climbers" as we hurriedly packed. Oops, our camera, wrapped in a towel for warmth, fell on the cold cement floor and broke into pieces. It was a goner. We agonized for a few seconds, then shrugged it off, filled our bags and headed for the door. We were greeted by a beautiful sunrise. The summit remained socked in. As we hugged

Mohammad and Sana I said, "We almost made it, but we didn't allow Kili to kill us!"

CAT TRAX Days 146 & 147, Down and off Kili! Anxious to escape the cold thin air, we were almost jogging. No more pole, pole we wanted a real bed under our backs, and bikes under our butts. We were back in the streets of Moshi in just a day and a half.

Though we were running short of cash, we upped our tip to $200. Genesis and the boys had worked so hard for so little. Funny how, once again, people we'd known only for a few days felt like family. Especially Genesis. He was one fine person. We hugged, promising to stay in touch.

Chapter 19 Kilimanjaro to Tanga, Tanzania

CAT TRAX Day 148, A Fantastic Day at Hotel Impala We were so sore, we dedicated a day off to recovery. Our toes were blistered, our tired legs ached. Due to our late arrival, we were given a small run-down room. As we ate breakfast, the young man who'd checked us in on our first day asked how we were doing. We replied, "Tired but fine, however we're disappointed we didn't get a better room." After we finished eating, he led us to a beautiful suite. The bathroom was huge with tub and shower. Delighted, we happily moved when he told us the price was the same.

We needed, nay deserved luxury. Cat immediately took a long hot shower rinsing away the grime of Kili. We went exploring, shopping for water and food, then enjoyed a picnic lunch sitting on our patio overlooking the pool.

CAT TRAX Day 149, Another, Even Better Day at Impala. Cash day, we'd need enough to get us through a couple of weeks between Moshi and the next banks. We'd asked the Impala to advance cash on our Visa card, they declined. We needed an ATM. We discussed our dilemma over a hearty breakfast near the pool. Our only option was to take the hotel shuttle to Arusha and Barclays Bank.

Our plan: get to Arusha, get cash, and have lunch before returning. Unfortunately, the shuttle was booked by students at the International School, so we had to wait forty minutes in the bus. That shredded our plan. We'd only have a thirty-minute turnaround. When the bus reached the Arusha Impala, Cat asked the driver to drop us at Barclays Bank. Just as he agreed, a woman stuck her head into the bus to tell us the bus to Moshi was leaving right then. We explained our need for cash and the entire bus journey we'd just made to get there.

The woman took us to the other waiting bus and told the driver, "You must take this lady to Barclays Bank before starting back to Moshi." Whew, a very close call. The shuttle stood idling, waiting for us at the bank. We withdrew cash, then were headed back to our Hotel Impala.

CAT TRAX Day 150, On the Road Again, 64 Ks Moshi to Mwanga. It was 11:30 when we said goodbye to the friendly staff and cycled out of the Impala. We rode into town to bid adieu to our friends at Mauly Tours. They told us Genesis was so tired he was taking a few days off. It was 1:30 and hot by the time we finally started pedaling up the hill and out of Moshi.

At a roundabout, we asked a local girl for direction to Hino. She stared at us and squinted. The blank look told us she wasn't connecting with our pigeon Swahili. A couple of girls walked up. They were from the US, there in Tanzania on a Mission of some sort for a year. They confirmed the right turn was the main road to Hino, Dar es Salaam and points south.

We stayed on the bike seats until 6:00 p.m. with only occasional stops for a stretch or trip to the bushes. Mwanga was a dusty wide spot on the highway. Tired, we got soft drinks and sat on the steps of a teleboutique. The girl there told us of a place, Hotel Anjelika. She suggested a guy lounging nearby, Omar, would guide us for 1000 Shilling ($1.00). Exhausted and tired of getting nowhere, we hired Omar. He immediately lit a cigarette assumed a posture of importance and began to swagger, leading us down the side street.

He spoke to every passersby as though he was accompanying royalty. Cat began to get nervous. The road deteriorated to dirt. Omar couldn't communicate with us at all. A slick-looking guy sidled up and spoke in English. He assured Cat that we were headed in the right direction. He also chatted with Omar. We felt he was trying to get a cut of Omar's 1000 Ts. Then as suddenly as he had appeared he pointed and said "Anjelika Hotel, goodbye." and disappeared into the bush. Omar puffed up his chest, puffed on his cigarette, and bragged to the staff about having led us there. The room was tiny but clean. We had our own toilet and shower. Cat called it a haven in an otherwise hideous place.

Tired, we felt as though we'd lost our stamina due to trekking and being off the road.

CAT TRAX Day 151, 57 Ks, Mwanga to Same (Sah-may). By 8:30 we were on the road again. A goodbye to the nice people there, although few could understand they all joined in saying, "bye, bye."

A tall, lanky guy, bare from the waist up, staggered across the road in front of us. He was talking to himself, we thought he was mentally impaired. His right leg was swollen, the ankle huge. It looked like he had Elephantiasis, like we'd seen in Genesis' book.

It was 1:30 when we rolled in to Same. A policeman directed us to the Elephant Hotel. The young clerk could barely see over the desk. The room and price were small, too, 15,000 Shilling.

Both of our tail ends were scorched with saddle sores. We had really gotten soft during our Kili hiatus. A generous application of antibiotic cream soothed and cooled our tail feathers.

CAT TRAX Day 152, 115 Ks, Same to Mombo. Monkeys watched from the trees as we downed our breakfast. They put on a show, swinging branch to branch. They witnessed the rolling out of our bikes. Perhaps their first cyclist sighting.

A slight drizzle felt great. Not wet enough to bother us, but enough to cool the air. We passed by several possibilities for food, so it was 2:00 p.m. as we pulled into a wide spot in the road known as Buiko. A young guy Nuru, suggested a shack for food. He was a student at Mazinda Day Secondary School. It was market day and lots of Maasai Warriors drifted in and out. Several young guys were dressed fit to kill. I tried to get a picture, but they made it clear they didn't want to be a part of our memoirs. They didn't ask for money, they just turned away or covered their faces.

Entering Mombo, the Liverpool Bar and Restaurant drew us in. We sat in the shade, sipped soft drinks and chatted with locals. They all agreed the best hotel in town was nearby Saldina Inn. Cat checked the room came back and said, "If that's the best, I'd hate to see the worst." The room was stark and dingy. The toilet and bath across the courtyard were even grimier and slimy. The squatter toilet had an aroma that hung in the air. The best features were an oscillating fan at the foot of the bed, and the mosquito net draped over it.

Sleeping was tough in the $2.50 room. Thunder, lightning, and rain interrupted sound sleep. Buckets of rain pounded down on the tin roof. Deafening at first, it soon sounded soothing. We slept soundly.

CAT TRAX Day 153, 68 Ks, Mombo to Segera. I asked a guy about bridges down or mud blocking the road. He shook his head, "No, is okay, road is okay." We were either coasting down or "Granny Gearing" up all day. There were no in-betweens. We cycled forty-three Ks into Korogwe by 11:30. With a fading feeling and gnawing stomachs, we decided on lunch. The Transit Hotel was also a bus station. Noisy buses, their engines roaring, were coming and going every few minutes. Same luncheon fare of rice and meat.

Was it day four syndrome or the thick warm air? For some reason we were both experiencing terrible saddle sores. We took turns powdering each other's butts behind trees. Entering Segera our spirits dampened. Albert, a teacher, pointed to a shack for soft drinks.

Natasha was cooking coconut with beans and fish and had cold drinks. She also gave out great news in her Maasai/Swahilli, accent. "You find motel, one kilometer." We were ready to call it a day. She was correct, and we were ecstatic. The room at Segera Highway Motel had a bath, TV, and AC. Alas, our room had all the aforementioned but no electricity. The clerk Mohamed said, "We have this problems, but will come back, electricity." Cat hit the cold shower hanging above the toilet. I averted a catastrophe by grabbing the toilet paper before the downpour began.

Good news, they had pizza. Bad news, no alcohol. Mohamed pointed out a stand where we could buy beer. We watched chameleons scamper up and down the walls slurping up their dinner of pesky mosquitoes. Pasta and pizza made up for three days of skimpy rice and beans. Bugs by the thousands began to swarm around the restaurant lights above us. Mohamed apologized, "I turn

off." Not very appetizing to pick flying termites from your pasta.

CAT TRAX Day 154, 75 Ks, Segera to Tanga. The day started with a good breakfast, we needed fuel. Walking back to the room in the hazy morning sun, we came across a huge insect crawling on the sidewalk. The gardener called it a jumbo. It was a centipede nine inches long with a thousand legs moving in sync.

The road was ups and downs, the scenery small patches of farmland worked by families with hoes and machetes. The area resembled Louisiana 150 years ago. Cat thought the people looked like slaves chained to the tiny fields tilling the red soil by hand.

Lots of cyclists on the road. Locals with large yellow plastic panniers hauling water. Another group carried bulky loads of cut grass. On an uphill, one of them broke from the pack and challenged us. In fact he passed us, standing bare foot on steel pegs where there once were pedals. He'd probably never heard of Lance Armstrong but for that moment he would have led Lance and the rest of the peloton up that hill.

The Hotel Ambassador and turnoff to Pangani were in Muheza. Lunch was good, the hotel dreadful. The toilet was an outhouse, one of the worst I'd ever seen or smelled. I suggested that Cat "hold it." A nice tree would be preferable. The best of the Ambassador was the meaty, tasty, rice and beans.

The afternoon temperature was climbing into steamy heat. We'd cycled through a banana-tree belt and now began dropping toward the Indian Ocean. A cool breeze blew softly into our faces. We picked up a fellow cyclist, Abdullah. He was soft spoken but spoke no English. His bike squawked with every turn of the crank. Along with the clicking of Cat's broken pedal clip, it drove us nuts. We pulled up to get a drink and let Abdullah go past. He waved, then as I checked Cat's pedal he turned and returned. We shared colas with him, then departed the snack stand together, squawking and clicking a syncopated symphony. Finally he waved, picked up his pace and squawked away.

Our downhill run was in uphill wind. Traffic thickened as we neared Tanga. We spotted the DHL freight office and stopped to check on our camera being sent from home. While there we met a guy, Marty, who lived down coast. A seventh-generation Afrikaner, he'd lost the lease on his farm in Zimbabwe.

He said, "Robert Mugabe the President of Zimbabwe started a program returning land to native Africans. The plan was simple, if a white farmer left the land locals could claim it. They threatened my family and me with death if we stayed. We left our land, sold it for small dollars."

He'd been living in Tanzania for six months, managing what we thought he'd called a sizable estate. "No, no," he said, "a sisal estate." He explained, "Sisal is hemp used to make rope. It was a big product during sailing vessel days. Today, auto manufacturers are beginning to use the natural fiber to replace petroleum-based nylon in floor mats."

At dinner, we met Karl, an American from Ohio. He was a recruiter with Bowling Green University, placing five Tanzanian students annually on four-year scholarships. He also farmed 3000 acres on a 99-year lease. Sort of a sharecropping deal with local farmers. Karl certainly had a lot of irons in the fire.

Chapter 20 The Pirates of Zanzibar

CAT TRAX Day 155, 52 Ks, Tanga Town to Peponi Lodge. Our guidebook described boat trips to Zanzibar, the Spice Island. Rather than cycling six days to Dar es Salaam, we decided we'd visit Zanzibar if we could find a boat.

Mr. Maphingo, a stately gray-haired African man at DHL said, "You should not cycle to Kigombe, you might be robbed." Seeing our expressions, he backed off a bit, "There haven't been robberies but there could be. Also, don't take a boat. They too are dangerous."

Cat sent an e-mail to Marty, the farmer we'd met, asking his advice. Later that afternoon he responded, "Go to a place called Peponi Resort. The road is dirt but safe. They can find a boat and it's a nice place to stay, too."

At dinner we asked a couple of Irishmen what they were doing there. "We're installing a malaria wing at the hospital," one said in thick Irish brogue. "The equipment and cost of labor have been donated by the Bill and Linda Gates Foundation." The other said. "Malaria's the worst disease of all, in Africa."

Cat told them about the ragged dirty man we met in Kenya. "He'd held his hand out begging, not for money, for an ass-per-een, an aspirin. He had chronic malaria."

I called Peponi, and Denys, the owner, urged us to come. "Sure, we can get a boat and you will love our place, will you camp or stay in one of our Bandas?" We chose Banda with bath.

The road was littered with trash, traffic stirred up dust. The sign directing us toward Peponi marked the end of what Tanzanians call *"tarma",* pavement. As Marty had warned, a road crew was busy grading, turning the surface into soft sand and rocks. Our overloaded bikes dug in and squirreled around, requiring all our strength to keep control. We finally ended up on a footpath that ran close to the doors of rural huts.

At 22 Ks we entered a village where Denys had said we'd find food. The guy inside a small store yelled out, "No sodas, no food today." Hopeful there'd be another store or restaurant the answer came in a shout. "No more, until Pangani." That was another 30 Ks and beyond Peponi.

"I'm burned out, tired and hungry," Cat said. Ducking and dodging rocks had beat down our upper bodies. Struggling she said, "I can't go on, I don't see any sign of a hotel." As though by divine intervention we sighted a sign and arrow pointing down a two-track pathway to Peponi.

Denys and his wife, Gilly (pronounced *Jilly*) greeted us. First things first, Gilly made sandwiches and served them with chips and a cold bitter lemon. "We started with just a tract of bush. It took five years to carve out our wonderful little Peponi beachfront resort," she said, with pride.

After we ate, Denys led us to Banda Zebra. It was at the end of a white-sand walkway near the beach. It was primitive but comfortable-looking. A two-room hut of woven palm fronds and sisal poles. There was a toilet and tiny shower. Mosquito netting draped the twin beds.

I took a dip in the warm Indian Ocean then followed Cat into the shower.

Cat Trax, Day 156, Peponi Resort. We awoke at 6:00 a.m. completely rested. It was the first uninterrupted night's sleep we'd had in weeks. Denys joined us at the breakfast table. "I spoke with Mwashondie, our dhow captain" he said. "He's sure he can arrange a pirate's boat to Zanzibar tonight, or early in the morning."

"Did you say pirates?" Cat queried, "Are pirate boats safe?"

"Not exactly pirates, actually smugglers," Denys replied. "They usually run under cover of night, buy duty-free sugar in Zanzibar and return, cheating the government out of the 10% tax. Although Tanzania and Zanzibar are one country, they operate as two separate tax districts." Continuing, he explained, "Tanganyika and Zanzibar were merged as Tanzania, in 1964. You guys will be illegal cargo on the voyage across and illegal aliens when ashore. Law requires you have your passport stamped, upon entry. When you get to Zanzibar, take a Dalla Dalla, a truck bus, to Zanzibar City and get your immigration stamp."

"Okay," said Cat, uneasy with the prospect. "Even though they aren't exactly pirates, are you sure we'll be safe?"

"Safety is probably in the eye of the beholder," Denys told her. "I've never heard of a dhow sinking, passengers being robbed or hurt during my five years here. It's illegal for them to take passengers, they have sail power only, no motor, or safety equipment."

"What's a dhow?" I asked.

"A five-thousand-year-old Arabic designed sailing boat. It has a triangular sail that's shifted back and forth, to catch the wind." Denis replied, making it sound almost romantic.

Mwashondie told us the boats leave at 4:00. We walked down the beach to meet the captain and crew. A language glitch led to finding they were talking about 4:00 a.m. the *next* morning. The price 30,000 Tanzanian shillings for both. We talked in a low whisper, then agreed. We had a deal. Mashwondie would come for us at 3:30 a.m. We were set to go.

CAT TRAX Day 157, Peponi to Dar es Salam. At 3:00 a.m. we

185

were awakened by rain pounding down on thatching. We lay and listened as it intensified. Huddled together in one of the little beds we held each other close. Lightening lit the stormy sky, thunder shook our cozy Banda.

"I don't want to go in this storm," Cat whispered.

"I think it'll pass." I said, attempting to bolster her courage. "It's just a tropical squall."

She wasn't convinced. "I see us stuck in that boat, wallowing in stormy seas, soaked and miserable for eight to twelve hours," she moaned. "Maybe longer."

"Okay, if that's the way you feel we won't go," I conceded.

We were just drifting back to sleep when Mashwondie knocked on the door. I stepped outside and stood shivering in the driving rain. "The beach is mud," I said. "We won't be able to get our bikes down there."

"Road is okay," Mashwondie said. "*Hakuna Matata*, no problem, and I will help."

Back inside, we talked again. I felt we should go. Cat remained fearful, remembering times when she'd sailed in the stormy Pacific. She didn't want to risk it in such a remote place.

"Come on, you can do it," I urged.

"No," she argued. "I can't, damn it."

I went out and told a disappointed Mwashondie that we weren't going.

He made a feeble last effort, then shrugged and said, "*Lala salaama*." (Sleep well.)

Once we began considering our options, we couldn't sleep. The big problem as usual, money. Down to our last shillings, we thought we'd find a hotel on the Zanzibar side that would accept one of our credit cards. We had enough cash to pay Denys and Gilly for our stay at Peponi but little more.

"We can't just sit and wait for perfect weather," I said.

Setting off for Dar es Salaam on the bikes wasn't feasible either. The trip would take four or five days, we'd be broke in a day or two. Near dawn we came up with a plan. We'd take a bus to Dar es Salaam get money and pick up our new camera to replace the one broken on Kili. Once the plan was in place, we fell back into each other's arms and fitful sleep. Cat had a nightmare about heavy seas and a terrifying boat trip.

186

Denys was shocked when we came in for breakfast. I told him the story and explained our plan. He agreed to keep the bikes in his shop and save a Banda for us when we returned. We threw our light bags into Denys' cousins' cute little Suzuki 4WD. They dropped us at the bus station in Tanga. The bus was comfortable and air conditioned, although leg room was limited. We'd picked up soft drinks and had the sandwiches Gilly had prepared for the boat trip. We were surprised to find they provided water and drinks for passengers. By 6:00 p.m. we were checked in at The Peacock Hotel in Dar es Salaam.

CAT TRAX, Day 158, A day of biz in Dar. After a bit of hassle, we got our new camera and Cat's prescription drugs released from customs. Loaded up on cash from Barclay's Bank, we even had new WorldRiders2 business cards quickly printed.

CAT TRAX Day 159, Return Bus to Peponi. On the return bus, the driver's assistant made an announcement. Swahili first followed by, "You may urinate here." Most of the passengers did just that. The men walked twenty paces off the road and turned their backs. The women squatted in the taller grass their heads still visible. A crowd of local merchants gathered, selling everything from soda pop and nuts to toys and gadgets. It was obvious this was a regular pit stop, confirmed by the overpowering smell of urine in the hot afternoon sun.

A group traveling in an African tour truck had set camp at Peponi. Their tents were at the edge of the beach. They were doing their own cooking. Most were Austrian or German and kept to themselves, although four did venture inside for beers and a game of darts.

Again, I slipped into Cat's twin bed that night.

"I'm still afraid of the boat, and pirate crew." She said. "They have no schedule, Denys isn't even sure when the next one will leave." We hugged and talked about giving up on the boat and just cycling down coast.

"I hate the idea of being out there in the dark," Cat whispered.

"Night's scary," I agreed. "As a kid, I was afraid of demons in the dark under my bed."

CAT TRAX, Day 160, The Pirate Boat to Zanzibar. At 6:00 a.m. we heard a soft knock and murmuring at the door. We thought it was Denys, checking to see if we'd like to go fishing. At second call, we recognized Mashwondie's voice.

"A boat leave soon. You want go?"

The three of us jogged down the beach to Kigome, the tiny mud hut village, and tried to communicate with a man who said he was the captain. Mwashondie argued with him then said, "He take you to Zanzibar Island, 35,000 T-Shilling."

"That includes both of us and both the bikes, right?" I asked.

The captain nodded, and Mwashondie said, "Yes,"

We shook hands, then hustled back for the bikes and bags. Gilly had our bill ready. She gave us a bag of bananas and two bottles of water. We only had a pack of cookies to accompany the fruit. Gilly gave Cat a Dramamine pill and offered one to me. I told her no, I never got seasick.

As we pushed the bikes through the sand past the truck camp people peeked out of their tents. They seemed shocked seeing our fully-loaded touring bikes. They swarmed out flashing thumbs ups and shouting encouragement.

Mwashondie helped Cat push her bike. He pointed out a boat lying just off shore. The vessel was constructed of rough-hewn lumber and looked like it had been around for most of those five thousand years Denys had spoken of.

The sun was already hot. Sweat trickled down my forehead and my back. I was nervous. Twenty or so guys gathered around us. Their stares seemed evil as they contemplated the two strangers and their even stranger-looking bicycles.

We had long ago become accustomed to languages foreign to our ears. However, now it felt like we were being talked about. We couldn't help wondering what was being said. Paranoia like that could lead to paralyzing fear and we knew it.

I whispered, "Remember, 98 percent of all the people in the world are good people."

Cat gave me a sideways glance. "These are pirates. Are they good pirates?"

Mwashondie shook our hands and said, "Safe voyage," then ran back toward his dhow full of waiting fishermen. A sinister-looking guy stepped out of a hut and said something that included, "Le Capitan." We began putting two and two together. The guys we'd made the deal with were foisting us off onto another boat and crew.

The dhow lay anchored about twenty yards off shore. The barefoot Capitan waded into the water then motioned for me to bring the bikes aboard.

"Hey," Cat said. "Wasn't that part of the deal."

Then, as though scripted, two muscular young guys appeared and in pidgin English said, "Me carry, Boss, 5,000 T-Shilling."

Cat objected. I negotiated.

"Two bike," I said, pointing at both. "Two bike, 5,000." I held up five fingers. The two nodded approval, grabbed Cat's bike, hoisted it above their heads and waded toward the dhow.

"Your friendly pirates are screwing us," Cat said.

"If you want to be terrific, be specific. We weren't. They meant two people and two bikes. Nothing was said about getting aboard. It's worth $5.00," I retorted. "The bikes and bags weigh almost 100 pounds each, no way we could carry them?"

As the young men carried the second bike, we waded out and climbed aboard.

"I hope this isn't a huge mistake," Cat said.

"We'll be okay, I know we will," I told her, mustering my courage and sizing up the crew.

Once on board, "Le Capitan" asked for 5,000 T-Shilling in advance. We watched as he slipped it into the dealmaker's hands. So now we knew there were pirates, even among pirates. We were illegal aliens going to Zanzibar with smugglers. They were charging us small dollars because their boat was almost empty. As Denys had said, the pirates were taking chances too. If caught with us on board they could be fined, arrested, or even have the boat confiscated.

That dhow was an amazing craft. The hand-hewn hull had a tree trunk mast and a sisal pole attached by rope for a cross arm. When the crew began hoisting the sail, they invited me to help. A wondrous feeling of history flowed through the rope and into my hands. Dhows, the workhorses of the Indian Ocean, had been moving people and freight for centuries.

Powered only by wind, we caught the tail of the morning tide and the heavy wooden hull was soon plowing its way through rolling seas toward Zanzibar. Denys had been right, they had no emergency equipment on board. No radio, no lifeboat, not even a life  jacket. If we wanted to sail in a dhow with pirates, we'd be taking our own chances and paying our own dues.

Other than two crazy cyclists, the cargo headed to Zanzibar consisted of two bags of rice and a few tomatoes in a bamboo basket. Cat took a seat on a rice bag. I began to feel queasy and was soon flat on my back on the deck, wishing I'd taken that Dramamine pill Gilly had offered.

Le Capitan, the eldest of the crew said, "I cook now." His barbecue was made from an old car wheel. He fired up charcoal, using cotton balls soaked in kerosene. Then he dipped a large beat up old pan into the sea, swished it a couple of times, tossed the water, filled it again, and put it on the fire. When it was boiling, he threw in several big handfuls of rice. As he stirred and thickened, he added half a bottle of olive oil. He sat another pan on top the pot and filled it with coals to keep the rice hot. Very clever.

The first mate on the tiller shouted, "*Dolpheen!*"

We watched as a school of fifteen of the graceful mammals played in the wake of the bow. By that time we were surrounded by sea, no land in sight.

Cat whispered, "Do you think this where they throw us overboard, and steal our bikes and bags?" For a moment I was sorry I'd taken pictures and shown them to the crew. Our camera was probably more valuable than their dhow.

Le Capitan and two of his five-man crew took shelter in the shade of the rough decking and nodded off to sleep. Cat sat on the rail, dipping her hand in the cool water. The first mate manned the tiller. I lay back on the bags of rice and soon joined the pirates in sleep.

I dreamed of darkness and monsters lurking, a nightmare. The crew tied my hands behind my back and threw me overboard. There in the darkness, I waited, knowing that an ogre was moving in for the kill. Saved, I awoke when Cat shouted, "Land ho!"

She was the first to catch sight of Zanzibar. That stirred the crew back into action. Le Capitan uncovered the rice and garnished it with slices of mango and our bananas. The crew crowded around the pan and began scooping up handfuls of the rice. We watched as they rolled it into balls and popped them in their mouths. Le Capitan squinted at us, then with a wave of his hand invited us to dig in. Cat pulled the package of cookies out of our bag and offered it. He tore the wrapper off, took a handful, and passed them around to the crew. They wolfed them down quicker than we could say "Zanzibar."

Following their lead, we ate with our fingers. The rice was tasty, and calmed my queasy stomach. The Spice Island seemed to pull the dhow toward shore. We finished the rice while enjoying pidgin English/Swahili table talk.

Le Capitan said in very plain English, "You pay now!"

In my best sign language, I made it clear we'd pay when we were safely on the beach. The Captain's smile seemed wise and friendly. "Hakuna Matata," he said as the thick wooden bow crunched into the coral and white sands of Zanzibar. Getting ashore was tough. Cat jumped into waist-deep water and cut her foot on the coral. Her wallet and passport went completely under. Barefoot, she struggled as I jumped in and felt the sharp coral under my feet. The crew passed the bags holding the camera and computer to us.

The two strongest struggled in the surf with the bikes, one at a time, above their heads. Amazing, they got both onto the beach without dunking them in the surf. I handed the balance of 30,000 T-Shillings to Le Capitan. He complained, asking for more. We'd  already decided to pay an extra 5,000. It had been an experience of a lifetime, well worth it. As I paid, a stranger walked down the beach toward us. Le Capitan took the extra Shillings, winked, then wadded up the note and put it into the stranger's hand. Without a word, he slipped the wadded T-bill into his pocket and ambled away. "Another middle man in a local Mafia set-up," I said to Cat.

The two crewmen pushed the heavy dhow out and swung her around. As those in the water scrambled aboard, the others hoisted sail. Then, like the end of a movie, they stood at attention waving like parting friends. We all knew we'd just shared an extraordinary adventure.

"I don't get what you just said," Cat queried.

"Remember the first guys we made the deal with," I asked. "They were the kingpins. They don't do anything but seal the deal, then get a piece of it. Then there's another guy waiting on shore in Zanzibar. He holds out his hand and gets another piece. If we hadn't paid 5,000 extra, then our crew, the guys that did all the work, would only have gotten 25,000 T-Shillings."

As we struggled through the soft white sand pushing our overloaded bikes, a couple of guys walked out of the jungle. The tall one stood in our pathway and said, "Police." Then he held out his hand, "Passports!"

Remembering what Denys had warned us, Cat said, "We're supposed to take a Dalla-Dalla into town to get our passports stamped." I sized the guy up and decided he was bluffing, trying to get a couple of bucks out of intimidated tourists. "Show me your

192

identification," I said.

"No my identification, you give passports," the guy persisted, leaning into my face.

"No identification, no passports," I said with conviction as I began pushing my bike.

"What are you doing?" Cat called out. "Don't get us in trouble!"

"I think this guy's a fake," I said loudly as I turned to the guy. "You follow to hotel. We'll ask them about identification." That stopped them in their tracks. The shorter one, in ragged clothing, said something in Swahili as they drifted along beside us. As we neared the hotel they stopped and stood watching as their would-be pigeons flew the coop.

"So they weren't real?" Cat asked.

"Not real cops," I muttered, "hard to tell if they're members of the local Mafia or just two-bit crooks trying to horn in on the action."

We propped the bikes against each other and hugged. We'd done it again. We'd survived the dangers of a pirate crossing and foiled a scam. There's something arousing about having flirted with danger and escaped. Perhaps an overdose of testosterone brings the need for closeness. Whatever it was it drew us into each other's arms.

"As your mother always said," Cat whispered, "all's well, that ends well. Let's get a room."

Chapter 21 Zanzibar, Stone Town

CAT TRAX Day 161, 68 Ks, Nungwi to Stone Town. With the anxiety of Pirates behind us, we resumed our bicycle tour. Our first stop, a wooden boat hull under construction. Amazing, they were hand building a dhow. An open air boatyard on the white sands of a

beautiful beach. The shipbuilders were friendly and loved having pictures taken of their nautical art.

Roadside, we ordered chicken and fries. The fries arrived, covered with hot sauce too spicy to eat. They took them away and put a fresh order into the boiling oil. When the new fries arrived, I asked how long it would be before the chicken was cooked. The young guy looked at us quizzically and said, "No chicken, haf no chicken." Language, ain't it wonderful?

Half full, we rolled onward to Zanzibar Town. The locals called it Stone Town. Finding Zanzibar Serena Inn was easy. We filled out the guest form, then, as they called for approval of our Visa card the girl told us their rates started at $250 per night. Ouch! Cat waited in the shade while I set off on another hotel hunt. Just outside, a car pulled up and the driver said, "I see you on the road from Nungwi." He decided to take it upon himself to help us find a room. Don't you just love that kind of kindness?

Since it was a weekend, the first two places he led me to had only a room for one night. I hated the thought of moving. He understood and led onward to The Shangani Hotel. A decent room at a decent price, so I took the deal.

Back at the Serena Inn, I said, "Hey Cat, this guy saw us on the road and helped me find a room." She looked at his car and said, "I don't remember that car." Had he hoodwinked me? Locals called guys like him Ticks because they stick to you like a tick. He had been helpful, but when he held out his hand I told him we had no cash, only credit cards.

He continued to stick like a Tick, following us back to the Hotel Shangani. When the clerk there tried our Visa card it was declined. The lurking Tick pointed out a telephone stand and said, "Calls cheap there." The money exchange closed at 5:00 p.m.. I had to find Tanzanian Shillings or we'd be broke and homeless all weekend. The call to Visa went through immediately then they put me on hold for ten nervous minutes. Finally, a person in Security filled me in on the problem. Someone had used our Visa card, there were mysterious charges. Electronic gadgets and flowers sent to an address just one block from our home in Oxnard.

The really bad news: they were cancelling our card. She said, "We will issue a new card and ship it to you." I begged, and they finally agreed to allow an hour before cancellation.

I sprinted back to the Money Exchange, Tick in tow and burst through the door. The clerk looked doubtful but placed the call again. When he put the receiver down he said, "Sorry, they have declined again."

Another three block run, more shuffling through phone security then a woman said, "I don't know why they didn't lift the hold, your conversation is right here in the computer." She promised the card was good for the hour. I ran through the heat, sweating bullets. If the card failed again we were definitely in deep doo-doo.

The door on the Money Exchange shop was closed even though it wasn't yet 5:00. I pounded, yelled, and pounded some more. The guy slowly opened the door and agreed to try one more time. He smiled then began counting Shillings. We'd be able to pay for our room and meals.

My pal the Tick was still hanging, hoping I'd reward him. Still worried, I told him our cash was too short. He looked sad, then smiled, shook my hand, and wished us well. I feel guilty every time I think of him, wondering why I didn't give him something for all his useful help.

We needed a calming glass of wine. Stone Town was 95% Muslim, which boded badly for wine lovers. Fortunately our guidebook listed an Italian restaurant. We decided to shower, dress up, and hit the wine bar. The server there said, "Sorry, we are Italians but we're leasing from Muslims. The lease doesn't allow alcohol." Sensing our disappointment, she pointed down the street to La Fenice.

They not only had wine, they served us on a patio overlooking the sea. We savored a couple glasses of French white, along with French cuisine. A dhow sailed past as the sun set into the Indian

Ocean. We toasted, "Life is good!"

We walked back to The Shangani Hotel, a huge yellow moon in the African sky. A magnificent ending to a very fretful day.

CAT TRAX Day 162, A Lazy Day in Stonetown. The streets of

Stone Town were narrow, winding, and full of interesting people. In our wanderings, we found Mercury's, an oceanfront restaurant named in honor of local boy Freddie Mercury. Born there, but of Indian decent Freddie studied classical music in India and took that training to stardom as a founder of Queen, the group that produced hits like "Bohemian Rhapsody," hard rock with classical overtones.

Gilly at Peponi had urged us to eat at Fodorhani Gardens, a group of food stands where local specialties were prepared and sold by chefs and venders. A bonus: we'd seen posters touting a Music Festival. As we ate local foods, we were treated to local sights and sounds.

CAT TRAX Day 163, Spice Tour of Zanzibar, The Spice Island. How could we travel to the white sands of Zanzibar and not tour the Spice Island? We joined Mr. Mitu's Tour, a Dalla Dalla filled with folks of international flavors. A couple of Italian girls, a couple from Norway, Erica from California, and Tammy from Milton, Canada. She was amazed that we'd cycled through Milton less than two years earlier.

Fiad, the guide, was terrific. His accent "spiced up" the info he dished out. He walked to each tree bush or plant, explaining how it was grown and how the spice was extracted. There were children at each stop selling trinkets. At the final stop, a young boy took Cat by the arm. He'd made a frog from a palm frond. He didn't speak English, but he indicated it was for her. He hung it around her neck on a strand of the same fronds. I was suddenly generous, and felt guilty not

having slipped the Tick a tip as I handed the boy 200 TS.

Chapter 22 Tanzania, The Road South

CAT TRAX Day 164,   Rain delay in Morongo. The news that evening on BBC reported a militia in Uganda had killed 183 villagers. It was confirmation that we'd made a good decision to skip Uganda and the Silverbacks. Another local news flash: the car carrying Robert Mogabe, President of Zimbabwe, had been attacked in Tanzania. Both Marty and Denys had said they were surprised Mogabe hadn't already been assassinated.

CAT TRAX Day 165, 105 Ks, Morogoro to Mikuni Park. At

9:15 a.m. we rolled out into mud puddles. Traffic was heavy, and the drivers discourteous, blaring their horns. A motorcycle policeman pulled up from behind, honked and waved us over. He asked, "How far you come?" When we told him from California, he quipped, "You must be very tired." At the next village another policeman pulled us over and asked, "From California?" We thought the other guy had radioed ahead, then realized it was the same guy. I asked to take his picture. He shook his head, "Not allowed on duty." There was a group of Maasai nearby, he said, "Take theirs." I spun the camera around and caught them unaware. The Maasai usually expected payment for pictures.

Stopping for soft drinks, we sat near a group of Maasai. They were friendly, especially one woman. I wanted a picture of a great-looking guy but as I raised the camera he held out his hand asking for money. Cat started a conversation with the Maasai woman. When I asked for a picture she nodded and stepped nearer to Cat. Cat was tired of her soft drink and offered it to the woman. She accepted with a huge smile. We were pushed for time. I believe if had we'd stayed a bit longer the guys would have posed without payment.

We had good food in a tiny restaurant in Mkata Village, but we couldn't spend enough time digesting as dark clouds were gathering. Under the threat of rain, we got our first glimpse of that infamous sign, "Entering Mikumi National Park," with the warning, "Dangerous Animals Next 50 Kilometers." Suffering from indigestion ourselves, we hoped the beasts weren't hungry!

The baboons we'd worried about ran into the bushes. The warthogs waddled away as herds of giraffe and zebra nonchalantly grazed. Let's not forget that elephant family that turned tail. This was the Africa we'd dreamed of, the Africa we'd wanted to experience.

Soaked to the skin, we were met with something less than a welcoming. The gate guard pointed toward a guy seated inside a kiosk. Standing in the rain, we told him we were booked at the Park Hotel. That meant nothing to him, he demanded a $15.00 entry fee and said, "That hotel, not part of Park." We argued, but he stood his ground and said, "I retire soon, I'll not risk breaking any rules for you." I asked to call the hotel for help. "Call is 1000 Ts," he smirked.

When I told him that was a lot of money, he shrugged. Thinking he hadn't understood, I pleaded. "We need their help."

His reply, "First, you give 1000 Shilling!" Divine intervention came in the form of a couple who had paid earlier but came out of the Park and wanted a refund. They complained that in the pouring rain they couldn't see any animals. An argument ensued. In the midst of it a guy from the hotel drove up. As the tourists were losing their argument, the hotel guy told us we'd have to pay the entry fee. When Cat threw the 30,000 Ts onto the desk the kiosk man snarled, "Park rules forbid pedestrians, bicycles and motorcycles." Then he picked up the T Shillings and asked, "What is this?" Cat responded, "Our entry fee."

He smirked again, pointed to a small sign, and asked, "Can't you read? I accept only US Dollars."

A woman, the boss who'd been called to the gate regarding the

198

refund, said to the gatekeeper, "The rain, is an Act of God, you must return their money." She also arranged to exchange our Shillings for US Dollars, satisfying the grumpy gate guy. Then she said, "Your cycles will be stored safely in the museum."

A driver in a Range Rover wearing a red beret pulled up. The hotel porter helped us throw our bags into the Rover. There was no room for the porter so he clung to the back of the Rover in the rain. Mr. Red Beret, who hadn't lifted a finger or ventured into the rain, drove slowly down the muddy trail. Again the porter unloaded as we went inside. Mr. Red Beret watched. Guess drivers drive and porters port.

The five-star hotel was as upscale as the price. The desk clerk offered a fruit drink, I gulped down a couple. The porter got the bags inside, then disappeared. We were in Banda #4 called Twiga. We were in a hurry to get inside so carried most everything ourselves. I asked the clerk about hot water, he said it was being heated. Then he asked, "May we serve you dinner, now?" Shivering, Cat almost screamed, "No, not until I have a warm bath!"

Geez, one of the most expensive places we'd ever stayed, yet they acted like they were doing us a favor. Ah, a bit of civilization they did serve wine. We had a glass as the water warmed. *Après* bath, we were the only diners in the restaurant. The food was good enough, considering the remote location. However, for the price it was a disappointment. The total cost for park fees, room, dinner, and breakfast was $168.00.

CAT TRAX Day 166, 25 Ks, Mikumi Park to Mikumi Town. I was up half the night, suffering the return of African Guff-Guff. Damn those two fruit drinks. The Banda had no glass windows just drapes. When Cat pulled them back early in the morning she whispered, "Get the camera we've got an elephant on the lawn."

There he was a huge tusker, grazing, as we assume they must most of the time to gather sufficient sustenance for their huge bodies. Then and there we agreed, "Rate had its privileges." The right place at the right time was worth the cost.

Once again, we had the

dining room to ourselves. The others were already exploring, the early birds get to see animals. Breakfast was filling. We repacked, then hauled our own bags to the Range Rover. Mr. Red Beret watched as we loaded, then without a word, he drove to the gate. Again he sat waited and watched as we off loaded. Drivers drive!

The bikes were as we'd left them, leaning near an elephant skull surrounded by stuffed animals that were doomed to an eternity in that stuffy room. As I pulled the bikes out and installed the seats, Mr. "About to retire" sat quietly, looking unfriendly.

It was sunny and warm by the time we got onto the highway. Our goal was to get free of the Park and its animals, then ride the short distance to Mikumi Town. As we pedaled a semi-truck pulled up. The driver shouted to us in Swahili. Cat said "I think he means elephant?" He leaned out the window and yelled, "Yes, yes, Olliphante, tembo on road!"

He pulled away, we cycled a short distance, and there they stood a tusker protecting his herd of a dozen, just off the road. They calmly grazed, lifting their heads to gaze for a moment at the strange beings pedaling past as fast as they could. In our minds we were certain there was a lion lurking behind every bush. We set our personal best record for that 25 K ride.

As we cycled past the sign "Leaving Mikumi National Park," Cat breathed a sigh of relief, "We made it!" she exclaimed, and relaxed, until I reminded her that lions and elephants can't read. They roam anywhere they want. We dared not let down our guard.

The Genesis Hotel in Mikumi Village seemed okay for healing. Our necessities, a bed and toilet. Cat shrugged and said, "Well it's only for one night." She took a walk, as I lay on the bed watching the blades of the oscillating fan. Good dinner, but slow service. It didn't matter as everything I ate was destined to quickly drain out my backside. Cat asked Cyprian, a young guy that spoke English, if he had medicine for bad stomach. He ran to the doctor returning with a few pills wrapped in newspaper. Written on the newsprint were directions, 2 X Daily. Cyprian said they were fragile. We thought he meant Flagyl. I quickly downed one.

CAT TRAX Day 167, Riding out the African Guff-Guff. Except for toilet runs, I slept through the afternoon and all night. Breakfast, another pill, then back to the bed. Cat went walking. When she got back, she said, "The young guys called out Sista or Momma, as I passed."

Lunch, we ordered chicken sandwich. The girl went to the kitchen, returned and said, "We have no bread." Cat asked, "Can you get some at the store?" She left, but returned empty handed, "No bread in Mikumi Town." We asked for a bowl of rice, she left came right back and said, "No rice, power out!" We decided to walk to the Internet Cafe. They had a generator as well as rice and meat in casaba leaf. Cat hit the computer, I took my fourth Flagyl pill and headed back to the bed feeling fragile.

We walked for dinner to a restaurant Cat had spotted. A bowl of pasta went down better than local food. Walking back in the darkness we felt safe.

CAT TRAX Day 168, Doctoring in Mikumi. Still queasy, I wanted to move on; Cat was anxious to get going. Two days there

had been two days too long for us both. Ohhh, stomach pain and quick trip to the toilet. Yikes, another just two hours later. Still feeling way below 100% we decided to find a doctor. Cuan, (*Kyoo-ann*) a fellow we'd met earlier introduced us to William, an Irishman living in Mikumi. When he heard the problem, he said, "Get in my pickup truck, I'll take you to our family doctor. It's Dad's day, I've got the kids along, Sarah, Kathryn and Harry, you guys jump in the back."

Dr. Lushino, a delightful man, discussed my problem. He decided to get stool and blood samples. Blood was no problem he drew some. Stool was a bit more difficult. He handed me a plastic tube with a little spoon attached to the cap. I worried it might be days before we got results. He laughed, "We can do the work here and have results in thirty minutes." He and his wife also ran the laboratory.

William invited us to his home. We met his wife Anne, and sat in their back yard watching the kids play on their swing set. They'd been in Africa eight years. We asked if they missed Ireland, he said "In Ireland, you never get a drip on the end of your nose, the wind blows it right off. We plan to live out my contract in Africa, then buy a home in Spain."

William took us to his office and traced our route on a large scale map, estimating a five-day ride to Mbeya. He called his friend Joel to get his opinion. I had another bowel movement and caught a sample in his restroom.

We dropped the sample at Doctors Lushino's office, then went to lunch. Back in an hour the doctor was out. His wife said, "You must see doctor." We asked questions and she spilled the beans, "Stool sample was negative, but you blood test have positive result for Typhoid Fever."
Cat gasped, "Typhoid Fever, we thought that was ancient history?" It sounded serious, Typhoid killed millions around the turn of the twentieth century (remember Typhoid Mary?).

Mrs. doctor, sensing that she'd gone too far said, "You must wait for Doctor."

He came in with the air of a busy man. We waited anxiously as he and his wife spoke in Swahili. He took us into his office and calmly explained. "We don't measure for Typhoid in your blood, we account  for the antibodies you are producing to kill the bug." We dug our Inoculation Certificates out to show him we'd had Typhoid shots. He explained, "You have twice as much anti-body as would be normal even after inoculation." Then another revelation, "Typhoid is a form of Salmonella."

His prognosis, "Since you don't exhibit symptoms, I will prescribe Cipro, an anti-biotic. It has a positive effect on several organisms that might show up." His recommendation, "Take the Cipro with you, if symptoms don't ease or become worse in the next few days, begin the Cipro." He also recommended Fladagazole in place of the Flagyl that had been so tough on my stomach.

Amazing, his bill for the office visit tests and Lab, 15,000 T/Shilling, about $15 US. The Cipro was an additional $10 US. We joked later that at those prices he'd never be able to afford a Mercedes like our doctors back home. We followed up the visit with our own prescription, white wine and a toast to better health.

CAT TRAX Day 169 Mikumi to T-Junction Comfort Hotel 114Ks

CAT TRAX Day 170 Comfort Hotel to Iringa 36Ks on bikes, 40 Ks in Range Rover

A 9 K hill ground us down to a push. Sun bearing down, we remembered the big push in Malawi but continued. It took three hours and twenty minutes to summit. Slowed by the heat and African Guff-Guff, we rode at a snail's pace. After 4 1/2 hours I found a grassy area, lay back and stared at brilliant blue sky and puffy silver clouds. I'd had it, we called it a day.

Cat stopped the car of a couple we'd met earlier. They volunteered to give us a ride but there was no way we'd all fit. I flagged down an SUV. Raphael and his wife Natalia helped us load in and we were off to Iringa. After a short conversation about religion and their acceptance of our Mother Nature theory, we settled in to small talk. They even went out of their way to drop us at the Iringa roundabout. We quickly unloaded, got handshakes and hugs and in pouring rain went searching for the hotel. They hurried away to get to Raphael's church meeting. Rain began to pour as we searched for a hotel. Ask, ask, ask and by the time we found the M R Hotel we were soaked.

CAT TRAX Day 171 and 172 African Guff-Guff in Iringa

CAT TRAX Day 173, 86 Ks, Iringa to Mafinga. We were so anxious to ride that we hated having to wait for breakfast. By 8:30 a.m. we were ready to roll. Argh, I had a broken brake spring on the front wheel. I asked about a bicycle repair store. The young bellman said, "No, but there are boys that can help." I disconnected the brake, then pushed around the corner. There were half a dozen young guys working on bikes in the shade of a tree. One checked out the bike and introduced himself, "Me Salum."

I showed him the broken spring and asked, "Do you have this

part?"

"We no have, I can make!" Salum picked up an old spoke and began bending it using the broken spring as a pattern. Soon he had installed his work of art. He wanted to straighten the wheel but it was already 10:00, so I decided we'd hit the road and wobble into Mbeya. (Salum's handmade part worked all the way to Cape Town, South Africa.)

At a small store we shared a Bitter Lemon. Mathew, the owner, was a talker. He said "Mafinga is the new name, it was called John's Corner. Nobody know John so we change." We drank and listened, then as we prepared to leave he said, "Why you don't buy two drink? You from California, everyone there be rich!" Then he asked, "What you get for doing this?" When we told him we got nothing, he asked, "Why you doing this?"

"We're here to meet nice people, like you," I said, as we started toward the road. Cat was already there and mounted up.

He grabbed my handlebar and said, "You come to Africa to see monkey people?"

That one shook me. "What did you say?"

He repeated, "The Monkey People, that's what Germans called us during Colonial Days."

Sure that my jaw had dropped, I said, "We believe we're all the same under our skin and in our minds."

He agreed then I quoted a sign we'd seen "The Earth is One Country, and Mankind It's Citizens!" We shook hands vigorously, using the Tanzanian shake, grasp, clasp, grasp, shake then I hustled off to catch The Cat.

Our guidebook described a Stone-Age prehistoric site. The sign pointed to a turn off. The road was mud. Cat wanted to call it off, but the further we went the more intent I became. The site was anti-climatic. A small shack with a few stone tools that may or may not have been 60,000 years old. The guide explained, "Local people know of this place for many years. In 1950s Chicago University come, and excavated in 1957." One Guestbook entry said it was an easy bicycle ride from Iringa. They must have ridden on a dry day.

CAT TRAX Day 174, 113 Ks Mafinga to Makambako. It was 4:40 p.m. when we reached Midtown Guest Lodge in Makambako. It was a strange looking place with animals made of concrete lined up out front, some on the roof. Grace, the girl who greeted us with an infectious laugh said yes to all our questions. BBC? "Yes", restaurant? "Yes", wine? "Yes"! We were at home. Good news the room only cost 7,000 T Shillings ($7.00) and it was clean. The French wine cost 8,000, but was well worth it.

A power outage caused lukewarm showers. The brown stains in the tub and thick brown water made the lack of light a blessing. A glass of wine and The Cat began to feel better. The generator kicked in just as we walked to dinner. Chicken soup sounded good it turned out to be a bowl of hot water that tasted like a chicken had been boiled in it. They served a chicken leg on the side. A generous sprinkling of salt made it edible.

Main course was Roasted Chicken and Chips. The chicken was tough, the chips were good, the wine was great. Dinner cost an astounding 4,600 TS. ($4.60)

As Grace collected our rent our liking for her grew. I asked about a telephone, she laughed and said, "Not here, but close by, I will take you." We had decided to call Joel, William's co-worker, to ask about a place to stay in Chimala.

She led us out the gate around the corner and into a candlelit stall. The girl there collected 3,000 Shillings. Grace looked at Joel's phone number and said, "You know my friend, Mr. Masharubu?"

She told me it meant "mustache" in Swahili. When Joel answered I asked, "Is this Mr. Masharubu?" He stammered so I asked if he was Joel.

He said "Yea to both." Then asked where I was calling from. When I told him Midtown Lodge he said, "I think you must have met one of my friends there." I told him it was Grace. He said "I don't know a Grace." Then he added, "The only place worthwhile in Chimala is Chimala Guest House. Mention my name and ask for room #7." We promised to meet when we roll in to Mbeya.

CAT TRAX   Day 175, 124 Ks, Makambako to Chimala. Breakfast was greasy chapati. Two Tanzanian businessmen took seats in our bungalow. They were curious, wondered how we compared Africa to California. We told them the people in Tanzania had been extremely friendly, we hoped when they visit California they'd receive the same treatment. They both insisted our ride, though long, would be easy. "It is all downhill to Chimala." We could only hope.

Grace came out, smiling as usual, and told us that she was leaving. She had worked five straight twenty-four-hour days and now, had a day off. We took a picture with her and a cement monkey that was flipping the finger. She was so full of life. When we told her Masharubu didn't know her she said, "My Swahili name is Neema. He know Neema."

The Tanzanians were right, we literally sailed down almost all the way to Chimala. The terrain and trees reminded us of Oregon. At 80 Ks we arrived in Igawa. Our plan had been to stop 8 Ks from there, up a dirt road off the highway. Cat was still feeling weak from the African Guff-Guff. She toughened up, we keep rolling downwind and down the road.

We ducked into a cool, dimly-lit fly-filled café. The cool felt good, we dealt with the flies. The only food we found was rice and beans, again. An interesting group stopped talking and stared for a second, then continued arguing. One guy hit another hard on the arm for some reason. The guy that got hit shouted, then threatened a woman and her kids. The pecking order we assumed. Lots of interaction, all with an angry undertone. The lady that cooked and served took a little BS from her husband who just sat and complained. Once we were served she dropped the top of her dress and began nursing her baby. There was little joy in the food, however her smile and watching the social interactions were delightful.

After 30 Ks Cat began to fade. I had another broken spoke. At last we limped in to Chimala, sick, lame, and wounded. No one spoke English at the Chimala Guest House. The place was minimal, but so was the price. We took two rooms #7, Joel's choice and 8 just across the hall. We would work on and keep the bikes in #8. They had no wine, we made do with slightly cool Kilimanjaro beers. We sipped as Cat swore she wouldn't bathe in the chocolate-brown water. She reconsidered and was soon in the shower. It didn't look as brown when raining down as it did draining into the squatter toilet she had to straddle. Ah, may we never forget the odor and ordeal.

Three broken spokes, two mine, one of Cat's. It took three beers and an hour to complete the work. I was a greasy mess and ready for a stinky brown shower.

They offered beef and chips. We took seats at a table in the dirt courtyard amongst the locals. The moon cast a silvery glow through the clouds. Mosquitoes nibbled at our ankles. We washed the chewy beef and cold fries down with a couple more Kilimanjaro beers.

CAT TRAX Day 176, 50 Ks on Bike, 25 in Matatu, Chimala to Mbeya. Anxious to get to Mbeya and a day off, we were pushing

out the gate at 8:00 a.m.. Cat suffered another attack of African Guff-Guff and her breakfast didn't set well. Tree branches placed across our lane warned of a hazard ahead. Rounding a corner, we saw that a truck and bus had crashed head on. The injured and casualties had been removed. It was easy to see that the truck driver and some passengers must have been killed. The driver's side of the bus was ripped open, seats dangled out the gash. They say bus travel is one of the most dangerous things to do in Tanzania.

Cat's rear derailleur broke loose from the frame. When I tried to tighten it, the remaining threads in the soft alloy stripped. My worst nightmare had occurred. Our friend Brad with the bike company was sending something he called a "Nutsert" to re-thread. It wouldn't arrive for a couple of weeks. We continued cycling, but Cat was limited to only the three front gears. In her weakened condition, we walked and pushed up hills we would normally have easily ridden. We limped into the next village. I began searching for a bolt that would fit through the hole. A tiny Auto Spares kiosk looked like a good bet. My vision was a bolt with a head thin enough to clear the chain. Oliver David a young guy who spoke English came to our rescue. I explained the problem and he translated to the guy in the shop. We tried all possibilities but none of the bolt heads were thin enough. Then Oliver David said, "I have sent a friend, to bring a man, he can grind it to fit, for you."

The man, Said, (Saw-eed) looked and listened then took a bolt that fit through the hole back to his shop. Returning, he'd ground the bolt head down but not enough to clear the chain. He left then returned. I tried to help. The bolt was so hot it burned my fingers. He felt he'd ground as much off the bolt head as he could without weakening it. It still wouldn't quite allow the chain to clear. I was ready to give up when Said suggested a washer. I had one I'd carried since  given to us by Fireman in Greenland. Said placed it on the axel and voila, it worked.

Oliver David and Said joined us for a soft drink. We paid for the bolt and offered Shillings to Said. He refused them, only allowing me to thank him and shake his hand. We were impressed by Oliver David's abilities and command of the English language. We urged him to get back to school and learn about computers, positioning himself for a job with real earning power.

Cycling on Cat became very sick. We hailed a minibus. It was already overloaded. The driver and conductor were adamant they could squeeze us in. Most call these buses "One Mores." They could always pack in one more. Cat objected, I worried we'd be stuck there the rest of the afternoon. I stripped off the bags, they piled them in on bags of grain.

The next big challenge was Mbeya Bus Station. As we pulled in the sellers of things and guys claiming to be guides surged around. We were stranded, our bikes and bags strewn on the ground. A guy that I thought was the driver said, "Give me 10,000 Shilling." I did and he quickly disappeared. Then the conductor said, "You must pay 20,000 T Shillings." I told him I'd already paid the driver. He pointed and said, "This is my driver." I told them the guy I paid wore a Sadaam Hussein t-shirt. They knew him, caught him and drug him back. He reluctantly handed back the 10,000 TS.

Then came a shouting match with the driver and conductor about the fare. They finally agreed to take the 10,000. Cat was pretty upset but too weak to fight.

Bags on the bikes, we pushed to a telephone stand. I tried to call Joel but his phone was in a different area code. A guy with a Duke University t-shirt muscled in trying to listen. I turned my back, told him it was private. He wouldn't take private for an answer then followed us as we walked to Hotel Mbeya Peak. Cat finally made it clear we didn't need help and wouldn't pay. That did it, he spun around and headed back to the shark tank they called a bus station.

Hotel Peak was atop a hill. It looked like a Sovietski hotel. Later, I read that the Tanzania government had been modeled after that of Mainland China. Hotel Peak looked like Chinese places I'd stayed in 1989.

CAT TRAX Day 175, R and R in Mbeya. Joel had his driver Khalid pick us up and take us to his home. We played our band Acadiana's CD while he ate lunch. He grabbed his harmonica and played along. Then told us, "I'm originally from the Missouri Ozarks but I've lived most of my adult life in Africa. I was married to a local woman we had two daughters. She moved with the girls to Berkeley, California. We divorced some time ago. My girls are in their twenties now and studying at the University." Suddenly, he said, "Hey, I've got to get to my bank, you guys want to come along?" Bad news for us, his bank's Manager said, "There is no way to get cash with ATM or credit cards in Mbeya."

CAT TRAX Day 177, 15 Ks, Mbeya to Stockholm Hotel. As we ate breakfast, three men with two teenage boys drifted in. One man stood behind me and said, "What are you doing, Old Man?" I spun around and said, "What are you doing, Old Boy?" I almost said "Fat Boy," but thought better of that. It took him by surprise. He introduced us to his twin sons as he sucked down three shots of booze in little plastic tubes chased by Coke. Wow, what a way to start a day.

Joel convinced us to move to The Stockholm Hotel. As we rolled past the bustling bus stop, the Duke University guy came running. I said, "Mr. Duke, what do you want?" He backed away as I took a picture of the bus station then said, "You must pay for taking photo." Sorry, Mr. Duke, you lose again!

As we cycled into The Stockholm, Robert, the desk clerk, rushed out and said, "Masharubu has told us you would come!" Cat did the check-in duties, I changed out broken spokes and oiled up our machines. Joel taught us a way to beat the telephone system. We would call, ring once, then hang up, this was a signal to Joel, who would then call back.

We sat in a hut in the hotel garden and listened to Joel's tales and music. He played guitar and had a harmonica hanging from his neck. Blues and oldies were his specialties. I shot a video as he played and sang, "Corrina, Corrina where've you been so long." Viewing the video he said, "I've gotta start practicing again!" The afternoon passed too quickly, and Joel had to go. We walked him  out, then pulled together in a group hug. We knew we'd see Mr. Masharubu again!

CAT TRAX Day 178, Typhoid or No Typhoid, That was The Question! Pee break at 3:00 a.m., my right foot was numb. So numb I stumbled to the toilet. Back in bed, I wondered, should we ride? Would I be okay in the countryside for five days? I wished I'd gone to the clinic and taken a blood test. Soon I had a dull headache and ringing in my ears, but rationalized it was a sinus infection. I've

always had sinus issues in altitude and Mbeya is at 6,000 feet.

Tossing and turning, I decided to have the test done. Decision made, I slept soundly. Cat was anxious to get back on the road. I suggested, "Let's go to the clinic, have the test done then load up and go." She peeked out the window and said to expect a rain delay. I called and then waited for Joel's call. He understood my concern, called the Aga Khan Health Center, called me back and said, "They are open, go right in."

Robert was calling a taxi when another guest, a Tanzanian Army General, walked past. Cat caught him as he was climbing into his Range Rover and asked for a ride. The General looked nervous then said, "Yes sure, come get in." We were unprepared, I only had 25,000 T Shilling in my wallet. Thinking "I'll deal with that later,"

we jumped into the back seat.

The General said, "I'm General Nasser, my driver here is Mr. Nikiti." He drove fast. Other cars and pedestrians moved aside as he honked and swerved. Nearing the clinic, Nikiti stopped.

General Nasser said, "You get out here!" Was he concerned about being seen aiding foreigners?

Aga Khan Clinic was shuttered. We rattled the door and a muffled voice said, "Clinic open at 3:00." We did the Joel call trick. He said, "I'll come pick you up."

I had a partially crushed banana in my pocket. Instead of tossing it, I offered it to a street urchin. His eyes locked on mine, he grabbed it took two steps back, then spun and bolted up the street.

No Asante, no thank you but it made us happy anyway.

Joel pulled up, we piled in. He drove to the door, the open door of the same Aga Khan Clinic we'd just left. I told him the guy had said they opened at 3:00. He reminded us "9:00 a.m. is 3:00, in Swahili time. Remember, the day starts at sun up 6:00 a.m., so 9:00 a.m. is 3:00." We thanked him and apologized. He said, "Call when you're finished, I'll drive you back." Friends in need we were (again), and he was a true friend, indeed!

After a short wait the Lab Technician came in, laughed and joked then said, "Please take a seat, I must to use the toilet." I whispered to Cat, "I hope he washes his hands before taking blood." He motioned, I followed, he washed his hands in the lab then broke open a sterile needle. Quick and painless. He said, "Come back in forty-five minutes for results, you pay 1,500 Shilling." Forty-five minutes later, his conclusion, "No Typhoid!"

Joel drove us back to The Stockholm. Over lunch, we again talked of life and music. Hugs and goodbyes with promises to meet again, then he drove away. We were ecstatic I wouldn't have to take antibiotics.

CAT TRAX Day 179, 70 Ks, Mbeya/Uyole to Tukuyu. The wind was blowing, the sky full of clouds but no rain. Uphill was the word of the day. Granny gear, pedaling hard at 3 MPH. Carts, heavy-looking wooden carts with car wheels, were flying down as we did the "pole, pole" up. They were great to watch. Cat thought it would be fun to ride one. The driver hung on the wagon tongue and flew, his feet touching ground every ten feet or so. If he got in trouble, his only braking system was to rear back and let the tail of the wagon drag on a tire. Looked like a dangerous way to make a living.

The scenery was spectacular, mountains blanketed with farm fields of greens and gold. A fellow we met in a store worked with World Bank. He said, "Good news, a little more up then it is all down to Tukuyu. You should eat lunch in Kiwira they have a good restaurant in  the hotel." He was right, we topped out, then swooped down so steep that our hands and wrists got fatigued from clasping the brake handles. We flew right in to Kiwara for lunch.

The Landmark Hotel in Tukuyu was recommended by Robert from the Stockholm Hotel. He was right too, it was as nice as his.

CAT TRAX Day 180, 50 Ks, Tukuyu to The Malawi Border. BBC News aired an alarming story. A US chartered passenger plane was confiscated by the Zimbabwe Government. The US government denied any part in what appeared to be a mercenary invasion. The plane was full of guns, military hardware, and 64 soldiers. We'd need to keep a watchful eye on that situation!

We rolled through steep hillsides covered with tea plantations, bananas, and corn, with stands of pine and eucalyptus trees. Cat commented, "I bet a lot of people in the States would love to live here if they felt safe and could get all the modern conveniences."

We stopped in Kelya, the border village. A gutsy gal we met there, Inbar from Israel, was hitchhiking around Africa. Inbar was one brave chick. She flagged down a semi truck then waved goodbye as she climbed aboard. We lost sight of the truck in a downpour of rain. We wound our way through the rain, around puddles to the Malawi border.

Borders were all so similar. Guys come running, shouting "Change Money, change money." We shouted back, "No, no!" As we turned into the Tanzanian Immigration Office one shouted, "Thanks for nothing."

I yelled back, "You're welcome for nothing."

Exit stamps in our passport, we crossed toward Malawi. A Tanzanian soldier swung open the gate. After fifty days our Tanzanian adventure was in the history books.

Chapter 23 Malawi

CAT TRAX Day 180 continued, 50 Ks, Malawi Border to Karonga. By 1:00 p.m. we were in Malawi. No visa was required for US citizens. We thought that would make it simple. Cat went into the Immigration Office. Standing right outside, I could hear her conversation with the officer. She'd filled out the form and handed it to him. He scanned down then asked, "How much money you have?" Cat asked, "Why do you want to know that?"

He made it clear, "The question is on the form, my duty is to get the answer." I argued from outside the window behind him. That seemed to make him nervous. Did he think we carried a lot of money? Would he call friends and tell them we were coming? It was apparent he wouldn't clear us to enter until we disclosed our cash. He said, "Our country needs to know you will be able to pay for food and shelter while in Malawi."

Okay, we decided we'd play the game his way. Cat said, "We have 559,000 Tanzanian Shilling," He wanted to know how many US Dollars we had. We told him honestly, we had none. He sighed, then said, "You must go back, change the Shilling to Kwacha, before entering Malawi." He was adamant that banks in Malawi, would not change Shillings to Kwacha. We asked if someone there could change the money, we had just run the gauntlet through the piranha pool of Tanzanian money scalpers and didn't want to go back.

He whispered, "I cannot officially be involved in exchange of currency." We quietly asked him to help find a fair person. He said, "You wait, I will find him." When he returned, he told Cat to come around the building to room '9'. We decided I should go. As I walked down the dimly lit hallway he came toward me, we met at room '9'. Inside was a sweaty heavyset guy. Mr. Sweaty Big Bucks spoke in the local language, and the officer living on the fringe of legality said, "The rate of exchange is 1 Kwacha for 10 Shilling." That was better than Robert at the Stockholm had told us to expect. I said "That sounds fair." Mr. Big Bucks pulled up his pant leg and pulled a wad of Kwacha out of his sock. (Kwacha socked away!) The counting process was an interesting riffling through piles of money. Our 559,000 shrank to 55,900 Kwacha though we still had the same purchasing power.

Tom, our now-friendly immigration officer wished us a safe journey. We asked about a restaurant. Pointing to a shack just outside the fenced area he said, "You should eat there." Why would we doubt him? We pushed across the muddy area through a gaping hole in the fence then up a muddy, slippery slope to the café. Loud music and a dirt floor were signs that life in Malawi was going to be pretty much the same as Tanzania. A guy sitting nearby listened as we complained about the music, then shouted to the waiter who turned it down. The rice and beans were as good as any we'd had and no more expensive. Tom was right again.

The road was flat, surrounded by rice paddies framed by hills in the distance. We got an occasional glimpse of Lake Malawi on the left. Our map made it appear we'd be riding along the shore, but we were far from it most of the time.

It was 4:30 when we reached Karonga. We followed an arrow-sign, pushing through dirt and sand to Club Marina. Hot water and cold beer, not all bad. Well, unless you consider getting only one towel bad. We asked for another they said, "We have no more." We share everything else, why not a damp towel?

CAT TRAX Day 181, 90 Ks, Karonga to Chitimba. Ready and anxious to ride, we hit the restaurant. The guard said, "Open at 6:30." As we complained, the staff walked in. Sounding upset the cook said, "Food soon, few minute." We walked to the muddy lake shore, then turned back. The cook, walking toward us, said, "I watch you, come to warn you, mud is deep and trap you." Sounded like quicksand. She emphasized, "You could sink under, completely, very dangerous!"

Flat road, then hills. Road kill, fauna of various breeds and sizes. A huge lizard lay tits up, wondering, "What hit me?"

At a small village Dennis, a neat young guy, offered help. He led us through alleyways, searching for food. He kept saying, "The cafes are temporary" and they looked it. One woman told him she would have rice in thirty minutes. We decided to get a cold drink and move on. I bought Dennis a Coke, he was in seventh heaven. Locals gathered around. He swaggered, telling his rapt audience how he'd helped. He wanted our address. I asked "Do you have e-mail?" He didn't know. His friend Cuthbert McCarthy Manata explained. I called them our guide and teacher.

A quick lunch down the road at Chilumba village, rice and beans, of course. We wondered whether we'd passed into a different time zone when we entered Malawi. Our watch read 3:00 p.m. The wall clock said 2:00. "Yes," a boy named Malcolm confirmed, "now 2:00 p.m., here." That made us feel badly about the way we'd treated the staff at breakfast.

Typical, the way those who don't cycle describe roads. The group consensus: Chitimba was 10 Ks away on a flat road. It was twenty with two steep hills. Cat's tail feathers were ablaze with saddle sores. We'd sweat, get rained on, then dry in the hot sun, then the process began again.

We were in Chitimba by 4:00, Malawi time. The Chitimba Camp was another tough ride/push in dirt and sand. A young girl ran toward us to hold the falling-down gate. First stop we swigged beers, well, Cat a beer, for me ginger beer. The official greeter was a guy named Precious. The place was decorated like a surfers paradise sans surf, no surf on the lake.

Precious pushed Cat's bike through the beach sand to our lakefront room. The shower was dark the water cold. Cat saw a big black bug and huge wasp in the darkness. I came to the rescue. Oh, the 1,000 Kwacha rent ($10.00 US) didn't include towels or toilet paper.

We headed to the bar, seeking cold wine. There were several others there, elbows on the bar. John the owner, was tending bar. He and his ex-girlfriend Della had been backpacking, saw the place and bought a good deal. He seemed tired of the routine and there was still a lot of work to be done. Another guy, Tom, from Maynooth, Ontario, Canada, owned a backpackers hotel there. He spends summers working his tail off then takes the winter months to explore southern climes. By 9:00 we were snuggled down under our mosquito net.

CAT TRAX Day 182, 51 Ks on bikes, 29 in pickup truck, Chitimba to Rumphi. Voices wafted in at 5:30 a.m.. Fishermen launching dugout canoes were setting off next to the hotel. A wondrous photo opportunity! The orange sun streamed through thunderhead clouds, setting the scene. A moment of beauty created by brave men and Mother Nature.

The road was flat, 14 Ks to Chiweta. At a traffic stop, the officer asked Cat, "Are you armed?"

Cat asked, "Armed, what do you mean?" Thinking he wanted to confiscate weapons, she said, "We don't have guns!"

"There are bad people on the hill ahead. You had better find a weapon," he said in thick accent. Cat jokingly suggested they should come along for protection.

He said, "We have warned you, that is all we can do," in a very serious tone.

We'd heard so many warnings, we just took it in stride. The climb was 16 Ks and steep. The road swirled out of town and up into the clouds. Hot sun burned our necks. After an hour clouds covered the sun, that felt great. We pushed our heavy steeds most of the day, making extremely slow progress, we rested every few hundred feet. The clouds became mist, the mist drizzle, then a tropical downpour. We donned our ponchos. They kept out the heavy rain but caused us to sweat. Cat's tail was so painful it hurt to walk or ride.

Near the summit, a kiosk in a small village offered soft drinks. As Cat bought drinks, a group of tough-looking young guys milled around, playing soccer on the road. One began dancing to blaring music coming from a nearby building. He danced, flaunted himself with his moves, then he dropped to the ground and did pushups. He jumped up in front of me flexing his huge biceps. I clapped and said, "Fantastic!"

Cat said, "The woman in the store warned me, we should leave quickly." Then the strangest incident we'd ever witnessed. Termites began to swarm from a hole in the dirt. The biggest brawniest guy squatted down and began flapping his arms and crowing like a rooster. As the termites surfaced, he scooped them up and ate them. Even the other guys seemed awestruck, he was definitely their leader.

When Cat returned the bottles, the woman warned again, "This is a terrible place and very dangerous. You must ride as fast as you can, away from here!" Cat was terrified, I began to plan our escape. The best I came up with, in case they attacked, was turn tail and sprint back downhill. I urged Cat to turn and ride off if the guys got in my face.

The local toughs parted, allowing us to push our bikes through. They chattered and made cat calls, but didn't try to stop or touch us. Their threatening comments were meaningless to us. We pushed as fast as we could up the hill. The idea of riding up fast was a joke, the grade continued at 10%. We rounded a curve above the village and saw three of the boys walking behind us. Then two more guys started down from a side road.

We felt trapped! Cat flagged down a passing car. Two young guys that looked like inner city gangstas listened to our concerns. The driver said, "You don't have to fear, we will follow." He got out and pretended to check inside his trunk, then walked around inspecting the wheels. We pushed as fast as possible. They began slowly driving behind us. Once we were safely beyond the side road they honked waved and drove on. A true act of kindness extended to a couple of Mzunga, strangers.

Climbing and pushing had taken 4 hours and 20 minutes to cover the 16 Ks. We were bone tired and facing another 50 Ks. It was getting late. Based on the time change, sunset was coming earlier. We rode hard in rising terrain next to a river. Exhausted, we stopped and opened a can of corned beef. Cat said, "This tastes like dog food." We spread it on bread and forced it down.

At 5:00 we pulled into a tiny village. With the sun hovering just above the hilltops, we decided we'd be safer hooking a ride into Rumphi (Rumpee). The police at the road block below had warned, "It is not safe to cycle on this road, after dark." A big pickup was parked in front of a cafe/bar. Cat approached the driver who was drinking beers with friends. She asked, "Can you give us a ride to Rumphi?"

They looked at each other then he said, "We haven't room for you and cycles." Slightly deflated, Cat went roadside hoping for another passing truck. As I stood near the two guys one said, "If you can get the bikes and baggage on the truck, we will drop you in Rumphi."

I hollered at Cat and began tearing down the bikes. Under their watchful eyes we lay the bags on their load of firewood. They helped lift the bikes up and I strapped them to the truck. As we put our handlebar bags helmets and water bottles inside they started getting in. When we'd asked we thought they were worried about allowing strangers in their truck. We didn't know they were all riding in the truck, they really didn't have room. Our addition jammed seven of us into a five passenger cab. Holding our bags and helmets, we squeezed in and were off to Rumphi.

The driver, James and friend Edward dropped the others off then took us to the door of the Countryside Inn. They and the staff helped us unload. I slipped James 500 Kwacha, he seemed embarrassed. I said, "For petrol."

He shrugged and said, "Thank you." Thanks to him and Edward we were in a safe place just as darkness closed in upon the valley.

The large bed took up most of the room. The bath and toilet were tight, everything got wet when we showered. However, hot water at the end of a very harrowing day was a luxury for only 600 Ks ($6:00 US).

We later learned the young ruffians on the hillside were underground miners. Imagine their dangerous lives, which they will live out in dark tunnels. How fortunate we felt pushing to the top of that hill and onward, in our adventuresome lives. The two guys in the car we trusted our lives to had looked like gang bangers from a ghetto. Though they wore stocking caps low over their eyes, we had no time to judge them by their looks. As Cat always says, "The most difficult times, make the best memories." We had accumulated some humdingers!

CAT TRAX Day 183, 63 Ks, Rumphi to Mzuzu. A good night's sleep, a bountiful breakfast and we were ready for the road. However, our legs were shot. We decided that in the future when faced with a huge hill we'd catch a ride. Crazy to be wearing ourselves down pushing. Between the fear factor and fatigue we felt justified taking the ride in to Rumphi. There were no rules except rule #1, Cat's call! Safety first!

It was pleasant, cycling through small rolling hills and fertile valleys. A line of women with babies on their backs piqued our interest. Ah, a clinic. The doctor was weighing babies in a hanging basket. Rudimentary medical care, however, we were told they offered the women advice, and even hospitalization if they were sick. Nearby, an open air school packed with kids stopped their lessons to shout and wave. The teachers also seemed to enjoy our passing.

The crops were a patchwork of corn and tobacco. We stopped and spoke with Anthony, a farmer raising both. He admitted, "Tobacco has taken corn off local's tables, but tobacco is my money crop." He gave us a tour of his tobacco-drying

shed. Riding away, he yelled out, "Go in peace!"

Passing by Ekwendeni village another cyclist, Pastor Arthur, began to pace with us. He told us, "Every other week I rides my bike to Mzuzu village and buys twenty milligram of maize, our only affordable food. Our village have no corn. Today my wife have three children and are out of food." His wobbly bike looked older than his thirty-five years. The chain jumped off three times.

Arthur said, "I am Pentecostal Pastor, in my very poor parish. I takes small jobs to get by. My dream is to go USA, study." He continued, grimly, "They change to free markets here, it allow rich to charge whatever they want for corn."

I asked why he didn't get land and do farming? He replied, "I have land but it need fertilizer, we cannot afford fertilizer." Then he began using the word capital. "If I had capital I could buy fertilizer, but I have none." His poor-me attitude was beginning to wear on us.

I told him my grandmother was Pentecostal and she taught me, "The Lord helps those that help themselves."

I asked, "Why don't you bring back some of the corn to sell to neighbors? Friends that also need food but aren't strong enough to cycle." He was skeptical, but kept repeating the saying, "The Lord helps those..."

I gave him another idea, "Rather than ride empty to Mzuzu take tomatoes, potatoes or other greens to sell. Never go with an empty bike."

He rode with us past the maize market to a BP Station. He was a bright young guy, so maybe the ideas would sink in. If he helped his neighbors and made enough profit to afford fertilizer he could farm his own corn. We bought three Cokes and savored the moment with him.

At The Sunbird Mzuzu Hotel we met two girls working with Code, a non-profit from Canada. Yvonne, the Executive Director, told us they provide African students with books and kits containing pencils, an eraser, a notebook, a ruler, and a personal note from a friend in Canada. Their brochure says, "Literacy = Freedom." Ain't that the truth!

CAT TRAX Day 184, Much Needed R & R in Mzuzu
CAT TRAX Day 185, Getting Well and Getting Ready to be Ready. A brisk walk to breakfast at Cafe Velo. When we told the waitress "velo" means bicycle in French she said, "Oh no, this mean LOVE, in Tumbuka language." Gotta love our bicycles!

The mist became rain on the way back. We scooted-building to building, tree to tree-trying to stay dry. Rain poured down, so we were very happy to stay a second day in our Mzuzu sanctuary.

That afternoon we felt the room move under our feet. We got that good old California feeling. The desk clerk said, "Yes, earthquake, we have occasionally, no big one for twenty year."

CAT TRAX Day 186, 54 Ks, Mzuzu to Nkhata Bay. It was 7:45 a.m. when we approached the door of Stanbic Bank. The Monday morning crowd thickened. About fifty folks laden with weekend receipts were anxious to make deposits. We were the first to reach the Visa window. I filled out the forms then the teller said, "It can be at least two hour before we receive approval."

Anne's Cafe and Butchery was next door. Once we were seated inside, Mr. Mulambia told us "My wife owns Anne's Cafe." Thinking for a moment, he continued, "I retired from police, I give politics a try, threw my hat into ring, but my party merge with another, their incumbent was running I had to withdraw." He was well known, people coming and going would bow, often urging him to run as an Independent. He said, "I might."

Then Mr. Mulambia told us a story that shook Cat's confidence. "The owner of our local internet cafe traveled to Zimbabwe. He took what he thought was a taxi, but ended up in the bush, robbed at gunpoint." Ah, retired policemen are the most cautious people in the world. I pointed out this type of robbery probably occurs twenty times a day in Los Angeles.

When Mr. Mulambia heard we were from the US, he summoned his son. Maimba was studying engineering. Papa wanted him to get a scholarship to an American university. We gave him the phone number for Kurt, the guy that distributed scholarships for Bowling Green University.

At 10:00 a.m. we got 40,000 Kwacha, enough to get us to Lilongwe the capital city. The rain poured down in torrents. But by the time we were loaded and ready to roll, the sun was shining.

Another day of up and downs. The dusty streets of Nkhata Bay were awash with people, all trying to sell wood carvings, art, or drugs. We felt uneasy. The road took a turn to the right, then turned to dirt. We stopped to survey our possibilities when a great looking classic motor home pulled up. Chris and Sonja were from South Africa, their rig was a converted 1979 Land Rover.

222

As we began climbing in the dirt and rock Chris and Sonja roared past then stalled out. We got to them just as she was putting rocks under the wheels to keep from rolling backward. Chris got out, crawled under then decided it may just have jumped out of gear. We pushed onward they roared past, again.

The road to Nkhata was rough and rocky, we had to push. The afternoon sun filtered through clouds bringing heat and sweat. At last a steep down and we rolled into the parking lot. A pleasant surprise the '79' Rover was there. They had vacancies, chalets on the lake and cabins above the restaurant and bar. The chalets had shared toilets. Cat chose a cabin, it was only 1200 Ks and included toilet paper, towels, and a shower with hot water.

Checking in, we met Tony from England and Amy from the US heartland, Leawood, Kansas. The waiter called himself "Food

Man," the bartender "Drink Man." Food Man's voice was wonderful, his laugh and the way he said "Yeah" were infectious. We sat on the deck looking out on the lake, enjoying pizza and beers and new friends.

CAT TRAX Day 187, Nyala Lodge, Nkhata Bay and the Rain! Our sleep was interrupted at 5:00 a.m. by brilliant flashes of lightening followed by rafter-shaking peals of thunder. The rain came down by the bucket. It was 7:30 when we finally drug ourselves from under the mosquito net. Hating to push in mud, we hired a truck to get back to the junction.

The rain continued to pelt down. Our 9:00 a.m. truck was delayed and the price went from 800 to 1000 Ks due to mud hazard. There were no other guests and as rain continued it was unlikely there would be others. It continued pouring rain and the next dry room was 40 Ks down the highway. We resigned ourselves to the fact that we were marooned in the mud.

CAT TRAX   Day 188, 120 Ks, Nkhata Bay to Ngala Beach.
Food Man and Bar Man came out to see us off. They were the highlight of our stay. Always joking, laughing, and spreading joy. A tip, hell yes, they deserved it! Also their food was great and the wine was fine. Passing by they shouted, "Happy St. Patrick's Day."

It was cloudy but the rain had subsided. We loaded the bikes on Paul's old truck. The road coming in had been terrible, now with mud, it was impossible to cycle. I saw him studying the lay of the land as he parked on a little hill. He had a broken starter. We got in, ready for him to roll back and pop the clutch. He couldn't get the truck into reverse gear. He pulled the cover from the transmission. The glove box was full of wrenches. We were scrunched up in the seat, he somehow got the linkage working, so we rolled back and the old relic fired up.

The road was a rough, rocky, muddy mess. Uphills felt especially treacherous. He'd gun the ancient engine then up we'd go slipping, sliding, and fishtailing. In town, we bought drinking water and a five-gallon container of gasoline for Paul, part of our agreement.

At the crossroads, we lifted the bikes down, paid, and were pedaling onward by 9:30. Our first Rubber Tree plantation, interesting how they tap the trees: cut a groove in the bark, milking them. Young boys stood roadside, bouncing and selling handmade rubber balls.

At 40 Ks we entered the village of Chintheche in thick rain. Hungry we rode through the muddy parking lot to a café. The owner Agnes, was holding court over a group of young guys. When she heard we were American she said, "My cousin live in the Bronx, New York. I think I visit him next year." She asked for our address and said, "Maybe I stop to see you, when I visits my

cousin." We tried to explain that California was 3,000 miles from NYC, she just didn't get it.   As we were leaving, she gave us a carved wooden salad fork and spoon, and a wooden wine goblet. What a nice gesture, we hadn't had anyone offer a gift since we could remember. At least not without asking for money.

Rain slowly drizzled until the sun overtook the sky. We were at 90 Ks and struggling when a little pickup truck pulled up. The driver Aaron, offered cold water and mileage advice. "It is twenty kilometers, to Ngala." That was a crushing blow. Cat was running on reserves. Aaron offered to haul us in. She clearly wanted to. I suggested she take the deal, I'd finish the ride. That was an absolute no deal. I did ask him to send out a search party if we weren't in by 6:00.

The scenery was spectacular, our legs were drained. I turned our taillights on at 6:15, hoping Aaron was on his way back. While installing the headlights, my bike took a tumble. There in the darkness, a vision, a sign reflected in the headlights of a passing car. Ngala Beach Lodge 400 meters. Then another apparition, a voice, "I am night watchman, Aaron told us we look for you, this Ngala Beach, follow me."

Riding in, I heard something fall from the bike. It was the salad spoon. The watchman found it. Damn, the fork was nowhere to be seen. Lost on the highway, no doubt. Ngala was a neat place. Our room was two bedrooms, one down the other above with a balcony. Craig, the proprietor assured us there was a lake view in daylight.

It was pizza night at Ngala. I asked if they had any white wine. Craig looked along the back bar and said, "Bad news, we're out." I pulled a bottle out we'd been carrying and asked, "Can you throw this one, in the freezer?" He did then said, "How's about a beer? We have Carlsberg Brown or Green. I recommend Green, tis' St. Paddy's Day ye know!"

The gang, all locals were there for pizza and a pool tournament. We sipped wine, nibbled pizza, and got acquainted. Graham, Tony, and Angus all worked at a sugar plantation twenty Ks down the road.

CAT TRAX Day 189, 94 Ks, Ngala Beach to Sani Beach.
Breakfast was great, strong coffee, eggs and toast. I discovered I'd
lost my sunglasses in the bike crash. We rode slowly back to the
highway, looking for them and the salad fork. We pulled up under
the sign where my bike had fallen.
The disturbance was there in the dirt.
The sunglasses and fork now had new
owners. Onward, into the glare.

Seeking food we stopped at a tiny
store. "No café," said the clerk. We
found cold pineapple sodas. As we
sipped, a young girl sitting across from
us began nursing her baby. Talking
with Cat, Unity said, "There is food, I
show you." We followed a few doors
down into a shabby little hut. We
asked for rice, Unity said "All they
have is Nsima, corn flour mush."

After we had eaten, Unity asked,
"Can you make photo, of me with
baby?" As I did, a crowd gathered. A
man pushed through when he saw the
camera and gruffly said, "Big man,
take photo of mother!" He, Royce,
was the type I tended to ignore. His
mother was a darling. He brushed kids
aside making sure it would be just he
and mom in the photo. I asked her to
smile, she remained stone-faced. I
used my fingers to trace a smile on

my face. She got it and grinned ear to ear. When they saw the
picture Royce said, "My mother is very smiling now." He pointed to
her heart. They nor Unity asked for a copy of the pictures, just
seeing them was enough.

Fatigue coursed through our bodies. We had asked a lot of them
the two previous days. Heat also took a toll. In late afternoon, we
pulled into the BP Service Station in Nkhotakota. Cat found cold
water. As we sat drinking, Andrew and Junio, artists/Rasta

men/salesmen displayed their wares for us. They called me Father  and Cat Mother. We explained we couldn't buy anything we had no room to carry. It would have been refreshing to just sit and talk had we not been so tired. Asking about the Pottery Lodge they thought it was 15 Ks, ahead.

We set off, climbing hills we didn't need. By 4:00 p.m. the heat had become unbearable. At the top of a steep climb, we saw a sign, Sani Beach Resort 4 Ks. We took the dirt turnoff. Another night watchman led us in. He said, "Sani good, you like." The sun was sinking fast. We got into Sani at 5:30, slightly ahead of darkness.

Dog tired almost to the point of illness, we were surprised to see Gary and Cathy, a couple we'd met the Stone Age Site in Tanzania. We threw the bikes into our room and hit the bar, trading stories with them as they ate. It was cold beers and a battle with a swarm of ants for us. They headed back to their camp, we went for a shower. The desk clerk said, "Showers have only cold water. You can use toilet and camping showers." Cat hit the ceiling. He apologized then suggested, "I bring for you, hot water, in bucket."

So bucket showers, then back to the bar for dinner. We watched a woman washing dishes in the lake. She carried them into the kitchen. Perhaps they had no sink or, no water.

CAT TRAX Day 190, 15Ks, Sani Beach to Nkhotakota Pottery. A knock on the door awoke us. The fellow from the restaurant said, "Breakfast" then loped away. We hadn't ordered breakfast.

We walked down to visit with Gary and Cathy. They had an interesting lifestyle. Just putt putting along the lake for the next few weeks until she flew out for Wales. He planned to drive south to his home in Zimbabwe. He assured us, "If you go to Zim, you will have no problems."

Breakfast was cold. The waiter said, "I warn you it ready one hour ago." The bill was a shocker 3500 for the room and they added 1500 for tax and tip ($50 US). I complained, pointing out that our Guide Book quoted 2400 for the room.

"Sorry," the manager whined, "New owner, change everything."

I wrote on one of our cards "The Rip Off in Malawi" and left it for the new owners. So much for a day off. We decided to put our weary butts back on the seats and move on.

Our bodies were spent, it took forty-five minutes to cycle 4 Ks to the highway. Our muscles were burning, Cat was feeling nauseous. We picked up a bike buddy, Isaiah, along the way. He led us to a store. We wanted drinking water and he ran down a steep bank below the road to check. He returned with plastic bags, the kind locals bite the corner off to suck out the water. I went down into the store to pay and bought three pineapple sodas. We stood savoring them with Isaiah, in the hot sun. What a nice young man. He was cycling to Chia Lagoon to visit a friend from school who was recuperating from Malaria.

We waved goodbye to Isaiah, cycled to Nkhotakota and Pottery Lodge then sat waiting as the room was made up. A couple came in carrying cycling water bottles. We asked if they were cyclists. He said, "Yeah, typical American cyclists we haul the bikes around but rarely ride." Sam and Johanna were Jehovah's Witnesses there on a three year Mission.

During our conversation, Sam asked, "Did you see any big animals on the road?" We told

them about meeting the elephants in Mikumi. He said, "I bet you wanted some help, do you believe in God?" I replied, "Not exactly, we believe in Mother Nature, if she wanted us returned to nature at the behest of one of her finest creatures, then so be it." We laughed together then Sam said, "Here's our phone number in Lilongwe, call if you need anything!"

Our chalet, on a sandy beach, was nice. I jumped into the shower only to discover there were no towels. Cat went towel hunting. I decided to dry using the bath mat hanging nearby. When I pulled it down a huge spider fell out and skittered across the floor. It was three inches across, as big as a tarantula. I hit it with the mat, that made it angry. It charged, I jumped, and flailed. Finally a direct hit, toilet paper and a flush, and the battle was over. I decided Cat needn't know! I've often thought what a funny video that battle between a skinny naked guy with weird suntan lines and the huge spider might have been.

Romantic lunch overlooking Lake Malawi. I wanted to go for a swim. It was hot the beach inviting but, what about Bilharzia? Our guidebook said Bilharzia was a disease caused by tiny worms in the water. It infects humans and water snails transmit it. A sign on the beach stated "Bilharzia" is a very low risk? A girl we met at Nkhata Bay had said, "You really should take a swim just to be able to say you've done it." When I asked about Bilharzia, she laughed, "You

 just assume you have it, wait a month then go in and take the treatment!" I passed on the swim, no telling where we'd be in a month or what medical facilities would be available.

The Pottery Shop was a big operation. They ship internationally. Charles a young guy, was throwing clay. We told him he was an artist. He smiled and said, "I love this work, I feel good for it, and I make some money." His smile got us, we had to buy a small pitcher he'd just made.

CAT TRAX Day 191, 108 Ks, Nkhotakota Pottery to Salima. At breakfast a young, light-skinned girl walked past, pushing a bike. I said "Hello," then asked, "Do you live here in Malawi?" When she said yes, I said, "You sound more British than Malawian."

She laughed and said, "I'm American, I've been here three years." She told of a difficult childhood, a dysfunctional family, lots of moves and school changes. "Mom and Dad divorced, Mom married money." Justine seemed to be rebelling. "I disliked their phony world. I live in a small village. My mom and stepfather came for a visit. They shunned my village, and stayed in the most expensive hotel, on the lakeshore."

229

Justine, on holiday from her Peace Corps duties, was cycling the length of the lake. We got the bikes out, posed together, then headed toward Salima. Our overburdened bikes and tired bodies were no match for her strong young legs and light load. She soon bid us adieu and pedaled away. Later we caught her in a village, talking with a group of young boys. As we pulled up they all jumped on the begging bandwagon. "Give me money!"

She scolded them in a local language. I told her we usually joked with kids about how old we were and that they were young enough to work. She said, "That's a good way to respond, make a joke, it leaves those begging slightly embarrassed. They may hold back, not ask next time."

Justine took Cat's bike to see what riding our heavy weights was like. Back on her skinny steed it wasn't long before she was waving goodbye, again. At Benga as we slowly rode in looking for food we found her. She was seated in the shade eating cookies and holding court with local kids. They all found it hard to believe that she spoke their language. Justine rode on while we found sudsa, that gooey stuff.

Cat had developed a taste for sudsa. I found it mushy, tasteless, and hard to swallow. She loaded it up with salt. I ordered chicken and was served only backs and necks.  The sauce added a pinch of flavor. We joined three others, rolling balls of the white corn dough and dipping it in the sauce. They all wanted to talk. One of them, Sampson, had a fair command of the English language. Sampson and the others were unemployed. Sampson was married and had two children. He worked in farming but said, "There are no jobs, now."

We asked for bottled water.

Sampson said, "There is none in Benga." Justine had told us she felt the "Bore Hole" water was usually drinkable and Sampson led us to their well. A group of kids pumped as I used our filter, hoping for the best. We emptied our remaining mineral water into one bottle on each bike, then filled the others. We were hesitant, unsure about drinking it.

We arrived at the crossroad to Salima and Lilongwe at 5:30. Surprise, as we rolled into the service station for a soft drink Justine shouted and waved. She'd been befriended by a girl from Denmark. The Danish girl worked at Kuti Ranch, Malawi's first wildlife breeding station 7 Ks down a dirt road. They urged us, almost begged us to throw the bikes on a pickup and spend the night. Our friends Gary and Cathy were camping there, too. It sounded like great fun, except it was tent camping and self-catering. That meant getting there, then setting the tent and cooking. It was already 6:00 p.m. and dark.

The Mal Tsalani Motel was in the heart of the village, near the PTC Supermarket. That would fill all our needs: wine, water and shelter. We had survived without drinking the Bore Hole water. Rain that had threatened all afternoon finally kept its promise. The motel was dark, a village-wide power failure since early morning. I stood the watch, mosquitoes nibbling my legs as Cat checked the room. It was adequate, the hallway was lighted by candles and a kerosene lantern.

Cat went for the shower and discovered there was no water. We complained, the clerk explained "All water from tank, have been used, electric pump is idle, due to outage." As he spoke, the power surged back to life. We drank a couple of beers then headed toward the bath. Cat got a cool shower. I jumped in just as the pressure surged and gurgled. I had warm water that turned brown as it swirled around my feet.

Chapter 24 Malawi to Mozambique

CAT TRAX Day 192, A Bus Ride to Lilongwe. Mozambique was another cash-strapped country. Our plan to cycle south required US Dollars. We considered cycling to Lilongwe, however, it was an up and back trip and would take several days. Cat voted to take the bus, and Cat won! Fear of leaving the bikes caused another vote. Unanimous, we take them with us. Finding the bus station was

231

easy. Finding information about the schedule wasn't. The best guess, the Lilongwe bus may depart between 10:00 and 11:00. Fun to watch, as buses pulled in hawkers ran to them, holding their wares up to the windows. Surprisingly, they did a brisk business with soft drinks, fruit, boiled eggs, and fried dough balls. Some of the shorter sellers used sticks with a nail to get their merchandise up to window level.

At 11:15 the bus rolled in. I pitched the bags inside to Cat who stacked them in the rear seat. I climbed to the roof and helped as the bus company employees hoisted the bikes up. I strapped them down, taking no chances, then stood guard as other passengers threw their bags to the roof.

It was hot, we sat quietly sweating, waiting for the bus to move and stir the air. Traffic and hills slowed our progress it took two hours to travel the 100 Ks. (62 miles) Probably a two-day ride on our bikes. The Lilongwe station was teeming with guys offering help. I asked for bus company employees. We stacked the bags in front of a group of police officers. I tried to get their picture but they told us it was forbidden while on duty?

One policeman went with me seeking a taxi with roof rack. We found one who agreed to take us for the price the policeman suggested, about $2.00 US. He tried to drive inside the station but the guard wanted another $2.00 for entry. It took several minutes to load the bags on our bikes. When we got back out the taxi was gone. We pushed around the corner and there he was. He was disinterested but finally agreed and at the original amount. Loaded up we were off to the Riverside Hotel.

CAT TRAX Day193, Business in Lilongwe. Three young people in the lobby nodded hello as we left for town. We'd just missed the mini bus. As we sat waiting, the three of them pulled around and offered us a ride. Erin, Kelly, and Jamin were from Florida there with a religion-  based company. They analyze projects for various churches finding ways to consolidate and share the work. Nice kids: dedicated, working for small dollars, and doing something they believed in. We agree that there's so much to be done, it's a shame to duplicate programs.

Once inside the US Embassy's Consulate Office, we were told to wait. The girls at the windows were taking a long time. I asked for the forms we needed to register. Forms filled and at the window, the Malawi clerk struggled. Kiera, called out, "Come to my door." She took us in, shared info from the computer, and her own experiences. A nice gal, from Porterville, California.

The nearby Mozambique Embassy closed at noon. We got in the door just under the wire. A simple form, 1600 Kwacha each (a value as Visas go) and we were told to come back at 2:00.

 With several modern buildings in the area, we decided to take pictures to prove Africa was more than just mud huts. As I clicked, a security guard yelled.

A guy standing next to me said, "You're not allowed to take a picture of that building."

I asked "Why?" By then the guard was running toward me.

Courteous but forcefully he said, "Erase picture, please." I told him I couldn't. He yelled bringing another green uniform and guy in suit toward me. The suit said, "The building, with a sign for the Insurance Company, is headquarters, for US AID."

Unbelievable! The guy, Zizwani said, "Erase picture, or come with me." I didn't know whether it could be erased in any case I didn't want to. Cat, who'd walked on looking for the Zimbabwe Embassy, returned trying to figure out what was going on.

"I'm being detained by the United States Government," I yelled. She didn't understand, so I explained as we walked to the building.

Zizwani called a fellow security officer who told him it could be erased. I objected, I didn't want anyone changing anything. I didn't want to lose any pictures. At that point, I asked to meet with anyone from US AID who was from the US. Zizwani was hurt and held his ID Badge up to prove his rank. Not wanting to usurp him I said, "I'd prefer talking with a fellow citizen."

He called Joe, who explained why it was important (due to terrorism) to maintain a high level of security. I suggested they should post a warning on the otherwise ordinary-looking building. When I asked his position he said, "I'm in charge of security for the

US Embassy." I told him we'd just left there after meeting with Kiera. He chuckled and said, "I saw you. You two don't look like terrorists, I think we can cut you loose. Let me talk with Ziz."

Ziz seemed slightly upset, but soon became friendly. He said, "I love my job, I have work with US AID five year." He continued, "Follow, I show you where is Zimbabwe High Commission." We shook hands he said, "Sorry for inconveniences," then led down the street and pointed to it.

Cat told a guy who'd pulled up in a Mercedes that we wanted a visa to Zimbabwe. He said, "I am Shame', Zimbabwe's Minister Counselor. I will take application for visas right now." Unfortunately, we'd left our passports at the Mozambique Embassy. Cat asked her usual question about how safe it would be for a couple of people on bicycles. Shame' chuckled and asked, "Are you sanctioning Zimbabwe, too?" Not sure how to answer, we told him we didn't have our passports. He laughed and said, "I will see you tomorrow."

While at the Mozambique Embassy we met Linda. She told us "I'm a Missionary, I will be conducting a Woman's Empowerment class in Mozambique." Then she filled us in on her life. "Originally from Illinois, my husband and I have lived in Malawi twenty-five years. We have three children, all born in Malawi. We do get back home, every three years." What a different life they had chosen.

With visas in hand we asked directions, and Linda offered us a ride. "I know exactly where Ulendo Tours Office is." We commented on her new SUV. As we pulled into Ulendo parking lot Linda said, "We just received this big SUV from our church. It was embarrassing at first. It's the same make and color as the President of Malawi's. A lot of people stared at us, probably wondering who we were." Linda was a typical "salt of the earth" person and a treat to meet.

CAT TRAX Day 194, Another Day in Lilongwe. Shame' was his same outgoing self except he could only take our application. The visas were drawn elsewhere and would take twenty-four hours. He also allayed the fears we had, based on all the media's negative reports. He said, "Reporters can write anything they want."

He gave us a book, *British Betrayal of the Africans, Land, Cattle, Human Rights, A Case For Zimbabwe.* Then he continued, "When Cecil Rhodes and his private army came to Zimbabwe in

1888, he granted land to white settlers. Local citizens were told their ownership was protected for future generations. However, by the mid-1990s whites owned 70% of all farmable land, yet were less than 1%, of the population. They claimed white farmers were the backbone of the economy. Redistribution of profitable land to subsistence farmers lacking skills would have serious fiscal implications."

(*From Wikipedia,* In 2000 President Mugabe got a referendum passed granting land redistribution to War Veterans. The voting white populace responded with a resounding 'no'. Strange, the 1%, still controlled the vote. Between February and October 2000, 600 white-owned farms were seized by people claiming to be War Veterans even though many were too young to have been. Twelve white farmers were killed. Though the "War Veterans" were promised the land. Opposition media felt that about 1/3rd had been given to Mugabe's relatives and advisors. What a quandary for us. Our Real Estate background left us opposed to anything that might threaten Private Property Rights, yet what were the rights of those 99% whose families had owned and utilized the land for millenniums, long before the Rhodesians.)

CAT TRAX Day 195 , Day 3 in Lilongwe. Visa card declined our request for cash. That led to a struggle between Visa and our bank. Argh, too many rules. A waste of money on telephone minutes, too. It was a security issue. Damn, our two cards had different expiration dates. Cat jammed into a mini bus and went back to the bank with my Visa card and passport. Another turn down, not the card, but I had to appear personally and sign. Cat called, when I arrived we stood in line again. I signed and they allowed us the ability to request cash.

CAT TRAX Day 196, Help, we've been ROBBED! We went to

a foreign exchange office and bought US Dollars. They charged our Visa card $500 for a cash advance, then deducted a $70 fee. Highway robbery, however we feared getting into Mozambique without money. I zipped the $430 wad into my pocket and we cycled to the bus station. Guys called out, wanting to help. We kept our eyes straight ahead, looking for the gate of the secure bus station. Bad news: no buses until the next day. Anxious to go, we cycled to the Matatu area, looking for an alternative. There was a horde of hungry-eyed seedy-looking people standing waiting for a van, or a victim.

We found a mini bus to Salima in the hubbub of fumes and dust. The conductor assured us they would tie the bikes on top and put the bags inside. As we pushed the bikes, a van swooshed in and almost hit us. We were trampled and jostled by the crowd, trying to avoided being hit. I leaned my bike on the side of the bus, Cat went around to the front into a mob of helpers. Fearing they'd grab a bag and run, I called out to her. She couldn't hear me. Hating to leave my bike, I yelled louder. A guy standing near said, "Excuse me sir, your pocket, it is unzipped."

My heart sank. How could that be? The pocket was hanging open, all 430 of our US Dollars were gone. A very slick operator! I was worried about Cat, she was around in front of the bus unloading her bags. I yelled again to her to stop. She couldn't hear, but a guy carrying one of her bags toward me got the point. He called to her. She looked back and I yelled, "I've been robbed, our money's gone, put the bags back on the bike, watch your things!"

She couldn't believe what she'd heard. I yelled, "Get your bags on the bike, we need to get out of here." Bags on the bikes, we quickly pushed away. Cat wanted to know what had happened. I told her it was my fault. I'd felt safe with the money in my zippered pocket. I wished we'd split it up, placed it in several locations like we usually did.

Cat was really upset. I finally told her, "No use crying over spilt milk!" As we rode through the menacing-looking crowd we both yelled out "Thieves, thieves!"

A police officer standing nearby heard our shouts. "What is the problem?" he yelled. "We've been robbed, our money stolen" I shrieked, hoping the thief would hear. The officer asked, "Are you hurt, were you cut?" "No, but all our money has been stolen." I yelped. "So you're okay it was only money, you weren't cut or hurt," he repeated.

He was right, it was only money, a lot of money, but only money. Back toward Old Town we went, to get more US Dollars and make a new plan. The Exchange Bureau apologized, they were only allow one $500 draw per credit card per day. The woman suggested we try the bureau around the corner. The guy there was happy to see us and honor our request. He was also happy to charge an even higher fee.

Hiding around the corner from the bureau we spread the cash between our wallets and bags. The emotional strain and fears of what harm could have befallen over a few dollars left us drained and feeling hungry. Nando's, a fast food place seemed the perfect prescription. Planning as we ate, we determined we couldn't, nay wouldn't, go back into that snake pit called the Mini Bus Station. It may be unfair to generalize, calling people snakes, but that was how we felt. Still we believed 98% of people are good people, however our anger affected our open-mindedness.

We began looking for a place to spend the night. Cat wanted to return to the Riverside Hotel but agreed it was too far to get an early start. A policeman suggested Hotel Lilongwe, just a few blocks ahead. The price was high but they took Visa. I negotiated with the desk clerk. A young guy took me to see the room. He suggested a less costly cottage. We made a deal.

Showered and cooled down we went to dinner. The smiling manager gave us bad news, no wine. I told him I would walk to the store. He knew about our ordeal and said, "We usually don't allow that, but under the circumstances, it would be okay." I walked, we sipped, and they served. We were soon back abed while visions of pickpockets danced in our heads.

CAT TRAX Day 196, 65 Ks Bus to Salima then Cycled, 65 Ks, Salima to Mua, Anxious, we were at the bus station by 7:00 a.m.. Bags on board, Cat stacked them while I put the bikes on the roof. We offloaded in Salima at 10:30 and rode out ten minutes later.

What a pleasure to flee the city streets escaping into countryside. Stopping at a cross roads we learned the only food was 3 Ks down toward the lake. After a short powwow we decided we'd better do the down and back. No telling where we might find food again along the road.

The Modern Tourism Lodge looked rough. Closer inspection confirmed, the clientele was all locals. However the guy that greeted us, Alexander, was a rare and unusual treat. We asked what the sign above our table, meant. He laughed and said, "Eat well, and be strong." As we took a picture he said, "I am called Alexander the Great." Lunch with Alexander was Great! When he heard our story he went from table to table, pointing at us telling all the others in the room about our journey.

As he took our order he asked, "Why you don't order Nsima? It's our national dish." To us it sounded like another recipe for Ougali, Fu Fu, or Sudza. Cat asked how it was made. Alexander offered a demonstration. The restaurant kitchen was out in the rear yard. The cooks had a pot boiling over an open fire. Alexander took over, adding corn flour and stirring. Then he told us, "When you eat Nsima, it fill up you stomach. In morning when you go  toilet, *whoosh*!" That made us and everyone nearby howl with laughter.

A kilometer down the road another laugh. A tiny mud hut church had a sign above the door. An abbreviation, "ASS. of GOD." Was the board too short or the hut too small for full revelation?

Rolling down a small hill, we were confronted by a crowd of people. They spread across the entire road, stopping traffic. Another election group supporting the President? I was taking pictures when several people clucked their tongues displaying anger. We were in the midst of a funeral procession. I turned off the camera, and we stopped and stood reverently as they passed.

Alexander had said The Mua Mission was the only place to stay in Mua. We saw a small sign Mua Catholic Diocese, nothing of a Mission. Asking, a guy pointed back to the tiny village indicating we should take a dirt road to the left. It was steep. Pushing, our feet slipped and slid. Still not convinced we were on the right track we asked some young boys. They sang out in unison, "You must continue, just straight forward." We met another boy, Willard, a guide for the Mission. He led us directly to the gate. It was 5:30 as we entered the courtyard of Mua Mission.

Kenneth, one of the Priests said, "Our Mission is 100 years old, I'm the only Malawian Priest." We soon had cold beers in hand and a room for the night.

Dinner was served exactly at 7:30. Food was presented on a huge concrete table under a thatched roof. Fellow diner Irene, a woman from Norway, worked with an educational group stationed in Lilongwe. A Japanese guy, Naoto came in late. He was there working on some sort of project. Dinner was a buffet and good. The best of it, being in the company of the Priests, Brothers Serge, Buchard, and Brenden. They were terrific hosts, the wine and conversation flowed freely. Brother Buchard was famous for his woodcarving project. He'd begun in 1977 and had certified 194 carvers. Young Brenden, from Ireland, worried they weren't doing enough to recruit new parishioners. We told of meeting Sam and Johanna, the Jehovah Witnesses and the pride they took in helping build a Kingdom Hall every ten kilometers along the highway. He said, "They are taking quite a few

people, with their efforts." Then he chuckled and said, "We can't fault them, we were the originals at that, you know."

CAT TRAX Day 197, 101 Ks, Mua Mission to Balaka. Father Serge rattled around, awaking us as he set off to perform 6:00 a.m. Mass. The call of an Imam squawked out across the hillsides. Competition? Then the peal of bells, the call to Serge's Mass. We relaxed, listening to Mother Nature, birds calling, bugs chirping, all welcoming the new African day.

Breakfast was at a round table in the upstairs dining hall. We felt obligated to tour the museum with Willard. Darn, he wouldn't waive the $11.00 US fee. He told stories of the three major tribes in that region. Most were similar, just enough difference to keep them squabbling. They all shared the custom of drinking home-brewed beer together celebrating life when members died, married, or had new babies.

Walking back, we came upon a dozen woodcarvers plying their mallets and carving tools. Father Buchard caught us and insisted we visit his hotel project. A worthwhile forty-five minutes, he had completed ten rooms with carvings inside and out. When opened, it would house study groups and tourists. He was looking

for money just like every developer I'd ever worked with. The kitchen area was ready for appliances but refrigerators, range/ovens etc, etc, would cost about $20,000 US. They had to be imported and even the church was subjected to the excessive Malawian import tax.

Facing 100 Ks we rolled down the steep slippery slope and off toward Balaka. Lunch at a bus stop store provided tasty bread but little else. We opened a can of tuna, made sandwiches and washed them down with four soft drinks, as locals stared.

It was 6:00 p.m. and dusk as we rolled into Balaka. The service station staff suggested the Miambe Motel. The streets were full of blaring music and people. We found the PTC Market, a bottle of wine and the Miambe. The pulsating music continued throbbing inside the security walls. A group of rowdy guys in the bar, beers in hand were in the midst of a Pool Tournament.

By then it was dark as pitch. We took the last available room and felt fortunate to have it. Typical dirty place and cold showers. Tired to the core, we were well-fed and back in our not so cozy room and asleep by 9:30.

CAT TRAX Day 198, 70 Ks including 18 wrong way, 88 Total On the bikes by 8:30 a.m. we pulled past a roadblock and saluted the military. One of them called out as we pedaled past. Up, up then at the summit I realized we were riding in the wrong direction. Checking the map, sure enough. Aw, well at least the backtrack was downhill.

At the military roadblock the soldier who'd hollered loudly suggested we should have stopped and asked. Almost as though we'd broken some law. I questioned and he became even more adamant. "That's why we're here, you know," he snarled. Rather than argue, Cat took a peacemaking position, thanked him, and we rode on.

On a downhill run we met a struggling cyclist wobbling toward us. He had baggage strapped on the bike. We thought he was Japanese. We pulled up, he continued past. We called out, he stopped and turned back. He had a strange accent, "My name ees Meeltone, I from Sao Paulo, Brazil. I bicycling north to Panama, flight to Cape Town, Sou Afrique. I beeen riding north, for un month." At first, we thought he was having a hard time understanding English or had a speech impediment. We wanted to know what he'd experienced in Mozambique. He slurred out an answer. "No food, no water." Worried, Cat asked if he needed a drink of water. He laughed and said, "No, I drinks Chibuku, you know Chibuku, the local's beers!" He uncapped a plastic bottle and sucked down a huge swig. It was brown and dirty-looking. He said, "Some peoples geeves it to me." He held the bottle out, offering us some. We told, him we never start drinking before 5:00, it was only 10:00 a.m..

Milton continued drinking Chibuku then said, "I know Americans cycling. I meet in Ecuador, Tim and Cindie." Wow, another Small World example, we'd met Tim and Cindie on the Internet. They read our journal and sent an e-mail telling us they'd met Luis, our friend, in Spain! He had cycled from Argentina, his home, to Alaska. Now Milton, who'd also met them in South America was there in the heart of Africa. What were the odds?

Lunch in a poor village, Nsima with rice and cabbage. I had them throw in a little goat meat for flavor. Cat was beginning to like Nsima; to me, it still tasted blah.

Afternoon sun filled the road with heat. The ups and downs

filled our clothing with sweat. Our plan to reach Mwanza began to melt down. At a T-Junction we sought cold water. Every business was packed with people listening to the radio. Blantyre's football team was playing a team from Zimbabwe. It reminded me of my childhood before TV when we all huddled in front of a radio listening to a World Series game or the Indy 500 car race.

After three stops, we found cold water. The radio announcer's excited commentary was in almost understandable English. During a break in the action, we asked about a hotel. The consensus of the crowd, go left 1K we'd find a place. Sweat ran down our backs as we pondered calling it a day. It was another 49 Ks to Mwanza and 40 Celsius in the sun (100 degrees F). With our 18 Ks mistake Mwanza would add up to an impossible 127 Ks. Stopping at a police checkpoint we asked about lodging. One said, "Go back to village."

We told them the people in the village had sent us there, to a motel. They conferred, laughed, and said, "That place is not safe for you, it is for truck drivers, and girl friends!" So the local jokers had sent us on a wild goose chase to the local whore house.

Following police directions, we found a sign pointing to the Dalitso Rest House. A young guy Lenato, greeted us and offered two small rooms, one for us one for the bikes. Not only small they were also hot and cheap. Both for less than $7.00 US.

The room was sweltering, Lenato brought an oscillating fan that helped. It quit, I investigated and decided it was a problem at the socket. I unplugged it and tried to spread the prongs, one broke off.
Now I'd done it, Lenato would probably charge us for the fan. I called him in. When he saw the cord, he shrugged picked up the fan and disappeared. Back in just a couple minutes he had a replacement under his arm. He showed me that one too had been broken. He'd cut the wire leaving two bare ends exposed. He took the exposed wires and carefully inserted them one at a time into the 220v socket. Wow, dangerous but functional.

Another fellow Davis, said, "I am cook." We asked for cold beers he lit out on the run. Back in minutes he had four, all warm. He chilled them in the freezer while we showered. The outhouse had the picture of a woman Akazi, on one side a man Amuna, on

 the other. Inside were squatter "long drops" and a filthy floor. (Long drops are deep pit outhouse toilets.) Showers were buckets of cool refreshing water.

Davis said, "I have for you, chicken and chips." Fed up with that, we convinced him to cook a package of our pasta. He not only didn't know how to cook pasta, he'd never even seen or heard of it. We took a seat and sipped beers while Davis and Lenato struggled with the meal. When finally prepared it was very good. They had garnished our pasta with fresh tomatoes and chicken.

The big battle was keeping the mosquitoes and other flying bugs at bay as we ate. Their tiny radio played good old Rock 'n' Roll. It had cooled considerably outside yet the bedroom was still hot.
. With no mosquito net or screens on the windows, we cranked up the crippled fan to high and lay atop the sheet. Sleep came slowly.

CAT TRAX Day 199, 49 Ks, T-Junction to Mwanza. Sun streamed through the cracks at 5:30 a.m.. Life began to stir with the rising African sun. Packed and loaded by 7:00 Lenato and Davis had breakfast waiting. It was eggs with chips and a couple of soft drinks. No coffee, but we had packets pilfered from the Riverside Hotel. Pretty good, mixed in milk Davis had heated. Sitting in the little lean-to food shack with the cool breeze blowing through was nice.

Another village, another soft drink. The man in the store told us they had cold Lemon Twist then a boy lit out on the run, to find some. We were almost ready to give up and move on when the breathless young boy returned. A strange looking fellow walked up and sat on a nearby rock. Disheveled he had long dirty hair, black paint on his face and a glob of something blue atop his head. The running boy said, "He crazy!"

The strange man observed us then moved away under a tree. I couldn't stand it I had to talk with him. He spoke not a word; as I coaxed, he just stared. When I held up the camera he shrank back. I extended my hand holding out 200 Kwacha. He smiled then sort of bowed. Approaching him I was apprehensive. The soft look in his eyes told me there was nothing to fear. He took the money and gently touched my hand then shrank back into the bushes.

Hot, scorching hot, especially when pushing up for more than 4 hours. We'd drunk all our water by the time we rolled into Mwanza. The Mwanza Hotel was expensive, 3,000 Kwacha. ($30 US) But it had a shower, fan and mosquito net. We needed water desperately. Out of mineral water, they offered a pitcher of ice water they said had been boiled. We gulped it down and asked for another. Cat asked if that had been boiled, the boy said, "We try our best?" We weren't sure what that meant but hoped for the best as we guzzled it down.

Quan, a young Vietnamese guy rode up on a bicycle. He was working with the Malawi Red Cross on the HIV/AIDS epidemic. He had to go, so we made a date for beers at 5:30.

Quick cold showers then off to meet Quan. He was late, we were already soaking up a beer when he came in. He told us, "I was one year old when the US pulled out and Vietnam fell. My father had worked with the US Army. He was shunned by the new government. Our family had owned a small rice farm. He was allowed to work there. I only knew life in a Communist country, until I was 15 years  old. I think it was a good life, for a kid. My aunt married a US soldier, moved to California, took me with her. I graduated with Masters Degree from Cal Irvine. Since then I lived in New York before taking this job."

Quan was gathering statistics on HIV/AIDS victims in the area. I told him about the German doctors we met in Ghana. They'd told us there was a 4% AIDS incidence there with 'hot spots' up to 10%. He shook his head then shocked us. "In this area, 25% of the people are infected." Unbelievable, his explanation even more so. "This is a border town, truck drivers pick up prostitutes, bring them here, or take them away from here. They rarely use protection, therefore often spreading the virus." He continued. "There is no treatment, when diagnosed victims are sent home to die. They do have an auxiliary, made up of families of past victims. They make house calls, but all they can do is ease the pain and help victims prepare for the inevitable. The worst is for families with children. They know that within a short time, their kids will be among the thousands of orphans. Even worse, the kids may also be victims if the mother was positive when they were born." He seemed visibly shaken as he finished.

CAT TRAX Day 200, Pat Pulls Up Sick in Mwanza. During the night, I awoke feeling terrible. The African Guff-Guff was back with a vengeance. Thought I was going to throw up. Was it the goat, the dirty dishes, or Arthur's boiled water? Whatever it was, it hadn't affected Cat. Unable to eat, I left Cat at the table and went back to bed. I'd thrown in the towel, we'd stay another day. The kitchen didn't offer soup but prepared a pack of Cream of Chicken that Cat had found at the local market. I tried but couldn't eat. I retreated to the room and the darkness of sleep.

Cat was like a cat on a hot tin roof. Her energy overload was hard to control. She walked a ways up the road, taking a look at the hill we'd face ahead. I was sleeping soundly when she returned. Later, I was able to get a few bites of rice down. Cat ate and drank with gusto.

Chapter 25 Mozambique and Zimbabwe

CAT TRAX Day 201, 86 Ks on Bike, 20 Ks in Frank's Truck. Early to bed, early to rise. Breakfast a 6:45 am, I choked down some cereal. Cat ate like a truck driver. Thankfully, the hill was not killer. We crossed the Malawi border with ease, only to find that the bank was closed. We needed to get rid of Malawian Kwacha. The bank guard pointed to an Exchange Bureau. A low exchange rate but the only game in town, so we took their deal and moved on.

Mozambique's border was five Ks beyond. Immigration and the checkpoint were mundane as crossings went. A quick look at our passports and visas stamped by an automated machine. They collected a $3.00 fee and we were pointed toward the gate.

I began to feel badly again. Soft drinks and an interesting chat with a local. We thought he was a teacher, the kids all knew him. He had a small radio hanging around his neck playing rap music. Not a teacher just a local guy, he told the same story told to us by many. "This is a town with no jobs, no future." I asked why he stayed, he shrugged and said, "This is my home."

Fading fast, I dredged up energy enough to ride another five Ks. We found soft drinks and talked about our situation. We'd come eighty-five Ks, I felt weak and couldn't ride another twenty. Cat went to the road, hoping for a truck. Darkness was looming.

A big rig pulled up. The driver asked, "You need help?" Frank, the driver, and assistant Hampton lifted the bikes onto the truck. We climbed up into the cab, Hampton stood in the truck bed. We were off to Tete. Frank explained, "We drive coal into Blantyre then deadhead back every day. Malawians use the coal to dry tobacco." That seemed like a  waste of fuel and time but we knew tobacco was the "Cash Crop."

A nice man, that Frank. He told us with pride, "I have 6 years old daughter." When Cat asked if he wanted more kids he laughed and said, "I wants to make sure we can give her a good life, before we makes that decision." Pulling into the coal mine we figured it was the end of the line for us. Frank said, "It is ten kilometers more, to Tete." It was almost dark. He surprised us, "We'll drop the trailer here, then take you to the bridge, just outside Tete."

Our newfound trucking friends drove us to the outskirts of Tete. Hampton handed the bikes down. We stood in awkward silence as Frank wrote down his mailing address. Cat and I called out "Obrigado," in unison, as they pulled away. (Mozambique was a Portuguese colony until 1975.)

Woozy from the Guff-Guff and the truck ride, I wobbled into town. We cycled across the bridge over the Great Zambezi River and to Motel Tete. Our guidebook billed it as "The best in town," but failed to tell us it was two kilometers beyond town. Worse, it was fully booked. Back tracking, we found a dirt road to Motel Le Piscine. Dirt roads in darkness are always a challenge.

The motel had a rundown 1950s look. The owner appeared time-warped from bygone glory days. She was definitely Portuguese and definitely held court at a table every night. She had a room for us, no room for the bikes. An African boy took up our cause, explaining in Portuguese what we wanted. She finally agreed to keep the bikes in a storage room.

Le Piscine was half vacant. The namesake swimming pool, like the motel, was in a terrible state of disrepair, just a huge mosquito-breeding ground. The air conditioner worked, however the shower was cold and the bed sagged badly.

CAT TRAX Day 202, Another Day of Healing in Tete. Breakfast, then I faded and fell back into bed. We were doomed to another day at Le Piscine. Cat used her energy to walk into town. She reported back that it was an ugly place. We walked for lunch to a close-by café she'd spotted. Obviously a favorite, we had to stand in a long line. Grilled ham, cheese, and burger on a bun. It felt good to be hungry again.

Salvatore, a man we'd thought was Madame's husband, joined us for dinner. He straightened that out swiftly. "Husband, no! I live Portugal, I own three grocery store. I come Le Piscine to vacation." A strange place to spend time by choice.

CAT TRAX Day 203, 95 Ks, Tete to Changara. We rode the dirt road along the bank of the Zambezi River. I felt okay, but not great. Resting had been a good idea. In a short time we surmised Mozambique was arid and boring. Long distances between populated places, with plenty of ups and downs. Not a moonscape like the Western Sahara, it was a place of huge rocks, mud huts, and little else. But the locals were friendly. No begging or was it that we just didn't understand them? They spoke Portuguese in combination with local languages.

Tired and hungry, we stopped in a narrow valley filled with green farms. Sitting in a grassy field we opened a can of corned beef. Cat again likened it to dog food. I needed food, it went down easily along with bread from a small store. As Milton had warned, there was little food and no water. Food, rest in the shade, then back on the seat into the heat.

My body was gasping for energy. It was so hot I took off my cycling jersey. My browned arms looked almost black juxtaposed with my white torso. A real sight to behold for the locals. I didn't care about looks, I was hurting. Each breath exhaled felt hot enough to scorch my chest hairs.

Changara was a small, dirty, crossroads town. Vanity returned at its edge, and I pulled my jersey back on. We rode up to a bar. Cat sought shelter and food. I sat at first, then lay on the cool cement porch in the shade. A young guy in the bar, Gil, was trying to tell Cat about a place. When they came out, she was embarrassed to find me laying there surrounded by curious locals. The soft drinks she brought had a good effect. I sat up, sipped, and stared back. It was hard to be an Ambassador of Good Will when I felt so bad.

Gil led us to what he called a Rest House. The area and place reminded me eerily of Boron, California, the desert town where I'd spent seven years selling groceries. The Rest House was the only game in town. Still shaky, I sat in the shade as Cat checked the room. She returned with a two-word report, "Very bleak!" So small the double bed covered most of it. The best news: a mosquito net and fan. The really bad news: the toilet and bath were outside and had no running water. A cement slab with footprints to help your aim and a rectangular hole to squat over. The bathhouse was just a bucket of dirty water and a cup for pouring. Oh, and no lights in the outhouse with darkness closing in.

In fact, no power in the entire village until 6:30 p.m.. Gil spoke with our hosts about food. They would send out for chicken and chips. He helped jam the bikes into the room, then left us.

The lights flickered on, and the fan began to whir at exactly 6:30. We asked one of the guys about the food. He indicated we should wait. We took a splash and dash in the slimy bathhouse. Cleansing no, cooling yes. Finally at 9:00 p.m. chicken and chips arrived. Cat was starving, I was beyond hunger. I nibbled at the chicken but couldn't take the greasy fries. She devoured most of the chicken and all the chips.

Two guys, Owen and Sam, joined us. Owen spoke English. He said, "I learn English in Zimbabwe where my mother sent me during war years." Cat asked what the war was like. Owen sat silent for a moment. When he spoke we could see the pain in his eyes. "I was five years old, when war came to my village. Dead animals and dead people, lay in the street." Easy to see how the experience had permanently scarred him. The fear of death lingered still. When Portugal pulled out of Mozambique, the vacuum left several factions fighting for power. There were no winners, only losers, Owen was among them.

When we finished eating, Cat offered the leftovers to the boys. They ate every morsel and were anxious to hear more about our trip and stories of America. They had a burning desire to travel across the US. We hated to cut the conversation short but we were dog-tired.

The long drop toilet was dark save the small beam of our headlamp. A cadre of cockroaches added a new meaning to "quick trip." Cat went, I heard her yelp and I ran to her aid. There was a gigantic frog sitting in the corner. Convinced that it would do her no harm and might even eat a few roaches, she warily squatted as it warily watched.

Another discovery, the bed had no sheets. It was still so hot, we just lay on the bedspread listening to the bugs, birds, and whirring fan as we drifted off.

CAT TRAX Day 204, Hitchin' Rides to Harare. At 2:00 a.m. Cat began making trips, frequent trips to the terrible toilet. She was feeling the wrath of African Guff-Guff. She had to compete with the frog and roaches each time she made the dash, and I felt terrible for her. At 4:00 a.m. she threw up dinner. Not able to make it to the terrible toilet, she just let fly in the cornfield outside our door. It was a horrible night for Cat and an awful experience for us both.

Awake again at 7:00, we lay in bed discussing options. Changara was our final point of decision on whether to continue in Mozambique or cross into Zimbabwe. The route south would be four days of desolation. Also Sam the Grocer had warned, "Monsoon is start, Mozambique road are bad mud!" Though she feared Zimbabwe, Cat was too weak to argue. With only villages like Changara and Rest Houses we chose civilization-we needed a doctor who spoke English.

You can understand why food didn't sound good to Cat. I bought Owen breakfast as he helped me make a plan. "There are buses to the border." he said. "I'm sure you can take your bikes on them."

The kitchen and dining table of the Rest House was outside. I watched the cook, Uncle Andy, the owner's mistress, struggle with breakfast. As she cooked, she also washed corn kernels in a plastic tub. A neighbor's goat wondered in and ate some of the kernels when her back was turned. She shooed it away, but wanted nothing to do with a hungry donkey-she yelped, and Andy came running and chased it away with a stick. The floor show was so unlike kitchens back home yet there it seemed normal. I knew Cat would have loved to watch but she daren't get too far from the long drop. My eggs were cold, the chips greasy, but I got most of it down. My first substantial food in two days. A local remedy I'd taken, similar to Lomatil, seemed to be working.

Owen volunteered to help us get to the bus stop. I got the bikes into the courtyard. Cat was too weak, so Owen pushed her bike. I took pictures of Andy, his family, mistress and helpers. For some strange reason, we seemed to have developed a feeling of camaraderie. A feeling that overcame language and cultural differences.

At the Y junction, Cat found a seat in the shade and we waited. Owen was also going toward the border, to check on his family's farm. The first passing Matatu was packed. No room for us, let alone the bikes and bags.

Plan 2, I stepped out in front of a car. The driver pulled up and told me to step around to his window, away from his wife. A really nice guy from Zimbabwe, he'd been trying to find work and a life in Mozambique. His daughter became ill, his wife nervous. They were  heading home to Harare, to their family and doctor. He apologized, they had no room. A pickup truck came around the corner. The bed was full of items covered with a plastic tarp. Walter, the driver, lived in Harare. Working for an engineering firm, he had delivered and set up tractors for a farm.

The truck was small. Walter said, "Jump in, if you don't mind sitting on the load." We quickly stripped the bags off, threw them aboard, and lay the bikes across the top. Cat and I sat on a bag of rice Walter was smuggling home. Owen sat on the tailgate facing forward, taking the brunt of the wind. I handed him my sunglasses. He assumed the look of Rambo. "My uncle plays videos on Thursday nights," he said. "I love your old California Governor, Arnold, the Terminator."

He also loved the glasses. When Walter stopped at his family's farm Owen hopped down and handed me the glasses. I held them as we traded hugs then gave them to him. In disbelief he walked into the field put the glasses on and assumed a Terminator pose. Another wonderful person, one of the hundreds that had helped us over the miles. It always seemed miraculous the way help appeared in our moments of dire need.

Walter led us through Mozambique's Immigration. The people

at Zimbabwe Immigration were nothing like the horror stories we'd heard. No four- to twenty-four-hour delays, as rumored. Possibly due to Walter, our new Angel's help. He followed us across the border, then helped as we exchanged our Mozambique Meticaish for Zimbabwe Dollars.

He apologized, "Sorry, I'm not going to Harare. If I were, you would ride with me." He drove us to the bus station. Noticing a local bus pulling away, he ran to the door and explained our situation. Walter clarified to us, "This local bus makes many stops, in small towns. You may only arrive half an hour before the non-stop." But we hated to sit there three hours, so the driver helped carry our bags and the bikes aboard. We thanked Walter, hugged, then watched him drive away.

At a checkpoint, a policeman stepped aboard, looked at the bikes hanging from the rack behind the driver and laughed. The driver and conductor laughed, too, as he waved them through. Later, at another checkpoint, another officer waved them down. He came aboard and spoke to the driver. The driver argued, the cop insisted the bus turn back. We believed our bikes hanging behind the driver were the problem. I asked a guy across the aisle, he listened then said, "Don't worry, you didn't do anything wrong, he did." he said, pointing to the driver.

Back at the original checkpoint, the driver and helper got out, argued, then agreed to a citation. We assumed they were cited for partially blocking the aisle or some other safety issue. Our fellow passengers sat quietly, some grumbling but no anger. When the driver came back I asked about the problem. He said, "No problem."

Walter had asked the driver to drop us at the Holiday Inn. He pulled to the curb, then handed the bikes and bags down. It was 6:00 p.m. and dusk. We loaded the bags, onto our bikes and pushed into the parking lot. The attendant tried to stop us, telling us to leave the bikes outside. We ignored him as though we didn't understand English, and pushed through the front doors.

Our entry took the front desk by surprise. The rate was high, but we weren't going back out into the strange city in the dark. The Holiday Inn would be home for a couple of days. Cat started to ask about taking the bikes to the room but I whispered, "It's easier to get forgiveness, than permission." The staff stood staring with gaping mouths as the elevator doors closed behind us. The hotel's Spurs Steakhouse served great food and wine; we were almost too tired to enjoy it.

CAT TRAX Day 205, Lazy Day in Harare. The breakfast buffet was very nice and very, very expensive, $20 per person. A church group in the adjacent room filled the air with gospel song.

The streets of Harare were quiet, most stores closed. There were some impressive buildings and a surprisingly well-stocked supermarket. Most was home grown, imports were expensive and rare. Small stands offered lower prices on better-looking produce than the store. Bananas, a beautiful mango, and hard cinnamon rolls would do for our next breakfast.

For dinner, we walked across to a fast food strip. Exiting, the gate guard warned, "Be careful, there are thieves out there." That put us on high alert. The place was crowded, some of the customers looked suspicious. Three stood at the entry, flashing wads of Zim Dollars, suggesting good exchange rates. We had been offered 5,000 Z Dollars for $1.00 US. Buying in would have cut costs but we were chicken. There were stories of guys who would grab your money and run. Other horror stories, too, of police setups and arrests.

CAT TRAX Day 206, A Frustrating Day in Harare. We ate our bananas and mango in the room. There was a hot water pot, so I found the porter, who gave us four packets of instant coffee. I slipped him 1,500 Z Dollars about 35 cents. He was very happy, and the hard cinnamon rolls were okay when dipped in the coffee.

Looking for the bank, we happened upon the Zimbabwe Tourist Authority. Tsvakai, the clerk, gave freely of maps and info. She also called to verify that we'd find a room at our first stop in the village of Beatrice.

Getting into the US Embassy was simple. Typical surveillance, the guard asked to see our passports smiled and said, "Americans, you can go in." They held our camera and Swiss Army knife. We were whisked into the Consular Section Chief's office. Ellen, a dynamo from Pennsylvania, conceded, "You shouldn't have problems, traveling here." She told us she'd been in "The Service" for twenty years.

We talked about the situation in Zimbabwe. When I said that the boycott seemed to be hurting things she fired back. "The problem is Mugabe, he runs the country-or would like to run the country-like Castro runs Cuba. I worked in Cuba in my early years...When Castro took over, he surrounded himself with bright, young, patriotic followers. As he aged, he grew paranoid about a potential power grab. I believe he had many of them killed. Take Che' Guevara, was it a coincidence that he was where he was when he was killed?" I told her we didn't know about his death but it had made him an international hero. We'd seen him all over Africa on shirts and posters.

Banking was an exercise in futility. The first woman was sure we could use our ATM card for cash. The second looked over our ATM card and said, "This won't work. Try the ATM machine outside, the maximum daily advance is 2,000,000 Z Dollars." That was less than $50 US. We decided to draw 2,000,000 on Cat's card, then the same on mine. However, the machine rejected both cards.

My stomach was gurgling and rumbling. Cat said we probably had the same bug. The bank lady marked the location of Avenues Clinic on our map. We wanted to hail a cab there were none. Another walk. As I filled out a form at the Clinic they asked for a 3,000,000 Z, deposit before I could see a doctor. We couldn't gather that much but I flashed our Visa Card, and they accepted.

Dr. Rudo entered the exam room with an air of confidence. She was young and thorough. I told her about my recent bouts with diarrhea. She asked for stool samples and a blood tests. Cat asked what the tests would cost. "It's too bad you came in after hours," she said. "The

costs double after 4:00 p.m.." It was only 4:20, but before I could complain, Dr. Rudo suggested, why not wait, bring the stool sample in and give blood in the morning? That would save half and you wouldn't have the results until 10:00 AM anyway."

The guy at the admitting desk swiped our Visa. You guessed it, we were declined. He tried twice, then we dug out every Z Dollar we had. We covered the 141,000 amount, leaving none for cab fare. Walking back in the gathering gloom was tricky. The sidewalks were uneven, full of holes, and the lighting was poor. The big Holiday Inn sign was like a light from above!

CAT TRAX Day 207, Blood Test Results, then off to Beatrice, 56 Kilometers. Hoping to be first in line at the lab, we took a taxi. There was already a line. We checked in, I handed them the stool sample, and they took blood. The nurse said, "We will have results in one hour." We walked to the bank. The ATM was now anxious to honor our requests so we withdrew the limit on both cards. Next the E-Bank Center where we got cash on our Visa. We needed enough to support ourselves for the next nine days, but we were cautious, since we knew that if we overestimated, we'd lose 20% to a pushy moneychanger at the South African border.

The phlebotomist scolded us for being a half hour late. She said, "I've worked hard to have these results ready for you, on time." We used the taxis as our excuse. The Avenues Clinic was just around the corner. Doctor Rudo said, "Your blood test results were negative. The stool sample will take three days, you can call for that result." A taxi at the gate whisked us back to the Holiday Inn.

The hotel staff gathered around, offering route advice. One drew a simple map, routing us away from the main street through neighborhoods to the highway. As the businesses thinned, we found a Steer's Restaurant for lunch. The road onward was flat to rolling. By 4:00 pm. we were in Beatrice.

Our room at the Beatrice Motel was basic, a toilet and tub, but no warm water. The floor was teeming with ants. A girl brought DOOM, an insect spray. The little critters were soon doomed. Cat bathed while I fixed a broken spoke and changed a shifter that had become shiftless.

CAT TRAX Day 208, 86 Ks, Beatrice to Chivhu. On the bikes by 8:00 am. Buses and trucks almost blew us off the road a time or two. The center lane was full of Mercedes, BMWs, and big SUVs.

South Africans, most pulling boats (we found out later they were headed for a big Bass Fishing Competition). No villages, but plenty of kids calling out for money.

After a lunch stop, my bike began to sway. Argh, a flat tire. The good news: it was the front wheel. Tube out, patched and re-installed, only to have it go flat again. The patch hadn't held, it couldn't, as the tube had split apart at the seam. Damn, I hate fixing flat tires!

Cycling into Chivhu, we rode through the smoke of a burning truck. The cab was completely destroyed. They'd pulled the trailer away from the burning cab, saving half the cargo. The burned half was being scavenged by locals. They were pulling at the smoldering boxes, ripping away hot steel, dismantling the truck body. Cat thought there were bodies under tarps on the road. I thought it was cargo, but she convinced me not to take pictures.

A young guy suggested "There are two hotels in town. I recommend Chivhu Motel, it's the best place." It had the typical rundown dirty look but we savored cold beers and relaxed. It was 4:30 p.m. and we'd found a home for the night. A couple of young guys, Steven and Moris, came in. Steven had lived in the US for seven years. He said, "I loved Boston, but it was often too cold." Moris had only traveled to adjoining African countries. He said, "I am determined, God willing, to get to USA."

Steven insisted on buying Cat a second beer. He said, "I work at an auto parts store. When in Boston, I was orderly in hospital." We talked about the average American's concept of Africa. Lions and leopards behind every bush, naked natives carrying spears. He said, "I received a telephone call at the hospital from my mother. My fellow workers were shocked, to hear that we had telephones in Africa!"

They were curious about our opinion of Zimbabwe. Cat told them she'd been afraid to come. Moris said, "There was a lot of bad press, some deserved. The Land Reform issue burns hot on everyone's minds." To Realtors like us, it was hard to imagine the government taking property. However, it had been taken, originally, from locals. And using the democratic "majority rule", it made no sense for less than 3% of the population to own 90% of the land. Something had to give. Perhaps if white farmers had worked with the moderates it could have been a different story. The turbulence and violence might have been avoided.

Steven and Moris urged us to cycle the short route through Chaka. They knew of a place, The Golden Spider Web Hotel. We tried to call, but the phone rang and rang. Giving in but not giving up, we decided to try again the next morning.

CAT TRAX Day 209, 96 Ks (including a 13 K backtrack) Chivhu to Chaka. At breakfast we called The Golden Spider Web Hotel again, without luck. On the way out the desk clerk suggested we stop at the police station to ask about the hotel. The police knew nothing; it was out of their area. A nice fellow stopped us on the sidewalk and asked, "Where are you going?" After hearing our story, he told us, "I'm sure The Golden Spider Web is open. You should stop in Mvuma and ask. They would know, and if not, they have several hotels there."

We pedaled out of town on the horns of dilemma. At the crossroads we chose Mvuma, hoping for the best. There was a weather-worn sign "Golden Spider Web" pointing down the road. A cluster of buildings led us to believe we were in Mvuma. We asked two women. One clicked her tongue, the other shook her head and said, "You have passed Mvuma." Damn, we hated backtracking. We

asked a couple of police officers about the Spider Web. They were uncertain, suggesting we ask at the supermarket. Just around the corner at a telephone shop the workers were having a Scud party. Scuds were what had been called Chibuku Beer.

They were all in happy moods but sad to tell us phone service was out throughout town. One of the guys with a bottle of Chibuku in hand assured us, "Golden Spider is open." Back to the place we'd met the ladies then onward into unknown territory. We were intrigued by the name Golden Spider Web and hoping our Scud-drinking friends had been correct.

More ups and downs on sore butts. At 5:00 p.m. we limped into The Golden Spider Web. The grounds were absolutely gorgeous, the buildings whitewashed with thatched roofs. The reception area was beautifully furnished. We sat on one of the couches and enjoyed a cold beer. What a luxury. Jeremiah, the desk clerk, gave us a tour of the three rooms to let. The first two had tubs without showers-we wanted a hot shower. The third choice, a small finely-furnished hut.

Dinner's rump steak was not as great as the facilities but good. Dennis, the owner, joined us. He said, "This place was the dream of Betty and Don. They owned it, developed it, and she poured a lot of love into it." Her touch was evident everywhere. Dennis spoke of her as though she was his mother. Don and Betty had owned three farms and The Spider Web. Dennis said, "The Land Reform people had their eyes on this place, for a long time. They finally took two of the farms and The Spider Web. Don and Betty were left with one farm that had a livable house. She became ill with cancer. I drove her to the doctor in Harare, many times. They finally gave up, and moved away to South Africa."
Dennis applied to the government and was awarded The Golden Spider Web. He said, "I have also continued a cottage industry Betty started. She hired locals and trained them to stitch lace items, tablecloths, napkins, even clothing. It gives the women income and self-confidence." I asked how he got along with the squatters on adjacent farms. He shrugged his shoulders and said, "They harassed me in the beginning. Broke windows and punctured my tires. I filed complaints with the police, they put a stop to that."

Dennis said, "Don and Betty have lost everything. She clings to life, despite surviving beyond medical predictions. They live in Bloemfontein, South Africa." Again he spoke lovingly, as though they were his parents. We made a note to seek them out and hear their side of the story.

CAT TRAX Day 210, 70 Ks, Chaka to Masvingo. Dennis predicted we wouldn't find drinking water in Chaka or anywhere along the road to Masvingo. Jeremiah was supposed to boil tap water, but in the spirited conversations we all forgot. They quickly boiled a pot full, and put it in the freezer. We'd to only drink it if we ran out of bottled—we were tired of being sick!

A stalled truck had placed reflectors on the road. Cat accidentally hit and broke one. We stopped to tell the driver. He walked back, found it beyond fixing, and spent several minutes talking about his life. His name was Blessing which didn't seem to fit a rough, tough, truck driver.

Lunch was chicken pies from the Spider Web. The entire village we stopped in was partying. Everyone had a Scud in hand. We sat, observed, ate, and got the heck out of there. As we mounted up a young guy staggered over. He asked where we were from and where we were going. I tried to explain but he was three Scuds to the wind.

It was 3:00 p.m. when we rolled into Masvingo. Lost, following our map, we pulled up to a Chevron Station and into a wild crowd. We thought it was a political event. No, they were out of town soccer players and their fans, there for a big game with the locals.

At dinner we met Yash a Japanese guy. "I'm a water quality expert," he said, "I've been here for two years. My friend Ken and I are visiting the Great Zimbabwe Monument in the morning. Maybe we could share our car with you guys?"

CAT TRAX Day 211, A Day at The Great Zimbabwe. Yash and Ken had made an expensive-sounding deal with a guide. We discussed it over breakfast. The front desk recommended a guy Kenneth. His deal seemed much better. As we spoke, the guide they'd talked with walked in. They discussed his price and service.

Though his price was the same he was a driver not a guide. Kenneth came in, we fine-tuned his deal and booked him.

Kenneth said, "We will need four hours to see the monument." We thought that was a lot and questioned him. A woman at a nearby table,

Wendy, spoke up. "Kenneth is correct, we were there yesterday. You will need four hours to see The Great Zimbabwe Monument properly."

Kenneth's car wasn't his. He'd hired a guy to drive and his car was a clunker. The five of us jammed in, then went questing for gasoline. The two stations in town were dry. The fuel shortage was having a terrible effect. He drove out on the highway toward The Great Zimbabwe to another station. It too, was dry, but the driver and Kenneth wouldn't give up. They introduced us to the station attendants who were impressed by the story of our trip. Enough so that they found a 10-liter can of fuel. The driver paid double the going rate.

The name Zimbabwe comes from the Shona language meaning great stone houses. The city, once home to 20,000, was the capital of a kingdom that stretched from eastern Zimbabwe across Botswana and modern Mozambique into South Africa. The area was first occupied in the 11th century. Construction of the hill complex began in the 13th century and was completed over 100 years. We could see his pride as Kenneth described each area.

The tour of The Great Zimbabwe was wonderful. Kenneth really knew the place and added details that made it more interesting. He climbed with us to the top and we surveyed the kingdom, even sat in the King's cave where he would call for wives. "The

King," explained Kenneth, "had many wives, and would call out, when he wanted one. The sound echoed out of the mouth of the cave directly into the women's quarters below." How wonderful for the King. Here, like everywhere, as Mel Brooks said, "It's good to live in a kingdom, if you're the king!"

One of the important features, a 10-meter (35 foot) high conical

tower. At first it was thought to be hollow and full of treasures. Turned out it was solid stacked stone. Kenneth struggled as he  explained its significance. He talked about fertility, crops and cattle reproduction, then finally said, "It is a phallus!" He was embarrassed, but I couldn't let that one go so I said, "How'd they ever find a condom that size?" A stupid joke, but timely. Condoms were a very big deal there with all the deadly HIV/AIDS problem.

Europeans couldn't or wouldn't believe that the Great Zimbabwe had been constructed by Africans. Our guidebook put it thus: "Despite nearly 100 years of effort by colonials to ascribe the origins to someone else, anyone else, conclusive proof of the Bantu origins was established in 1932, by British archaeologist, Gertrude Caton-Thomas."

On the way back to town the clunker blew a tire. The driver pulled off the road into a ditch. I wondered how he'd jack the car up on that angle? Well he wouldn't-he didn't have a spare or a jack. We walked back to town. It was a long walk. Three men in a pickup invited us in to the back. Cat was reluctant, but I was tired of walking. They dropped us in front of the hotel.

 *CAT TRAX Day 212, Easter Sunday in Masvingo.* Our plan to cycle was thwarted by another round of African Guff-Guff at 4:00 a.m.. An added bad omen, it was pouring rain. The next hotels were 110 Ks away in Runde River. Cat was disappointed, but I needed rest. I felt stiff, sore, and fatigued.

Wendy, the gal who'd insisted we take time at The Great Zim, was having breakfast. She said "I was born, here in Masvingo, I met my husband and we raised our family here."

Hearing my health issue, she suggested we see her pharmacist,

John. "He won't be open, but he's always there. Look for his blue truck out front." She was correct, we explained my problem and John suggested Lomatil. I hated that stuff-it didn't cure anything, just plugged you up. John agreed but felt it important to take rather than risk dehydration. What a nice guy, it was almost like a consultation with a doctor. It was back to the room for me, I needed rest.

Dinner with Wendy was a delight, as we gained insight into her life and life in Zimbabwe. She said, "My husband worked in the meat-packing industry. When he retired, he planned to relax, for a couple of months, then find another job. Relaxing has lasted six years, and during that time, we've drifted apart." She was a talker, "I'm a social person, he's introverted. I like to go out, see people, enjoy life. We're still married, he prefers being at home, puttering with his car, or other mechanical things. I like having tea in the restaurant, every morning. I often come alone, for dinner." We had another emotional parting. We'd only known Wendy two days yet felt as though we'd been friends for years.

CAT TRAX Day 213, 110 KS, Masvingo to Runde River. Two years ago to the day we'd set off on this grand and wondrous Odyssey. Often it seemed like just yesterday, other times it felt as though we'd been away forever. We did miss family and friends, but were still convinced that our efforts, the exhilaration and pain we had experienced, were worthwhile.

Rain, ugh, we wanted to get moving The Cat was stir crazy. I began to have second thoughts about leaving. Cat stood her ground, "Let's go, it'll clear up," she insisted. As we pulled the ponchos over our heads I felt a shiver, maybe the cold or perhaps an omen. Thirty minutes of struggle then the rain lightened. Just as we began to think the worst of it was over, another sheet of wet blew into our faces. I was convinced it would stay drizzly or worse for the rest of the day. Cat pressed onward and shouted above the wind, "We've ridden in worse!"

Most of the ride was uphill, the scenery dry despite the rain. After an hour of cold and wet the sun broke through and the wind died down. We began a search for food. There were no service stations or stores. At 1:30 we pulled up at a rest stop. We ate pilfered rolls from breakfast smeared with peanut butter, washed down with water. By then it was hot under cloudy skies.

We crossed the Runde River bridge and rode directly to the Rhino Motel. The owner, a young Afrikaner woman named Sjaleen, expressed anger and disgust about the Land Reform Act and its consequences as she checked us in. Her family also owned nearby farms. She said, "The Africans often stop and threaten, or remind me that they could take our places. My family, we're confident we'll continue to own our property." Such uncertainty must be frightening. We were becoming convinced that something had to give. We felt there should be ways to mitigate the issues. Perhaps terming ownership out over time? Enough time for the government to amass sufficient money to pay reasonable prices for the land and improvements.

At dinner we met Donald, who said he was there with The Cotton Company, trying to help the new small farmers learn to plant cotton. Maybe that was a start in the right direction.

CAT TRAX Day 214, 100 Ks, Runde River to Bubye River. At

breakfast we met Atti and Anna. He said, "We've been farming here, since 1974. We aren't Rhodesians, we moved here from South Africa and bought the farm. Today we're on our way into town to pick up proceeds from the sale of our property. They pay us in Zimbabwean Dollars that are losing value daily. Also, can you believe, we need clearance to take our own personal possessions with us to Zambia." Though they'd lost most of their investment, the loss to him was much greater than money. "I love this land, and the things we've produced. Our main product has been cattle. We also expanded into the game farming industry. We had 80 giraffes, 300 Eland, and other small herds of grazing animals. This is the best grass grazing land in the world. I've sent cattle to market, fed only on this grass, and they were judged too fat."

Atti furled his brow and said, "The saddest thing, the squatters that took over are plowing the bountiful grass under. They're planting corn, the only crop they understand, the crop that will feed their families." He sighed, then continued, "It's too wet here for corn. The corn is mildewing on the stalk. We made our decision to move on, live with our children in Zambia, when the squatters cut our telephone lines."

"To keep you from communicating?" we asked.

"No," he said, "They use the wire to make snares to catch our game animals. They kill and waste them, because they break into the corn fields." Atti and Anna were sad, no doubt, but like the pioneers they were, they seemed to be taking it in stride.

A beautiful day on the road. The grassland Atti described surrounded us. Both sides of the road held endless expanses of knee-high grass and thick-bodied cattle. Fearing darkness, we ate a hurried lunch of rice and beans at a café in the Rutenga. The rest of the day was just a hot six hours of pedal or push. We enjoyed lots of honks and waves from passing cars and trucks.

It was after 5:00 p.m. when we rolled up to the Elephant and Lion Hotel. Peter approached as we pushed to reception. "We saw you on the road, you guys must be crazy! My wife Melanie and I are ferrying our  caravan (trailer) to South Africa, for my mother to use."

We sat on a patio in the shade, sipping beers and chatting with Peter. "I'm a transportation consultant," he said. "The current political situation is terrible. I'm confident change is in the wind. I believe the Land Reform will be changed, and farmers will be fairly compensated." We hoped he was right.

Three gals in the adjoining room, Pat, Karen, Ema and their kids, from Harare, were headed to Johannesburg for a shopping spree. Pat approached as they were leaving and offered to rent us a flat she owned in Cape Town. She gave us the address and manager's phone number.

CAT TRAX Day 215, 78 Ks, Bubye to the South African Border. At breakfast new friends, David and Melanie, introduced us to Boer Sausage. They loved it. For us it was tasteless dry beef sausage.

264

Loaded up we stopped to say goodbye. David stepped out of their caravan and said, "Here take this Top Ramen and canned meat, you'll need it!" What a kind thing to do. He continued, "Melanie is

making her professional opera debut in Johannesburg, tomorrow night." We told her to "Break a leg!"

She warned us, "There won't be any place for you to stop between here and Beitbridge, the Zimbabwe border town."

It was a day of strange road kill. As we rode through a small village, two kids were dragging a dead donkey by the tail. It must

have been a recent fatality, as it left a slick trail of blood. Then there were Cat's favorites, snakes. We've seen quite a few small snakes but that day there was an abundance. One in particular was at least 2 ½ meters (5 feet) long and it hadn't been flattened. It

looked like it could slither away.

Then bugs, millipedes a foot long and huge silvery boxy looking fellows 3 inches long. I wanted to get a picture of one and in my excitement I forgot to signal I was stopping. As I braked, Cat crashed into me then fell into the middle of the road. I threw down my bike and ran back. She crawled to the shoulder as I got her bike. She'd badly skinned her elbow and knee, and slammed her head on the road. Thank goodness for helmets. She was pretty shaken, but gathered her courage, climbed back aboard, and we pedaled onward. What a tough woman!

We were in Beitbridge, a typical dusty border town by 2:30.

We'd been worried about running short of Zim Dollars so we'd gotten an additional 9,000 on the way out of Masvingo. Now here we were at the South African border, where they'd have little or no value. We searched for a bank only to find they were all closed, still celebrating Easter. The guard posted in front of Barclay's Bank said, "You come back tomorrow." When I told him we needed to cross the border that afternoon, he asked us to wait and went searching for a moneychanger.

Cat was nervous, she feared being arrested on our last day in Zimbabwe. When the guard returned he was followed by a tall nice-looking African woman, Angela. She didn't look or talk like an illegal moneychanger. I liked her, Cat remained suspicious. Angela motioned for me to follow up the stairs and into the ATM area on Barclay's porch. We knelt down, she kept peeking over the railing as we counted out money on the floor. I did get a little nervous when Angela asked about our trip. As I explained that we'd been on the road two years she exclaimed, "You must have a lot of money with you?" I assured her that lying in front of us was all we had. Creative truth, we did have $350 US stuffed here and there, but of course I meant Zim money!

Compared to the size of our pile of Zimbabwe Dollars her stack of Rand was disappointing. We lost about 20% in the transaction. As she re-counted the stack of Zim bucks she peeked out again then whispered, "Duck down." I could see two men hanging around next door. "They're very bad guys," she warned, "They'll follow you to the border, pressing you to change money, then try to grab your wallet."

Back at the bikes, Angela said, "Be wary, avoid those bad guys, go straight to the border, don't stop for them!" That made Cat even more anxious, she was ready to get out of Zimbabwe. All border areas seem to share a lawless, dangerous feeling.

The Zimbabwe border was typical. Lanes full of idling cars and trucks sitting waiting for clearance. Cat went inside, I watched through the window. She wound her way through the maze, got the appropriate stamps, and we were on our way across the bridge into South Africa. Somehow we'd gotten onto the "vehicles only" bridge. Two policemen on the old bridge above, yelled and tried to get us to turn back. They wanted us to use the pedestrian bridge. No way, we were finally on our way into South Africa!

266

Chapter 26 South Africa to Johannesburg

CAT TRAX Day 216, 90 Ks, 12Ks in Zim, 78 in South Africa, Zim to Messina. South African border passage was simple. Again Cat went in as I stood and talked with the immigration officers. They were astonished to hear we'd cycled through Zimbabwe and 17 other African countries.

It was 4:00 p.m. Election Day. The streets of Messina were filled with shoppers. Though the polls were still open there was a feeling of celebration in the air. A guy on bicycle wobbled up and asked, "Way're ya gwone?" He was in no condition to be cycling. I told him we needed a grocery store and motel.

Otto led the way to Kwik Spar Market. He strutted around the store, slurring out our story to anyone who would listen. What a treat, walking through a store filled with good things. The nice gal at the counter directed us to the Impala Lielie Motel. The room was plain but large. The real treat: crackers and cheese, and a glass of good South African wine. We were back into the 21st century!

CAT TRAX Day 217, R & R in Musina. (Messina) We were two stiff, sore bodies. Cat doubly so due to the crash. We took our Monday Malaria pills, wondering whether to continue them.

We found The Internet Shop, it was also a Computer Store. The owner, Cameron, was an avid cyclist who wanted to know everything about our voyage. He was busy, otherwise we would have spent the afternoon trading cycling stories. He suggested getting together for dinner.

Messina on our maps was now called Musina. They had reverted to the original African city name. Many cities had taken their original names after Africans won the elections. Politics had made a difference. I found a pair of sunglasses. The store sold Icees, crushed ice covered with flavored syrup. I had three!

Cameron came to our hotel room at 6:00 p.m. with a bottle of wine. The three of us sat talking cycling and sipping. He'd competed in bicycle races. A broken arm and elbow problem had temporarily taken him out of competition.

About the state of the nation he said, "South Africa is going to be a tough place to raise and educate my children. I came here from England, I plan to move back in five years. I want my kids to attend good universities." The way he described his family left no doubt he was a proud and happy man.

Spurs Restaurant was his choice for dinner. Good food, better conversation, and, of course, another bottle of wine. Cameron insisted on buying—the first of many generosities we would experience in South Africa. It was a wonderful, albeit late evening.

CAT TRAX Day 218, 81 Ks, Musina to Ingwe Ranch Motel. Up early with slight headaches, the price of a late night with a great guy. We cycled to Cameron's shop for a farewell. He rode my bike and said, "Like driving a truck." We shook hands, hugged, promised to see each other again, then pedaled away.

After drinking two soft drinks I took the cans back in to throw in the trash. The clerk said, "You should take food and drink with you, as a gift." I told him we'd rather just take his friendship. He liked the idea and shook my hand vigorously. At Jay & Ash's Liquor Store next door we wanted a liter bottle of soda to take along. The older guy at the checkout said, "I insist, you take this cold drink, for the road." He pressed the large bottle of Lemon Twist into my hands.

The clerk from next door, Jayesh, came in. He and Ash his wife owned both stores. The older guy, Uttam, was Jayesh's father. Jay said, "I am African, born and bred." Uttam added, "I am first generation, Jayesh and Ash are second generation from India." Jay offered, "There is a motel part way up the hill thirteen kilometers from our store." We left with the big bottle of cold Lemon Twist and a wonderful feeling for Africans, especially those born and bred of Indian decent.

Ahead lay one hell of a hill and two tunnels. The first tunnel looked threatening. Cat decided we should walk the bikes. I wanted to ride, she insisted not. She was right, it was dark, noisy and tight. The traffic roared past, just inches from the tunnel wall. Reflectors jutted out two inches from the wall. Easy to see in car lights, painful when I snagged one leaving a gash and bruise on my leg.

Called the Hendrik Verwoerd Tunnels, the second was an even tougher walk behind the guardrail. At the other end, the guardrail curved and attached to the tunnel wall. Challenging two tired cyclists, we had to lift the bikes up and drag them over the two-foot-high rail. What a struggle, trying to balance them one at a time, while avoiding falling into the path of the speeding traffic.

Uttam and Jayesh's words held true. At 13 Ks we saw the Ingwe Ranch Motel up an incredibly steep driveway. Pushing was so tough I made it then went back to help Cat. The place was a pleasant surprise. Our room was a cabin. Tom, a local craftsman, was removing a window for remodeling. It fell with a crash, showering the steps with huge shards of glass.

Tom said, "Damn it!" Then collected himself and said, "My business is called Doors and Frames. I also have timber farms, I been logging for twenty-five years." His accent was intriguing. He explained the origin of the Afrikaans language. "Tis Dutch, left behind by The Dutch East India Company. They came to Cape Town area in 1652!"

CAT TRAX Day 219, Ingwe Ranch Motel to Mokopane, (Louis Trichardt) 16 Ks. We cycled down the steep drive, then up, up, slowly up pedaling, often pushing. The road was lined with peddlers selling avocado and potatoes. One girl offered thirty avocados for twenty-five Rand. Wow, eight cents each. How could she sell them

269

so cheap?

From the summit it was a fast downhill, into Mokopane. The mountain was covered with pine trees in neat rows. As we coasted in, Cat's front shifting cable broke and my auto shifter began acting up. We limped into town to the Tourist Information Center. Edina, the Manager, was very

helpful. She provided a town map then marked the locations of the Bicycle Shop and hotel.

Our first stop, The Cycle Center. They were busy. The lady said, "Our mechanic isn't working today, come back Monday." As we explained our trip, she called to the owner Mohamed. He listened then said, "Bring Cat's bike in, we'll figure out the shifting cable."

He and his helper Peter struggled getting the old cable off. Installing the new was a snap.

Mohamed was a great guy. He spoke of tolerance as he worked, "Eating dinner out last week, another family came in, and were seated. The waitress knew me and called me by name, Mohamed. The guy at the next table told me they were Jewish, then asked if I minded them sitting nearby. We got into such a warm, friendly conversation, that I suggested moving the tables together." Mohamed's story made us wonder why

governments can't get along like good people do? When they finished the bikes we took a picture in front of the shop. Mohamed, in what was beginning to seem like typical South African fashion,

270

refused to accept payment. We were appreciative but embarrassed. He also insisted on calling the best hotel in town to insure they had a room. What a wonderful human being and great new friend!

The Hotel Villa Grande was family owned and operated. The room was nice like the family. They didn't have a restaurant but the lady, Cora, suggested a couple. "A laundromat? Not in Mokopane," she said, "Give me your things, we'll wash them." Cat asked the cost and Cora replied "Oh, we'd never charge for that." More wondrous South African hospitality.

Famished, we stood in line at Kentucky Fried Chicken with a soccer team. Our first KFC ever! We'd eaten a lot of chicken and chips in Africa. This was delicious—tasty and hot. Sitting at a window seat we wolfed down chicken and enjoyed watching the team gobble and banter.

CAT TRAX Day 220, 107 Ks, Mokopane to Polokwane (Pietersburg). It took seven hours to get into Polokwane. Uncertain about direction, we were suddenly surrounded by cyclists, the Polokwane Pedalers. Gerhard, the founder and unofficial President offered a place to sleep, at his home. We explained we wanted a restful day off, he politely understood. He and Johan, the stoker on his tandem, checked our map, then set our course into the center of town. They made a couple of recommendations for hotels. The Holiday Inn was central, had a restaurant, and was within budget.

CAT TRAX Day 221, Day Off in Polokwane. First stop, the

bike shop that Cameron in Musina had recommended. Babu, the owner had a clean well-stocked shop. We bought gloves, handlebar grips, and a spare thorn resistant tube. In an adjacent store we found sox for Cat, CDs, and mini CDs for the camera; all items we hadn't been able to buy since beginning our ride in Africa.

Gerhard came to the hotel at 6:00 p.m. We loaded into his orange van for a visit with his family, wife Teresa and their two young daughters. We sipped a little wine and talked cycling. They had their tandem hanging from the ceiling in the hallway. Teresa served dinner.

CAT TRAX   Day 222, 62Ks, Polokwane to Mokopane. Breakfast buffet and directions, the recommendation was to take R101, the old road. We set off on R101, but found it too narrow and crowded. So, we swung over to adjacent N1. The wind began to blow, then howl, then scream. At the height of the storm, Gerhard pulled up. He offered a ride, we declined. We cycle and keep the wheels on the road as much as possible. He understood.

The skies darkened, the wind felt wet, then came rain. We pulled off on a ramp and into BJ's Café just as the deluge began. Sipping lemon twists, as we waited. Then like magic, the sun broke through. We cycled in sunshine on a long downhill run. It became a picture-perfect afternoon for cycling, and we were in Mokopane by 2:00 p.m.

Gerhard had insisted he'd find a place for us to stay. He was in charge of Mokopane City Parks. He'd booked us into The National Game Breeding Park. They had a small guest house on the property. All the animals and birds were caged and managed. They bred endangered species, also cared for sick and wounded animals. Mark, the manager, was a deep thinker. He spewed details of the Park, then wanted all the details of our journey.

Cat asked Gerhard what a Ladies Bar was. He said, "It's easier to show, than explain." We walked across to the Protea Hotel. The manager, Neil, was a character. He joked, laughed, and explained, "The name comes, from days when we had separate bars, for single men. Ladies Bar, was reserved for women, except those married, who were allowed to come in with their husbands. Today it's as integrated as the rest of South Africa. Anyone can imbibe, regardless of sex, color, creed, etc." Easily said, however there were no black people at dinner.

After dinner at the Protea we chose to walk back to the Game

Park. Mark had warned, "Take a taxi, walking at night can be dangerous." A warm, moonlit night walk without incident was a fitting end to a blustery day.

CAT TRAX   Day 223, 80 Ks, Mokopane to Modimolle. Breakfast with Gerhard. He provided detailed instructions about our route before bidding us adieu. Funny how parting with yesterday's

stranger could cause so much emotion. We said, "The best part of our Odyssey is cycling into the unknown, daily. The worst is saying goodbye every day!"

The old road ended abruptly at a T-junction. The shoulder disappeared at the edge of the paving, leaving a six-inch drop off. We got lost, realized it and altered our course to a "short cut." It was 5:00 p.m. by the time we got into Modimolle town. Thelma at the Pink Gables Inn greeted us with that now-familiar SA Hospitality.

CAT TRAX *Day 224, 80 Ks, April 22, 2004,* Modimolle to Carousel. After consulting with Thelma, we decided the N1 would be our best bet. A car pulled past, then stopped. The driver got out, waiting for us. As we approached with caution his smile shone brighter than the morning sun. Allan owned a game ranch just ahead. He invited us to stop and spend a day there. He was a cyclist and wanted to know everything about our ride. We had already booked a room at the Casino. The allure of a king-sized bed and luxurious surroundings beat out his wonderful offer. We have often kicked ourselves for not accepting a night at a game ranch!

With sun on our backs and a slight wind in our faces, we rolled along the wide shoulder of the N1. Flat and fast except for tollbooth stops. We passed by three, meaning we rolled around the booths and past the smiling attendants. They all waved, wishing us well. One rushed out, we feared he'd tell us to get off the N1. No, he wanted us to pass the sensor strips, avoiding a toll.

Signage led us to the gates of The Carousel Casino. They looked like a ticket booths at Disneyland. A guard waved us over and asked, "Do you have a reservation?" Our response, "No" brought a look of dismay. He made a call then said, "You must use the employee entrance."

We cycled toward a second gate. The guy there motioned for us to go back, we were in the exit lane. Another security gate. We were impatient, since we didn't understand what they wanted. Then, just as we thought we were finally getting somewhere, the security manager approached and said, "You must go back to the main gate. The guard there was mistaken."

Okay, we were tired and getting pissed. We rolled back around through the gate as though we had a reservation and up to the main doors of the Casino. The hotel was as glitzy as any Casino in Las Vegas. While checking in we met Liz, the Operations Manager. She'd heard of our entry problems and apologized. We asked about internet access, and she offered us her computer.

We accepted, then headed for food court. A sandwich, our room, a shower and rest. Liz's computer would let us view messages but not answer them. Perhaps her company's way of blocking employee access to the Internet.

Dinner at Giovanni's, pizza of course. Interesting, they had a separate area for us non-smokers behind glass. However, like most gambling joints, there were plenty of folk puffing cigs, pulling slots, rolling dice, and spinning the roulette wheel.

CAT TRAX Day 225, 65 Ks, Carousel to Pretoria. Checking out, Liz surprised us by cutting our room rate 50%. Then, in typical South African style, she hovered over our map helping us plan a route into Pretoria. She also forbade us to travel on the old highway. It would take us out of the way, the shoulder wasn't bike friendly and the townships between there and Pretoria were unsafe.

Another nice day, another ease of passage through tollgates.

Traffic on the N1 was light, the shoulder huge, the terrain flat. The sun was hot, so we sat under a bridge to eat our leftover pizza. A couple of guys stopped, asking where we were headed. Mark and Bertus were cyclists. They lived 100 Ks south of Johannesburg and invited us to stay with them. More SA hospitality.

Traffic on the N1 intensified coming into Pretoria. Riding along we sang, "Oh we are cycling to Pretoria, Pretoria, Pretoria. We are cycling to Pre-tor-ee-a today." Every on/off ramp was a challenge, evading cars and trucks. Often we had to stop, wait for a break, then scurry across.

Cycling on the streets of Pretoria was thrill a minute. No space on the road for bikes and no room in the minds of drivers, either. We were finally forced onto the bumpy narrow sidewalk. We sought the Arcadia Hotel, mainly because Arcadia, California was Cat's hometown. We failed, but a sign for Marriott Courtyard drew us down a side street. The girl was very kind and helpful. The price for a night was way beyond budget. She drew a route to the Protea Hotel.

Another good sign, a weekend special at the Protea.

CAT TRAX Day 226, 62Ks, Pretoria to Johannesburg. Greenfield's for breakfast felt like an upscale Denny's back home. We rolled away at 9:00 a.m. and up a long hill out of Pretoria. Now cycling on the N1 became very dangerous. Each on/off ramp left us with a heart-pounding rush. It was pull up, wait for a hole in the traffic, then dash. Worst of all, the two-lane ramps. The stream of side by side cars and trucks seemed endless.

A motorcade of black Mercedes Benz's sped past followed by motorcycle police, their sirens screaming and red lights flashing. President Imbeki, his cabinet, and supporters were headed for Pretoria and his second inauguration. Pretoria was the administrative capital of South Africa.

We decided to escape the N1 and turned onto Old Johannesburg Highway. Narrow, but traffic was minimal. The hilly road lined with pine trees became a study in pedal up, glide down. Midrand, midway between Pretoria and Joburg, reeled us in for lunch. We were feeling drained from our effort and tremendous anxiety. At a pub restaurant the waiters seemed more interested in our bikes than serving soup. Mounting up, I dropped my helmet. Broken, it needed a patch job. Chivon, at Beauty Haven, adjacent to the pub had glue and a smile. Like a broken fingernail she made the helmet whole again.

We veered onto Highway M1 and up to another tollgate. As we started slipping past the toll gatekeeper shouted. I turned and pushed toward her, straddling the bike. The cars in line were impatient, I blocked the lane. She said, "You owe toll." I yelled that we'd passed through all other gates without paying. She shrugged and said, "I will call the Metro Police if you don't stop arguing, and pay."

I pushed in front of several startled motorists, annoying them as I pulled up to the booth. She allowed us to pay a one vehicle fee for both bikes. The cost was no big deal, 4 Rand (about 65 cents), it was the principle that was annoying. I gave her our WR2 card and she glanced at it then held out her hand for the money. In a small protest, I took my sweet time digging out the money. All I had was a 50 Rand note. She frowned, gave me a handful of change, smiled, and raised the gate. Pedaling away, we decided paying the toll was a blessing. If stopped again, we had proof we'd been allowed to ride through.

Constant, ever-increasing traffic drove us off the M1 onto 6-lane Louis Botha Street in an industrial area. A young couple pulled up. She yelled out, "Where are you going?" Familiar with "Joburg" (as the locals call Johannesburg), Celia and Brett assured us we were on track to find our friend Cuan's neighborhood.

A while after we'd pedaled off, someone began blaring their horn. It was Celia and Brett signaling for us to pull over. They'd re-thought their advice, she said, "That area is like the Bronx in New

York, it's not a good neighborhood. You should get advice from the police, at the next corner." Then she added, "You should stay with us, when you pass through our town, we're 100 Ks south of Joburg." She handed us their address, we told her we might just do that. What nice people, so concerned about our welfare they'd spent half an hour circling and worrying.

The cluster of cops were involved in an arrest. The guy in handcuffs looked like he'd been drinking and was resisting arrest. A policewoman listened to our questions, had another guy listen, then a group gathered around and agreed we should continue about 6 Ks and turn at the Police Station. Out of options, we set off. The neighborhood began looking seedy and Cat became more and more nervous. A minibus pulled up at a stoplight. A guy leaning out the window shouted, "What do you have in the bags?" The people on the crowded sidewalks heard and seemed curious too. Paranoia surged-would they gang up, rob us, take our things?

We stopped on the sidewalk. A policewoman was seated near an open window, eating lunch in a small café. Cat asked her advice. She shrugged then said, "You should be careful in this place, there are some bad people, lots of good people, but some very bad." That did it, tired and nervous Cat was ready to call it a day and call Cuan (Kyoo Ann). She asked about a telephone, the policewoman pointed across toward McDonalds. Yes, Joburg had a Big Mac.

 Cuan to the rescue: he answered and told Cat, "You guys wait there, I know exactly where you are. That's a terrible neighborhood, I'll come pick you up." It was Saturday and, like back home the McDonalds was full of little kids celebrating birthdays. Tiny faces under cardboard crowns, faces covered with ice cream and cake. Most were screaming with joy.

Cuan pulled up in his classic Land Rover. A quick reunion, then we tossed the bikes and bags aboard. Cat jammed herself onto the back bench seat with all our equipment. What a great guy this guy Cuan was. We'd only met him for a short time in Tanzania yet we already felt like family. He had introduced us to William the Irishman in Tanzania, and Joel, aka Masharubu in Mbeya. We'd kept in touch via e-mail and he insisted we stay with him in Joburg.

Cuan and his girl friend Debbie had just become co-habs. He'd had several "near misses" but never got to the altar. She'd been married once for "a moment." What a beautiful couple they made. We celebrated our arrival with a glass of wine, zydeco music and hot showers. Cuan  and his sister Juliet had owned the house for eight years. It was a classic. With a separate guest room made up for us.

Melville was a wonderful neighborhood of Joburg, reminding us of Noe Valley in San Francisco. We walked to the main street and dined in one of Cuan's favorite places. Wine, laughter, and getting reacquainted.

CAT TRAX Day 228, At Home in Melville. Breakfast, what a treat. Fruit coffee and cinnamon raisin rolls with white icing. Debbie called them, "Chelsea Buns." We just called them tasty.

A shopping trip to an upscale Woolworth Market for dinner supplies. Cuan chose meat, we bought wine for the occasion. What a surprise, Woolworth's had died and gone to heaven in the US. There in Melville it was alive well and very chic.

Cuan was completing a bid for a UN project. Debbie decided to give us a tour of Joburg's trendy neighborhoods. She pointed to mansion after mansion. Retired President Nelson Mandella had one of the finer homes. This was not the Joburg we'd heard of and feared. The Market Place was a mall full of upscale shops. I spotted a yellow Ferrari parked amongst the Mercedes and BMWs. It didn't equate with Joburg, the "Crime Capital of the World."

Lunch at Spiro's, Cuan's favorite cafe. Many of the patrons stopped to talk and shake Cuan's hand. One group was worried about a friend. He had been feeling ill, and almost passed out.

Cuan fired up the Braai. (Barbeque) Debbie whipped up a superb salad and sweet potatoes. Cuan Qued a coil of Boerewors sausage (Beef Sausage) and lamb chops to perfection. We sat

outside on the patio table, enjoying the food and each other.

CAT TRAX Day 229, A Business Day in Joburg. Cuan drove us to his travel agent Jan's office to pick up tickets to Victoria Falls. Second stop, a bike shop. They took the bikes in for a checkup. The shop was so well stocked, we loaded up on supplies. Our old shoes had disintegrated. We chose new pairs from their huge selection, plus shorts, leg and arm warmers, and puncture-resistant tubes. The techs checked the brakes and wheels, and installed new mirrors and pedals.

Laureen, a friend of Cuan and Debbie's invited us to a supper party celebrating South Africa's Freedom Day. A house full of friends, free-flowing wine, and conversation. The Braai was near the pool. Yuppies, they talked politics, business, and social issues. An FYI, all were white.

Chapter 27 Tourists to Victoria Falls

CAT TRAX Day 230, Flight to "The Falls." Our borrowed suitcase was packed with our essentials. Cuan dropped us at the airport just in time to board. I was seated next to Graham, a cattle rancher and tobacco farmer from Zambia. He and his family had been shopping in Joburg. He said, "I feel badly for Zimbabwe's farmers, but I also agree with you, the land issue is unbalanced. The farmers, all too often, flaunted their wealth." Nice guy, nice family. The flight was smooth and we got back on the ground safely-my idea of a successful flight.

Chuckie (Chookee) from Bushtracks Africa held a sign with our names. We jumped into her van and were whisked away to The Zambezi Sun Hotel. Three teenagers in tribal dress played drums and sang African songs to honor our arrival.

The hotel looked like it could

have been in Scottsdale, Arizona. No view of The Falls but we could see the cloud of spray through the trees and hear the roar. We learned we'd arrived at the worst time of year. High water season, in fact flood season. Native Africans called the falls "Mosi-oa-Tunya, The Smoke That Thunders."

CAT TRAX Day 231, Big Day at Vic Falls. Cat wanted fresh air. When she opened the slider two cute little baboons sitting on the deck rail dashed into the room. Cat screamed as they ran directly to the coffee set up, stealing all the packets of dry cream and sugar. They jumped to a nearby tree limb and sat calmly opening and eating the sweets and treats. Obviously this wasn't their first raid, they knew exactly where to go and what to grab. It looked like they had smiles on their cute faces as they licked the packets clean. They finished their brunch, Cat closed the slider, and they moved back to their perch on the rail, awaiting the next opportune opening.

Breakfast was a huge buffet served poolside. As we were seated a burly male baboon jumped from the roof and grabbed food from the table of two startled ladies. The staff yelled and feigned throwing things. The old fellow took his time, nonchalantly climbing back to the roof then sat enjoying his pilfered breakfast. Wow, our second Baboon raid of the morning.

Out for a walk, Cat threw our rain ponchos into the bag as an afterthought. Nearing the falls we were glad to have them. In fact, there was a small stand renting them to unaware falls visitors.

Walking the trails was like hiking in a monsoon. Even with ponchos our shoes and shorts got soaked. Fear of ruining our new camera drove us to higher and drier ground.

Walking toward the Zimbabwe side of the falls, we passed dozens of booths offering woodcarvings and souvenirs. The Victoria Falls Bridge, built in 1905, shook like a 6.0 earthquake as thirty-wheel big rigs rumbled past. They allowed only one vehicle at a time.

The bridge was also a favorite bungee-jumping spot. We watched as the crazies soared into the mist, dangling head down, waiting for the crew to haul them back up. As one climbed back over the rail, Cat asked "How was it?" He flashed a thumbs up and said, "Fantastic!"

We wanted to visit to the Zimbabwe side of the falls. Our visas were still valid. There was no view from the Zimbabwe border. The

Immigration Police gave a friendly but firm, "No!" Our visas were single entry, so we'd have to pay $30 US each to return. We did our best sales pitch but failed. Deciding it was not worth $60, we walked back through the Smoke near the Thunder.

Another "Road Warrior" appeared through the mist. Christophe had cycled from France during the past five months. He'd ridden many of the same roads we had, carrying only a bedroll. Living off the land, he ate and slept with African families. He'd had constant diarrhea, amoebic dysenterary-even malaria, three times. Way tougher than we, he was fun to talk with.

At lunch another Big Baboon raid. Sitting eating in the sun, we were completely relaxed when suddenly, *crash* a huge male dropped onto the table next to us and began grabbing food. I jumped up and threatened him, but he ignored me. The women screamed as he continued to fill his hands with their food. The staff rushed out and sent him flying back to the rooftop. Once over the shock the women shared a good laugh. One said it was a "once in a lifetime event!" She didn't know this was our third-once in a lifetime episode, just that day.

We explored the riverbank upstream to The Royal Livingstone Hotel. A herd of zebra grazed on the lawn and a deck jutted out over the swollen Zambezi River. The pools at the top of the Falls were flowing too fast for even the most foolish people to sit in. We'd seen pictures of crazies lounging as though in a hot tub at the edge of certain death. Even the thought made me queasy.

CAT TRAX Day232, Victoria Falls back to Joburg. The morning sun and a beautiful rainbow greeted us as we pulled back our drapes. It hung in the mist-the smoke above the thunder. Our scavenger friends the baboons and monkeys were nowhere to be seen. We enjoyed another lovely breakfast, they missed that ,too.

The boys in the African greeting band were again playing music as we departed. Native apparel and instruments made them look and sound authentic. New arrivals gathered round clapping, taking photos and video and putting tips in their jar. Many of the tourists, less traveled than we, may have thought these young guys lived in thatched roof mud huts and protected their families from wild animals with spears. The young leader, Lufasi, told us, "We just began playing together, three months ago. We all recently graduated high school, this is our summer job." Four clever young boys, fun to talk with, fun to watch them perform.

Our Bushtracks Africa van departed the Falls at 11:30. The waiting area at the airport, was hot and stuffy. Another great flight and we were on the ground at 3:15 p.m. A successful adventure!

Chapter 28 Johannesburg to Port Elizabeth

CAT TRAX Day 233, Return from Vic Falls. We had the taxi pull in to the DHL Office at the airport. The Manager found the paperwork for our camera then sent us to the Customs Office. The clock on the wall at Customs read 3:57 the sign next to it said Closing Time 4:00 p.m. We thought we'd just made it. A dozen chattering women came down the hallway. We asked who we should see, the lead lady smiled and said, "We are closed for the day." I objected, pointing to the clock. Several chuckled as she said, "Sorry but we are closed, come back tomorrow." We couldn't believe it, they were headed out the door. When we told them we'd have to pay another Taxi 240 Rand ($37 US) to get back, they just shrugged and walked away.

Our cab driver Joseph was a gem. He tried to get the Customs employees to help us to no avail. He came with us into DHL and expedited their service. Driving back through rush hour traffic Joseph knew short cuts. We were at the gate of Cuan and Debbie's place by 5:30.

CAT TRAX Day 234, A Day With Cuan and Debbie. Cuan

called a taxi company he used and cut a deal to the airport and back for 200 Rand. Our driver was a nervous Afrikaner who muttered to himself and yelled at other drivers. As we waited at a stoplight, he pointed to a woman begging. She had that homeless weather-beaten look. He spat out, "Look at her, she used to be white as you and me, now she's no better than those other black beggars."

Whites made up 15% of the population as compared to 3% in Zimbabwe. Another large group were called "Coloreds": mixed race, black and white. The difference was white people lived at every economic level in South Africa. Gerhard was a middle-income guy. This woman was proof there were also poor whites. In Zimbabwe we found a few middle-level folks however whites had most of the money and the things money buys. Our observation was in no way scientific. In the other Sub-Saharan countries we met mostly black Africans, but in South Africa most of our social interactions were with whites.

We walked into the Customs Office, up to a window and pushed our papers under the glass. The officer looked at them and asked,

"Are you leaving South Africa soon." We told him we were. Then he asked, "Will you take the camera with you, when you leave?" As we nodded yes he stamped the papers. The understanding agent waived the import tax! Clearance in hand, we slipped over to DHL. The now-smiling women immediately released our package.

Cuan's taxi driver dropped us at the bike shop. The bikes were ready, the clothing and shoes in bags. Cuan pulled up and helped us load up his Rover. Back in Melville, it felt like Christmas. The camera was fantastic. Cuan, Cat, and I walked to Main Street. Again we took Cuan's favorite table on the sidewalk at Spiro's. One of Cuan's friends told him the guy who had been sick the week before had been sent home to prepare to die. He had full blown AIDS.

CAT TRAX Day235, Johannesburg to Parys 24 Ks in Cuan's Rover, 75 Kilometers to Parys. Parting was sorrow, not sweet. We enjoyed coffee and toast with Cuan and Debbie. Once again strangers a few days ago were now as close as family.  Although we didn't think it would be difficult Cuan refused to let us cycle through Johannesburg. He wouldn't take no for an answer. Hugs, a moment of emotion, then Debbie set off to work and we off on our adventure.

Cuan gave us a quick tour of Joburg. We cruised through downtown but were disappointed, the Nelson Mandela Bridge was closed. Gauteng was the Sotho word that meant, "Place of Gold." Cuan pointed out yellow hills throughout town, golf mine tailings.

That second airport trip had robbed us of the time for a planned visit to the Apartheid Museum and Soweto the township where the struggle to end Apartheid had begun. Both Cuan and Cat were pushing to get us going. He had to get back to work, we needed to hit the road.

At 10:00 a.m. we unloaded the Rover. The final hug of the day was a tough one. You'd think we'd be used to saying goodbye. Handshakes, bear hugs, then Cuan turned and walked out of our life, for now but not for good. They'd promised to visit us when we returned home. We had lumps in our throats as he drove way.

The guys at the tollgate waved as we rolled around the sensor strips. The neighborhood was definitely townships. Small shacks with corrugated tin roofs. We'd not ridden 2 Ks when I had a problem. My shifting belt tangled around the gears and broke. That was a first in more than 23,000 kilometers. (14,200 miles) I had to

remove the rear wheel, replace the belt then put it all back together. Locals sat in chairs near their huts watching the curious spectacle.

Back up and rolling but not for long. Soon Cat's front wheel began to wobble. A flat, she'd picked up a nail. Another quick fix and we were riding south. Hectic, not a great way to start the day. It was sunny but cool. Tall grass lined the route. Lunch at 55 Ks, Meat Pies in a BP Service Station. We asked a local farmer the distance to Parys. He said, "Ask my wife, out there in our Bakkie." (pickup) That prompted a typical husband/wife discussion. Bantering back and forth as we watched she said, "It's 20 Ks." When Cat sighed he said, "Why not just come over, and stay with us?" We appreciated the offer but if we failed to reach Parys we'd never get to the next town, Kroonstaad on the following day. It was a long distance between towns on the sparsely populated prairie.

Interesting, Parys was sort of pronounced Paris as in France. They said Parees in a very different accent than the French. They did fly French flags and even sported a miniature Eiffel Tower.

First stop was a grocery store. The clerk, Louie, was extremely personable. We asked for wine and he said, "That's in my liquor store, across the street." Walking over with us, he asked where we were going. He helped us choose a bottle, we grabbed two since the next day was Sunday and liquor stores would be closed. The cashier was checking out her register. Louie said,

"Liquor laws require we close at 5:00 p.m. on Saturdays." It was 5:10 and we were facing a wine-less weekend. Louie said "Bring the wine through." I told him we didn't want to cause a problem for him. He chuckled and said, "I can't sell you wine but don't worry, I'm giving it to you."

Man, more SA Hospitality. Louie told us, "My family came here, from Madeira, when I was five years old. I'm proud to be Portuguese. I work hard, besides the market and liquor store, I also own the Spurs Restaurant." A proud, confident, successful young guy. He pointed out the hotel above Spurs. Surprisingly, he didn't own it.

The Palm Court Hotel was a classic, more than 100 years old. Recently renovated, the shower was in a claw foot tub. We toasted to Louie's continued success. Dinner was at Louie's Spurs restaurant, life was good!

CAT TRAX Day 236, 101 KS, Parys to Kroonstad. Before leaving, we wanted a picture with Louie. The clerk at the market said, "Louie not ear, he be ear, in few minutes," in a blend of Afrikaner and Portuguese. We waited twenty minutes then asked again. He picked up the phone called then said, "Eee be ear, 10 minutes." I asked if he and Louie were related. His chest swelled as he said, "Yeees, eees may Son-in-Law, married may daughter." Who wouldn't be proud to have a Son-in-Law like Louie?

It was great getting to know Louie just a little. He said, "I don't spend all my time working, just most of it. I have a hobby, drag racing. My car takes too much time and money, but I love it." Obviously he was driven to win, in drag racing and in his businesses.

Louie suggested the old road would be a good ride and we'd save 20 Ks. It started narrow, no shoulder and lots of traffic. Just as we began to doubt Louie's advice we reached rolling countryside and had the road to ourselves. The scenery was grassland, brown grassland that time of year. Cattle were scattered in small herds nibbling stubble.

It was 5:00 p.m. when we rode into Kroonstaad. The Hotel Hacienda was aged. Cat wanted a shower, the newly renovated double rooms only had tubs. They decided we'd stay in the old section that hadn't been rehabbed. We were given a double room for sleeping and single for the shower. Ah, the old adage, "All things are possible, just ask."

CAT TRAX Day 237, 101 Ks, Kroonstaad to Winburg. The day began cold and windy. At breakfast a little kid walked right through one of the sliding glass doors. He was okay, the slider shattered. The wind was so strong that even sitting at the farthest table from the shattered slider's flapping drape was still cold. The food was

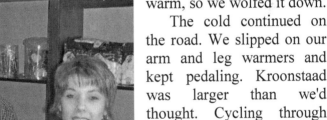

warm, so we wolfed it down.

The cold continued on the road. We slipped on our arm and leg warmers and kept pedaling. Kroonstaad was larger than we'd thought. Cycling through was tough, due to dense traffic and narrow streets. At the Sweet 'n' Spicy candy store Frans and Chantelle asked about the maps on our jackets. Hearing our story, they wanted a picture. He felt the local newspaper would like an interview. We told him we usually avoid press, not wanting to draw the wrong kind of attention. A person with bad intentions could easily find us on the road.

By 10:00 a.m. we were headed out into an unknown 100 Ks. Once free of the city, it was so desolate that at times we wished for a little more traffic. Ventersburg was halfway to Winburg. At Speers Restaurant, Mabel delivered burgers and fries. She joked about our jackets then became intrigued. When we'd finished the burgers, she insisted on a picture. As I raised the camera Mabel jumped on Cat's bike. She's the kind of person that made our photos and trip memorable!

The afternoon was a series of ups and downs through fields of brown. The sun was trying to slip away as we entered Winburg. It was ask, ask, time. Our first ask was a young girl. She pointed, indicating we should go ahead, then to the right. As 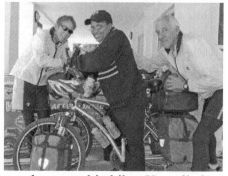 we started off her brother J. C. caught us on his bike. He called out "Follow me," and raced off down the street. He took us right to the door of the Winburg Guesthouse. It was dusk, we were cold, tired, and thankful.

As we checked in, Cat asked how many people lived in Winberg. Jock the clerk said, "2,500." Cat commented that it looked bigger. He astonished us by saying, "Well, there are about 30,000 blacks living here too." He added, "Some of them are out of work the mine laid off 1,500 today." He said it not with bias nor malice, just a statement. He was talking the talk and thinking the thoughts that had been the norm there before 1994. Some things die hard!

The Guesthouse, like Jock's thinking was old and tired. The owner was a local farmer his sister and brother-in-law ran the place. He'd recently purchased a second hotel down the street. It had been closed for several years. They were re-building and would soon operate both places. The sister served dinner. The brother-in-law was a cowboy who had lived in Texas and loved Country Music. The food left a lot to be desired. Nice people but they had a long way to go in learning the hospitality profession.

CAT TRAX Day 238, 115 Ks, Winburg to Bloemfontein. A cold, cold African night. We huddled under a pile of covers. Our bodies began to sweat, our noses froze. Breakfast was as poor as dinner. The Cowboy and wife were cordial. When they asked how the food was we just smiled and nodded. Hopefully, they'll get some help in the food service business, too!

The ride again was little ups and downs on a grassy prairie. There were trees along some of the riverbeds. Most of the scenery was grazing land and small herds of cattle. There was absolutely nothing in terms of stores, service stations or any services along the road. We slipped past the tollgate un-noticed, leaving town.

The afternoon passed quickly, maybe due to the distraction of friendly motorists. Most honked, waved, flashed their lights or gave us a thumbs up. At a rare Service Station/Mini Mart we had ice-cream. As we stood licking the cones, several people gathered around, talking travel and the world.

It was dusk as we rolled into Bloemfontein. A group of cyclists passed and waved from across the road. We made a feeble attempt to catch them to ask about lodging. They were too fast. As the sun sank a Holiday Inn sign lit up the sky. Damn, they were fully booked. They were busy checking others in but a desk clerk took

time to call another hotel. They, too, had no vacancy. She tried another then another with the same result. We were beginning to panic when she said, "Bring your things in, we'll make room for you." Bless her and the Holiday Inn. It was cold, dark, and foreboding outside. She couldn't guarantee that we could stay a second day. At least we had a home for the night. We'd decided to take a day off, so we'd make a move if we had to. There is nothing more wonderful than a hot shower after a cold day's ride.

The restaurant was called MacRib. The room was full of huge guys, Rugby Teams there for a tournament. So that was why the town was booked.

CAT TRAX Day 239, Day of Rest in Bloemfontein. After breakfast, as we savored our second cup of coffee, Clive came over and started a conversation. He and his wife Denine owned the restaurant. He said, "The restaurant is Denine's baby! She's only been open a month. I had been farming, lost interest and sold the farm. I'm dreaming of starting a "Quick Lube" place. Maybe even a car wash." Sounded like the farmer had the makings of a good entrepreneur. Actually aren't farmers the epitome of entrepreneurial spirit?

One of our goals was to have Cat's ears checked. Her hearing had diminished. She couldn't hear low-register sounds, like trucks bearing down on us. The Medical Clinic turned out to be the Emergency Room at the hospital. The check-in was the same as any hospital we'd visited anywhere in the world. Complete the paperwork then be seated and wait.

The facility was very modern. The doctor, a woman, took one look and confirmed my suspicion: earwax. She turned Cat over to a nurse armed with warm water and a wicked-looking syringe. Both ears flushed clean, a prescription for drops, and we were out the door for 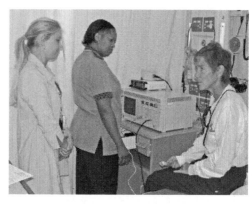 200 Rand, less than $40 in less than 40 minutes.

I found Don and Betty phone number by calling information. The phone rang and rang. I'd almost given up when she answered. I asked, "Is this Betty?"

She sighed and responded, "Are you selling something? I'm too sick to put up with this." I explained our journey and that we had stayed at The Golden Spider Web. She became angry, "They took my place away, they stole it, and gave us almost nothing." When I mentioned Dennis, how he had been keeping the place open and his high regard for her, she almost screamed. "He is just a thief, a kid I trusted, and he stole my place. I'm too sick to talk, you're upsetting me!" She hung up.

We sat and talked about the dilemma. Betty was pushed out of a business she had lovingly built. Dennis had said he felt like a son to Don and Betty. Neither made up the rules. It was the system that left Betty angry and hateful. Dennis was there when the opportunity arose, it was natural for him to step in. At times he spoke as though he expected Betty to return one day and he'd resume working for her.

CAT TRAX Day 240, Day Off in Bloemfontein. Breakfast at the Big Mac! Egg McMuffin! Yes, we were definitely back in Mickey D's territory. Klopper's Department Store had CDs and a memory stick for our new camera. At the check stand, we remembered Cat wanted a flashlight to replace the one lost in Guinea Bissau. The gal stacked our things aside and said, "You'll find flashlights on the second floor." A helpful fellow there led us to the shelf and

recommended one "Our best seller," he said.

The guy, Wouter Klopper, and his brothers owned the store. Their father founded it, they had grown up in it and grown it into a super store. Wouter was intrigued with our trip. As we paid he handed Cat a special tool. One of those "All in One" things with screwdrivers, wrench, even little pliers. Just another example of South African warmth, sharing, and hospitality.

CAT TRAX Day 241, 77 Ks, Bloemfontein to Edenburg. At 9:00 a.m. we pushed into a steady stream of traffic. Bloemfontein was a big city-population 380,000-and it felt like most of the residents were on the road driving that morning.

In a small shopping center, Cat sought food while I stood guard. A couple of guys seated nearby kept eyeing me. Thoughts of robbery crossed my mind. One walked over and asked, "Where are you going?" No robber, Chris said, "My brother and I built and own Blackwood Crossing Center. We completed it just 18 months ago, and are already 100% occupied." We filled him in on our trip then talked real estate. Chris told us, "We had owned and operated a chain of ice cream stores, sold them, and began buying and developing properties. This Center took eight years from conceptual approvals to completed project." Jeez, that sounded a lot like California.

The road divided then expanded into 4 lanes. The land began to look like desert. We were entering the Great Karoo. Wide-open spaces we'd been warned about. The relatively short ride had us in

Edenburg by 3:30. Country Lodge was a simple place in a simple town. Strange that even in small towns, maybe especially small towns, there were no black people in the bars or restaurants.

Charles at the adjacent table was quiet at first. Suddenly, after soup was served, he wanted to talk. "I'm 80 years old and an accountant. I still have quite a few clients." He paused then with pride said, "I just coming back from a 10-day holiday in George, on the coastal Garden Route. Such beauty, you must see it!"A wonderful evening, a terrific guy, we could have talked all night but fatigue set in on the three of us.

CAT TRAX 5/8/04, 71 Ks, Edenburg to Springfontein. Charles was already at his table when we came for breakfast. We assumed the same seats and resumed conversation. Susan and Michele, who'd served dinner, were back cheerful as ever and serving again.

As we ate, a gal came in holding a newspaper and said, "You're a bit famous now." Anita who we'd met in Bloemfontein had taken our picture and submitted the story. Susan had to read it to us as it was written in Afrikaans. Charles was quite intrigued and studied it carefully. When I started to add his name to our address book he took it and wrote, "Good Luck and good fortune, for your future travels," then signed it "Charles, 80 years old, Bloemfontein."

The consensus around the breakfast table was we should ride the old road. They said it was slightly shorter, less traveled, and more scenic. The surface of the old highway was rough, broken and patched. It paralleled railroad tracks. Other than a freight train passing, there was no traffic. The flat road across the prairie allowed us to bump along at a good pace.

Trompsburg was the halfway point between Edenburg and Springfontein. We found a store, bought lunchmeat and picnicked at a table. I opened conversation with Meshack a young guy who worked for the telephone company. We were surprised when he said, "I have work for phone company, more than 25 year. I also been marry 25 year, have two kids. My boy, he 23, my girl, she 20." He looked our bikes over then said, "Me strong cyclist. Me and group, we rides, from Springfontein, where I lives, to here and back, almost all weekend." Meshack's heritage was Xhosa. The Xhosa use tongue clicks as part of their spoken language. He said in Xhosa, "You're riding your bikes around the world? You must be crazy!" for our video.

Meshack was a product of modern Africa. His job was technical, he made good money. He owned two cars, a Mercedes and Toyota and drove a company Bakkie. He had raced bicycles in his youth and still loved to ride. He looked much younger than his 42 years.

Springfontein was small. It was Saturday afternoon, so the shops and markets had already closed. We asked a policeman for directions to a hotel. He informed us, "There is no hotel here, only a Guest House." We followed his directions and found the place. A small crowd of Afrikaners inside the bar were boisterous. The bad news: their restaurant was closed. The woman there didn't know of any other in town.

As we stood pondering, Meshack pulled up. Being a local, he insisted we follow him to a B&B. He said "It is much better, they make for you dinner." We followed, but when he pulled up it looked like a private home. He rang the bell then shouted, finally rousting a lady. "Yes," she said, "Ve haf room, you be only guest. Und, yes, vee do serfe dinner." Best of all they had a bottle of nice white wine. Meshack allowed a standoffish hug then drove away.

The Springfontein House was

very nice, our room was separated from the main house. The owner was away in Port Elizabeth attending a B&B conference. The two African women were nervous. They called him on a cell phone every time we asked a question. They were gracious, wanted to help any way they could. I hated it when they call me "Master." Cat thought it was a form of courtesy. I thought a holdover from the old days.

They cooked a wonderful meal for Master and Madam. Local TV announced that Brenda Fassie, a South African singer/songwriter was near death. More than a singer, she had been an icon during the anti-apartheid days. A strong proponent for human and women's rights, Nelson Mandela had called her a patriot.

CAT TRAX Day 242, 80 Ks, Springfontein to Coles. Autumn leaves of red and gold covered the few trees on The Great Karoo. As I crested a hill, I began sinking. Thinking the seat had come loose I stood and pedaled to the summit. Unbelievable, the top of the seat post had broken off. I was able to slip the sleeve over the remaining post and we rode on, but sitting low was tough on my knees. We rode up into Colesberg at 4:00 p.m.

The Lighthouse was a Guesthouse. Ettorina the night manager decided we should have a little house usually rented to families. She and her two daughters were cyclists. They had just ridden a 30 Ks fun ride and loved it. Plenty of room but only a bath tub. She solved that one too. There was a shower in an adjacent room. Wonderful helpful Ettorina!

Ettorina and her husband, Riaan who managed the Shell Station and Mini Mart called two brothers who worked at the bicycle shop. They came by to look at the broken seat. No way to fix it, but they would try to find a post that would fit. Nice guys to come out on Sunday night. They tried to force the larger of two posts they'd brought along into the frame. Failing that they asked to take the bike back to their shop. No problem.

While we were struggling with the bike, Cat talked with Ettorina. She was interested in Cat's perspective of our trip. "What have you gained from it?" she asked. After Cat shared her feelings about how much we'd seen and how we'd grown, Ettorina told her about their lives. "Riaan and I had been teachers but we were completely burned out. We just couldn't face another class, another year of the sameness, same books and subjects." I tried to explain my theory, how teachers touch lives well beyond the classroom. Not quite falling on deaf ears but it made me reflect on my own careers. I had taught many how to cut meat, run a grocery store, and how to achieve not just a career, but a profession in real estate!

"We work hard here," she explained, "You know, the Afrikaner work ethic. We're just slightly above middle income. I help manage the Guest Houses, juggle household duties and our two daughters activities. We are a Christian family." She took her bracelet off and gave it to Cat. It said, "Africa 2 Chron. 7:14," a Biblical Verse. She

 told Cat it meant, "Leave evil behind and God will guide and bless you."

At dinner we ran into a guy we'd seen at The Lighthouse. He stopped to talk, and allowed us to buy him a beer. Fletch had been in the South African Air Force for 11 years. Cat asked if he was a pilot. His answer, "No, I'm the guy responsible for keepin' em' flyin'."

The conversation became another lesson about the life of an average Afrikaner. "I've been married eight years, we have a three-year-old daughter. We have a nice home, in Louis Trichardt." he said with pride. When we mentioned the new name Mokopane, he scoffed and said, "They shoulda left well enough alone!" We invited him to visit when he gets to California.

He said, "I don't see ever havin' money enough, to get there." Our advice as always "Start Dreamin'!"

CAT TRAX Day243, 94 Ks, Colesberg to Middleburg. My bike was sitting on the porch of our little house. The boys had ground the bug post down to fit. It was solid. We were road ready!

Bianca and Brian were Managers of The Lighthouse. She

explained, "Father started the business, then died, a year ago. Mom begged us to manage the place. Our big decision, whether to give up our good marketing jobs in Cape Town. We wanted to start a family, Mom encouraged that, too." Brian said, "My days are spent keeping this 120-year-old building functioning. Bianca keeps the books, we struggle with costs and cash flow." He paused, then confided, "Taking over a family business doesn't guarantee success. It does mean hard work. The trade off, we're raising our family in a small town." Both were bright, we felt they'd do well.

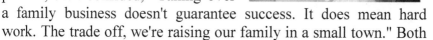

Colesburg's main street climbed up toward a small market. As Cat bought food, two young brothers approached, they were dirty, disheveled. I felt sure they would beg but they just stood and stared. I asked if they went to school. The older one said, "No." They seemed shy and backed away. I gave them our card and asked if they used the Internet. Again the elder spoke "Yes, in school." So, they did go to school, maybe they were out for spring vacation. Their look reminded me of my brother Jerry and me as kids. I told Cat, "On the last day of school we took off our shoes and wore our rag-tag clothes all summer."

Main Street circled around a church then really climbed. We huffed and puffed to the summit. Health Zone, the Bike/Weight Training Shop was near the top. We stopped to thank and pay J. P. for taking time from his Sunday evening to fix the bike. The shy young guy smiled, shook my hand, then pushed our money back toward me. I argued, he smiled then turned back to his work.

Down the road we met Allan, Brenda, Boet and Norma, two

296

couples about my age from Joburg, vacationing. They were camping in caravans (trailers.) They'd been sharing holidays for more than twenty years. The kids had grown, but they carried on the tradition. Allan called it "pulling their houses along." We hadn't seen many campers in Africa.

The Karoo Lodge sign was gold and hung on a white fence. Cute and a little over budget but breakfast was included. Desk Clerk Jenna introduced us to Alan, the owner. He and Jenna's mother were having tea. The gardens were expertly groomed, guinea fowl pecked at the ground, keeping bugs at bay. The house was more than 100 years old and wonderfully furnished.

The Karoo offered dinner, only if we'd reserved in advance. Jenna suggested the Farmhouse Grill, another old refurbished house. An enjoyable meal and conversation with Ari owner of Gauteng Leather Works. He was celebrating with clients from Italy. Ari invited us to stop by for a tour of the tannery.

They were joined by Rhona, girl friend of one of the Italians, who lived there in Middleburg. She was wearing exercise clothing. Ari introduced us, saying, "She's an avid bicyclist too." She said, "I just led a Spinning Class. I'm beyond avid, probably addicted. When I got divorced, I had to choose between depression, drink, drugs, or exercise. I chose bicycle riding." She reflected for a moment, then added, "Cycling is my life, I love my bicycle!"

CAT TRAX Day 244 , Day Off in Middleburg. The night was cold, almost freezing. As Jenna had promised, breakfast was terrific.

The stone fireplace and huge log ablaze was just what Cat needed to bring her body temp back to normal.

We walked through town then out to the Tannery. The climbing sun warmed the morning air. Inside the tannery we were escorted to Ari's office. He seemed less enthusiastic than he had been at dinner. Guiding us through his plant he warmed as he talked. "We don't actually tan the sheepskins here, we pickle them seal them in barrels and ship to buyers mainly in Italy." He walked us through the process from grading the rough skins to washing and removing the wool. When finished Ari said, "These are the best sheepskins for leather, in the world!"

Walking back was interesting, too. We skirted around the township, rough little shacks. Juxtaposed were beautiful older homes lining the other streets. Obvious, who lived in each.

When we returned to the Karoo, Cat was shivering and my feet were freezing. We went straight to our room and huddled under the covers. The chef, a woman, came knocking, asking if we wanted to order dinner. We passed, they were serving fish, and we wanted meat. When we told her we were freezing she asked, "Why don't you turn on the heat?" Heat, what heat? She pointed out a wall heater behind the desk. It wasn't instant, but we did feel heat as we headed out for dinner.

Back to the Farmhouse, we had another great experience. Lamb Shanks for me and Fillet Mignon for Cat. The only thing missing, the company. We were their only diners.

CAT TRAX Day 245, 99 Ks, Middleburg to Cradock. Our room was almost too warm, the little heater did the job. At breakfast we had company, George and Susan, on holiday from Johannesburg. Also, as we ate, reporters from two of the tiny local newspapers came in. Alan had asked, we felt if it had value for him we'd gladly meet with them. Alan asked, "Do you have digital cameras?" They both shook their heads and one said, "It wouldn't do any good, we don't have computers either." It was kind of fun but we were anxious to get back to the road.

Alan surprised us, grabbed his bike and played guide as we rode out of town. He warned, "There's nothing between here and Craddock." We stopped at the grocery, bought meat pies and soft drinks. He also pointed out both Rhinoceros and Table Mountains. He had recently climbed Table Mountain. Very active, hiking and cycling were his lifestyle. Another emotional parting.

Again we noted the difference in housing. The old classic homes were inhabited by whites. Blacks and Coloreds lived on the edge of town. Their homes ranged from cement block and corrugated metal roofs to newer small places covered with stucco. Each included an

298

outhouse. It brought to mind something Mark had said back in Mokopane. "The Government is adding 500 new homes everyday in South Africa."

Riding the Karoo was cycling in the desert. We sat at the edge of the road and ate our meat pies. The sun felt good. We enjoyed it and the attention from passing drivers.

Another cyclist pedaled hard uphill and upwind, toward us. I called out, he kept his head down and pedaled. We both called, he looked our way, stopped and stood, looking back. Slowly, he turned and rode back. Alex was headed toward Middleburg. It concerned us, it seemed too far for him to ride. What a strong willed interesting person. He set us straight, "Yes, I am mentally handicapped, but that doesn't stop me from living. I've cycled thousands of kilometers, around the Cape. I attended school for the handicapped." As though to prove that, he printed his name and address in our book then added his mother and father's names and signed the page. We stood watching as he rode away. I had a lump in my throat. Cat teared up.

It was a downhill coast into Craddock. A group of school athletes jogged past up the steep hill. Struggling up the main street, Cat spotted the Victoria Hotel. She went in, came back out, and said, "We are staying in one of their renovated classic homes, built in the 1800s."

She'd gotten a *home* called, "40 Something," with a living room, kitchen, bedroom and bath. Spacious, classic furnishings and within budget. The living room was our parking space.

We cranked up the heater then walked to dinner, a gourmet buffet that included an African music performance. During dinner three Xhosa women began singing. Ayabulela, Bulelwa and Noneca called their group Anointed Gospel. They mixed in popular music, accentuated by the wonderful clicking sound Meshak had demonstrated.

Back at "40 Something" we watched a TV special, The life of Brenda Fossie. From modest township beginnings to South African diva. She had struggled with drugs and emotional problems but she always worked promoting human and women's rights through her music and walking with protesters. I had moist eyes, Cat cried. We bought a CD, *Brenda Fossie and The Big Dudes.*

CAT TRAX Day246, 99 KS, Cradock to Golden Valley. Our day began climbing hills. The weather was cool and windy. After a long pull to the top of the first mountain, Cat had a flat tire. Not a great way to start a long cycling day.

Down then up and down and up. As we progressed, the wind picked up and clouds gathered. A quick ten-minute picnic at hill top had us huddled together in the cold wind. We donned our raincoats for warmth. We not only kept our raincoats on, we rode with the hoods up under our helmets to keep our ears warm.

Cat spotted the Golden Valley Hotel, a white two-story with lots of parked cars. She worried they might be booked. I couldn't imagine that, not on an off-season weeknight. As usual Cat was right. A South African Insurance Group was meeting there. At the desk a young girl said, "You could go to Middleton." She conferred with the manager Lizette, who said, "I don't think they're taking guests. They're converting the hotel into a youth center." None of that mattered to us it was too dark and cold to attempt cycling another 20 Ks.

We thought we were doomed to a cold tent on a freezing night. Then Lizette said, "You'll stay at my house." We were astounded; she was just ending a twelve hour shift. She added, "I'll cook dinner for you." That went way beyond SA Hospitality and was unreasonable. We suggested we eat there and sleep at her place. She called her husband Giel, and broke the news.

We ordered dinner. Lizette said, "I'm going to relax, have a drink, while you eat." The food was good, but the dining room was cold. She turned up a nearby wall heater and Cat huddled up to it.

We took clothes and toiletries off the bikes, leaving them in the hotel meeting room. Lizette's daughter, Lize (Leeza) drove us to their home, a farm 2 Ks from the hotel. It was a bumpy ride on a dirt road. Lizette, in her car, led the way. There she introduced Giel, her other daughter, Jolene and nephew Pieter. She went to work firing up the Braai. She'd invited another regular hotel guest who'd  also been shut out. Jolene played with baby ducks she kept in a box. She complained that her hand was sore. It was swollen, I said, "Our doctor told us the best way to heal swelling is R I C E." Before I could explain Pieter said, "Rest, ice, compression and elevation." I couldn't believe he knew about RICE. The others were equally impressed. He dismissed it by simply saying, "We studied it in First Aid class."

Cat went to a warm bath. Giel talked about their lives. He and Lizette had been married for a year. She'd been married previously a couple of times. "We set off together, with little and are struggling to survive financially," Giel said. "Teaching's a good life but doesn't pay well." He liked my immortality theory and that Cat and I dug ourselves out of a deep financial hole.

Jolene followed after Cat finished her bath. She came back out complaining, "There's no warm water." Giel told her, "Take a splash bath." Then explained, "The old water heater, doesn't recover very fast." Cat had used all the hot. I decided no to a cold splash so went to bed without a splash. The room was comfortable but cold. We huddled under heavy layers of blankets.

We talked about whether we would or even could be that generous? The decision as we drifted off to sleep, we would have to try when we got back home.

CAT TRAX Day 247, 89 Ks, Golden Valley to Paterson. Lizette was to awaken us at 6:00 a.m. so we would ride with her as she went to work. We were already up and dressing when she knocked. It was still dark and very cold. Giel and the girls were up, preparing for school. The old car sputtered, backfired and we were off. Lizette apologized about the aging car. I told her no one could understand starting over better than Cat and I. We were both down and out when we met, emotionally and financially.

Lizette made a pot of coffee at the hotel while we re-packed the bikes. She served a wholesome breakfast. Cat hovered near to the heater as we ate. We were ready to go by 7:30 but chose to wait for the sun. At 8:30 Lizette joined us in front of the Golden
Valley Hotel. We enjoyed a round of hugs and thanked her for the exceptional hospitality and friendship. We offered but she refused to accept money. Ernest one of the insurance guys took a picture of the three of us then we rolled away and she went back to work.

We flew through Middleton, considered stopping for a snack but it was too early. Cresting a hill a van pulled up from behind flashing its lights. It was Alan from The Karoo Lodge. He was headed for Port Elizabeth to watch his son's Rugby game. He told us that George and Susan a couple we'd met briefly at The Lodge were also coming and had a surprise for us.

Nearing the top of a tough climb a car began to honk, pulled past then in front of us. It was George and Susan they'd brought sports drinks called Naartjie for us. We stood and talked, he said, "I work with the Telephone Company." Then added, "They break the equipment, or it wears out, and I fix it." She worked with Regional Government. They were on a driving holiday to the Garden Route. More wonderful folks doing nice things for people they barely knew.

The toughest ride and push of the day, Olifantskop Pass. (Elephants Pass) At the summit we swept down a long steep grade and into Paterson. We were headed to Sand Flats, the Liquor Store,

Artists Shop and B&B. A couple, Rudy and Denise owned it all. The hot shower felt great, especially for me, my first in two days.

Lammince, a young girl from Holland working there asked, "Will you eat in the restaurant, or off the bar?" I asked the difference and she said, "You'll be alone in the dining room." I told her the bar would be great if she could put a fire in the fireplace. She stammered a bit saying, "We hadn't planned on a fire." Then said, "Yes, I make a fine fire, for you."

The conversation in the bar was interesting but hard to follow. Afrikaans sprinkled with bits of English. We could barely hear them above the roaring fire. It was a fine fire and evening.

CAT TRAX Day 248, 88 Ks, Paterson to Port Elizabeth. The chill in the air continued, the landscape changed, brown grass gave way to green farm fields. Nearing sea level, we spotted the villages of Colchester, Sundays River and the Indian Ocean.

Stopping for soup, sandwich, and warmth, we'd just been served when an announcer broke in to a TV Soap Opera. The room was silent as the World Cup Federation President held up an envelope. He said "The 2010 World Cup Games will be organized by—" then he pulled a paper from the envelope and shouted, "South Africa!" Mayhem broke out. Those in the café and on Television went wild. As we left the café, they poured onto the street screaming, celebrating, some singing the African National Anthem. We'd hoped S. A. would get the Games. It was almost as emotional for us as for the noisy South Africans. With 50 Ks to go we pedaled.

Riding in road construction had us cycling on fresh paving in lanes not opened to traffic. Good while it lasted, we soon found ourselves on a narrow shoulder in heavy traffic. Shortly we were thrust onto a busy freeway. There was no alternative, so we ducked

 our heads, gritted our teeth, and rode. Fearful, we took the first off ramp and escaped to a surface street.

A disabled truck limped along behind us. Rather than compete, we pulled over and let him pass. He drove slowly, lights flashing, then stopped and began to back

up. Curious, we pulled over to watch. A mechanic drove up, the driver jumped down and talked with him, then turned to us. He, Swiphiwe, said, "I blew three tires, and hit the guardrail, trying to get this 26-wheeler stopped. The tires were fresh, but re-caps." He complained, "I just bought them. By the way, I knew about you guys. All the trucks know about you two, we've all been watching your progress for days, sharing it on our radios!" What a nice guy, what a big problem he had.

Cuan had insisted we meet his family who lived in Port Elizabeth. They knew someone with a B&B. We stopped and called. His mom Jeanette answered and after formalities said, "You're on track, keep riding, call again, when you get closer to town." We stopped in half an hour at a shopping center and called. She said, "You will stay at First Avenue Lodge, keep going until you find First Avenue."

The oceanfront with shops and a pier reminded us of our hometown, Ventura. We easily found First Ave. Denise, the owner of the Lodge had a room only for one night. Disappointed, we told

her we needed a rest, wanted to stay three nights. She studied her reservations then re-confirmed the bad news. When we asked about other places she said, "Why don't you take a look at my cottage, across the street?" Though Cat loved it, Denise was apologetic and offered it for the same price as a small room in the main house. Cat told her we'd love to just relax, cook in and hide out.

The bikes lay in repose in our living room near the couch and TV. Also, we had a kitchen, breakfast bar, bath with shower and roomy bedroom. The piece de resistance, Cable TV that carried CNN and BBC. We'd found a new home in Port Elizabeth.

Rather than tell us how to find the grocery store, Denise insisted on driving. We bought chicken for dinner, fruit and muffins for breakfast. Feasting at the coffee table, we watched a movie. Life was good. Several times we had wondered if taking the extra five days to see the Garden Route would be worth it. That night it began to feel as though it might be the best of our African Adventure.

Chapter 29 Port Elizabeth to Cape Town

CAT TRAX Day 249, Day of Rest in Port Elizabeth. This day was the anniversary of the United States Supreme Court Decision, Brown vs. Segregation in 1954. Imagine, such a short time ago the good ole U S of A finally allowed black kids in the southern states to attend public schools. The TV in South Africa played and replayed scenes of whites cursing, jeering, pushing, and threatening the kids arriving for their first day at the "Whites Only" school. There were a lot of similarities between the footage of riots in Alabama and those in South Africa, both occuring at about that same time. The civil disobedience and riots in South Africa led to banning the ANC, the African National Congress and twenty-eight years of incarceration for Nelson Mandela. It took another forty years in South Africa before Apartheid would give way to the sanity of a Rainbow Nation. Shamefully, Mandela remained on the United States Terrorist Watch List until 2008.

CAT TRAX Day 250, Another Day in Port Elizabeth. Another

"just like at home" breakfast, spiced by CNN News. My job, get to FedEx to pick up the package from our bicycle company. When I asked Denise for a phone book she again insisted on driving, "I go that way, anyway."

I got back just in time to get to our meeting with Cuan's family, Jeanette the Mom, Juliet his sister and Shawn his brother-in-law. Lunch at The Oyster Catcher with an ocean view. Great food and a getting acquainted conversation full of laughs. Shawn was a musician, we talked music. He'd played guitar with some big names in Rock 'n' Roll. It was 3:00 p.m. when they reluctantly dropped us back at our little home. We hugged, did the cheek, cheek, kiss, kiss and promised to see each other again, somewhere, somehow, sometime.

I called Ema in Zimbabwe on Denise's phone to reassure her we wanted to rent her Cape Town flat. She'd offered it for 200 Rand per day. ($30 US for a 2 bedroom, 2 bath, fully furnished place.) So we'd have our own house in Cape Town, too.

CAT TRAX Day 251, 92 Ks, Port Elizabeth to Jeffery's Bay.
Goodbyes to Denise then down to the beach onto the N2 and into
heavy traffic. The weather turned cloudy and cool. We found
ourselves in nerve-wracking cycling chaos. Cars and trucks were
coming at us from all angles. Bridge construction slowed traffic but
left us without a shoulder. A helicopter hovered above. Cat yelled,
"They're probably talking about us, on the TV traffic show. You
know, "We have a couple of crazy bicycle riders out here on the N2
slowing traffic. Who are they and what the heck are they doing
there?" The drivers, especially truck drivers cheered us on.

Typical coastal ups and downs, lunch at roadside. We left the
N2 and cycled around St. Francis Bay to Jeffery's Baai. A nice-
looking hotel drew us in, the rate threw us back out and across the
street to The Beach Cabana, a Motel 6 kind of place.

CAT TRAX Day 252, 78 Ks on bikes, 24 on Bakkie, Jeffery's

Bay to Tsitsikamma Lodge.
Jeff and Linda the Innkeepers
at Jeffery's Baai had been
farmers in Zimbabwe. Their
farm, lodge and game park, all
that were gone. They had
cashed out for small dollars.
They'd tried to immigrate to
Australia but a member of
their family had been disallowed. Now all their eggs were in the Inn
basket. Their daughter served breakfast. She seemed mentally
challenged. Could that have been the reason the Aussies had turned
them down? Pretty lame if it was!

Jeff told us, "You'll find the first 75 Ks is flat." We found ups
and downs. Fairly fast downs into the wind and very slow, often
pushing, on the ups. Jeff was completely correct about one thing:
there were no stores or services along the route.

The red mileage numbers on our map didn't add up. Still on the
road and the sun was sinking below the Tsitsikamma Mountains, at
75 Ks we were deep in the Tsitsikamma Forest. It got cold and dark.
Tsitsikamma Lodge was visible only on our map. The road
narrowed, a scary thought riding it in the dark. Too scary, so we
made a "get off the road" decision.

We turned our flashing red taillights toward oncoming traffic and waved our headlights. Funny, when riding there seemed to be a constant stream of cars and trucks. Now we waited, hoping for headlights. A small bakkie slowed, looked us over, then sped on. Another, pulling a trailer, slowed, passed, then pulled over. Our evening Angel, Doug, looked at our bikes then said, "You're lucky I stopped, most people are afraid to pick up strangers out here." Yes, we were lucky. Lucky to meet nice people like Doug who'd take a chance, and lend a hand to strangers in the dark!

We hoisted the bikes onto the bakkie. Cat jumped into the cab with the guys. I hunkered down with the bikes. As Doug took off, I noticed our ponchos, still on the bags, were flapping in the wind. I was able to get my shoes and poncho but as I struggled to get Cat's it flew off into the darkness. I did get her shoes and tucked our map cases down. They'd been threatening to fly away. Then it was back to my prenatal crouch.

Doug was a rancher and general contractor from George. He was returning home from a job and offered to take us on into George. I told him of our "Keep rubber on the road" philosophy, and he understood. At Tsitsikamma Lodge, Cat ran in to confirm a vacancy. When she gave us the high sign through the window Doug and I lifted the bikes down. Thank you seemed shallow but it was the best we could do. Doug invited us to spend the night at his ranch when we got to George.

The Lodge was a wonderful place in the wilderness. The cabins and main buildings were built of logs. Our cabin had a loft with extra beds. It was cold, the heater crackled as it struggled to drive the chill from the room. Thankfully the shower ran hot and heavy.

Dinner, a buffet. The glow of the fireplace warmed the evening and our hearts. Yes, we were lucky weren't we?

CAT TRAX Day 253, 85 Ks, Tsitsikamma Lodge to Plettenberg Bay. At the breakfast buffet Morris the bartender at night became Morris the morning waiter. A warming blaze in the fireplace invited us to sit near. Morris became intrigued with our voyage. "I was in to mountain bike racing and doing pretty well," he told us. "I took some bad crashes, had surgery on my knee twice. That ended my racing career, but I still love cycling." We checked out, then Morris checked out our bikes. Of course he had to give mine a try. He'd never

cycled with baggage on board. He said, "Makes the bike feel like a truck."

The road was tight and bumpy, the traffic thick and unforgiving. They all seemed in a hurry. It was 16 Ks of high anxiety until we reached a wide shoulder. Pine trees and ferns lined the route. It was the beauty we'd heard bragged about by so many South Africans.

We saw bungee-jumping South African style. The world's highest jump, 216 meters (710 feet) from a bridge into one of the series of gorgeous gorges carved by scenic

rivers seeking the sea. The Jump Master said, "After the jump, the first bounce is a greater fall than the second highest jump, in the world." A group of climbers prepared to repelled down the massive cliffs to the Storms River below then white water raft to the ocean. Made our cycling look pretty tame eh?

The N2 pitched up and down, reminiscent of The Pacific Coast Highway. Hard to believe it had been two years since we set off up the coast of California. We'd come a long way, baby.

The hills were sapping our energy. We needed food. It was after 2:00 p. m. and we'd had nothing to eat since breakfast. At 50 Ks we rolled into a small place, The Cregs. The little store had no fresh food, not even a loaf of bread. As we pondered, a guy with a cast on his leg hobbled up and said, "The woman at the business next over is an American." How had he figured out that we were from the US? He quickly limped away. Were we that obvious? We'd never know!

Kathy, originally from Minnesota, had lived in California. She told us, "I taught school in Orange County. The School District hired me to teach an outdoors class to city kids. I loved the job, but budget cuts did away with my position. I followed my brother here and got a similar job." She sighed and said, "I fell in love with a local guy, and gave up teaching when we got married." She pointed to a building and continued, "We own that welding shop. The Cregs has been a Polo Clubs area, for several years. Recently, we were chosen to host the Worlds Polo Championship Games, coming here in three years. It's great for South Africa and for us! We're building the pipe railings, for all the new Polo Fields."

Kathy sent us to The Pie Place. Following her directions, we were soon lost. A young guy pointed down a dirt road. We hated to leave the N2, but hunger won out. Allan, owner of the Farm Kitchen, served meat pies and info about the area. He'd been there four years. "I think this area is preparing to become a Mecca for tourists. A Monkey Farm recently opened and several other attractions are planned." Allan's son published *Holidays in Africa* a slick magazine full of ads promoting hotels, restaurants, and fun things to do along the Garden Route.

The remainder of the ride was pleasant until we reached Plettenberg. The road and hillsides were lined with trendy homes. Greeted by a huge hill, we pushed all the way up into town. The Bayview Hotel was beyond budget, but we were tired, so we took the deal. Pizza, local TV, and early to bed. Ah, the life of bicycle vagabonds.

CAT TRAX Day 254, 44 Ks, Plettenberg Bay to Knysna. The main street turned right-and right up a steep hill. Pushing was a tough way to start the day. The N2 was lined with B&Bs, a sign we were getting closer to Cape Town. Lots of tourist attractions tucked into the pine forests that lined the highway. Carpets of lavender beautifully accented the colors of the forests. Yes, this *was* the Garden Route!

Seeing the Knysna Elephant Park billboard inspired my idea to go there with the bikes and ride near elephants. Cat almost laughed, saying, "You think they'll let us just cycle up to an elephant?" I reminded her of the adage, "All things are possible, just ask!"

We took the turn off and rode to the Park on a dusty, bumpy road. Inside the office I asked, and the girl at the desk looked at me like I was crazy. She yelled to Renee', one of the owners. After listening to our story she called the elephant handlers. One said, "I think the animals would be okay with it."

Renee' directed us through a gate, then down a road toward the forest. It was a tough ride on loose dirt. What a spectacle we made to the tourists riding past in trams. There were five adult elephants and five young calves in the herd. Victor the handler asked me to ride by slowly to see how the elephants would react to a bicycle. Elephants are quick, very quick for their size. We'd read they could run 40 MPH. Acting as confident and nonchalant as possible I prepared for the worst. What preparation would be adequate if one of the beasts charged?

On my solo pass, the adults paid little attention. The calves stirred and ran away. Cat and I made three passes, each time getting closer. The third time, we stopped in front of three of the adults. The big one, Harvey, stepped close, sniffing Cat and her bike. His trunk left a trail of mucus across the

top of her panniers. Exhilaration doesn't do justice to explain our feelings.

We'd never been that close to un-tethered elephants. Victor was always near, reassuring us and Harvey. Cat was thrilled when Renee' suggested she bottle-feed one of the babies. Even the little ones were big. Cat approached with uncertainty. The little one was only interested in getting the large nipple into its mouth. I almost had to drag Cat away. Victor told us that unlike Indian Elephants, Africans can't be trained. These had been raised around humans but weren't tame. The park was a great way for tourists to see Harvey and the others up close. The Park took in sick and wounded elephants caught in the wild or from other game preserves.

The excitement made the final 20 Ks to Knysna fly by. As the N2 thinned, traffic thickened. Cycling in was like riding on PCH in Laguna Beach, CA. Stores, shops, cars, tourists, it had it all. We stopped at a Tourist Info kiosk. The young girl, Celine, gave us a list of places to stay. We asked about the Wayside Inn, she pointed to it just across the parking lot. The price was high. Celine called to ask about availability. She reserved a room, even got a better rate.

The Wayside was a surprise, a new building that felt like the 19th century. We settled in, then walked to the Internet Cafe. Surprise, the young guy there told us Celine owned the shop. He was a nervous wreck. His first day on the job and he'd just been robbed. A couple of teenagers hung out until he turned his back, then grabbed money from the register and ran.

The waterfront reminded us of a miniature Pier 39 in San Francisco. Shops, restaurants, and tourists milling about. Dinner was at a place called Changes. We both gorged on Lamb Shanks.

CAT TRAX Day 255, Another Day in Knysna. Breakfast on the balcony and a walk to the waterfront consumed our day. It was a small version of Santa Monica, complete with a ferry boat ride and marina. A strolling band of old guys in bright red jackets played

Dixieland music. We loved this sign; "Travel Broadens The Mind, Friendship Is A Sheltering Tree!"

CAT TRAX Day 256, 61 Ks, Knysna to George. Up early, anxious to ride. The road was flat along the Knysna River. We could see the "Heads," the headlands of the river at the ocean. It was a wetlands area, tidal flats with flocks of birds in the water and on the wing. Ups and downs through pines and brush took all morning. Into Sledgefield for lunch at an Italian restaurant with realistic-looking paintings of places around the world. We started a memory quiz of places we'd visited.

The Eiffel Tower was easy, several others, too. On a trip to the restroom I saw one that not a lot of people would know. I asked the Chef/Waiter Devon if he knew the story. "The owner told us it had something to do with pissing on the city of Brussels, Belgium." It was Manneken Pis the one we called "Little Pisser." We enjoyed telling Devon how Manneken saved Brussels by peeing on a big fire.

The hilltop had a 180-degree view. From there we rolled down to the Diep River and the Sledgefield on the Sea slough. The road to George angled off toward the right, 10 Ks according to our map. We tried calling Doug our Angel on the road to Tsitsikamma. He'd invited us to stay and we wanted to make sure the invitation was still open. We left a message on his answering machine.

An old hotel looked closed, there were For Sale signs on the driveway. The nice girl at the desk offered a very reasonable rate, 220 Rand. ($34 US) Cat checked it out. As she always says, "It's only for one night!" We moved in, then called Doug again. Hoping to at least buy dinner to repay his kindness. Again, we could only leave a message.

CAT TRAX   Day 257, 56 Ks, George to Mossel Bay. The included breakfast was surprisingly good. Curious Realtors, we needed to know about the For Sale signs. The server said, "The owner doesn't really want to sell. He has to keep the signs up, until the end of this month." Our best guess, the listing agreement must have been expiring.

There were lots of scenic ups and downs on the way to Mossel Baai. It was 7 Ks off the highway. Several B&Bs along the route looked inviting but we wanted to see the sights of town. The Tourist Office was across from The Old Post Office Hotel. Pricey, but the only game in town. Cat checked, they gave her a tiny discount. Once again, "Rate Had Its Privileges." A great room, we took the deal.

CAT TRAX   Day 258, 90 Ks, Mossel Bay to Riversdale.

Breakfast was a treat. The hotel Manager Karen stopped by our table to apologize for the lack of hot water in the room. She insisted on making it up in the rate. We didn't object. I asked about the music playing in the restaurant, a classical sound with an African beat. She checked, "It's a group called the Soweto String Quartet." I asked where we could buy a CD. She sent one of the girls to look. She returned with a CD. Same group, different songs. I accompanied the girl back to the shop. They were sold out of the CD *Renaissance*.

Karen offered their scratched well-used copy. I wanted the jacket, the story of the music so I told her we'd find it later. We loaded up, pushed through the lobby of the elegant old hotel, paid our bill and got a picture on the steps with Karen. She was a gem, helpful above and beyond the call of duty.

Lunch in Albertinia, the Aloe Capital of Africa. An aloe factory was surrounded by beautiful plants with tall orange flowers. There were two service stations, the decision which to choose was easy-a guy at one shouted a greeting and waved us in. Andre the owner was curious, wanted to know everything about our journey. Inside their café he and wife Renee served soup and conversation. Renee invited us to spend the night with them.

Andre whispered, "We've sold the business, they should finish the transfer in just a couple of days. We've made an offer on two video stores." Those two daring entrepreneurs had previously owned a tire distribution center in Cape Town, but moved to the country for better schools for their kids.

After the first 28 Ks the road ran across canyons so deep that it became dip down, then struggle to push back up. On the second big dip, a bakkie pulled up. It was Doug our Tsitsikamma Angel. He leaned out the window and said, "I told my friend, Hanae, here, that you two had to be Pat and Cat." Then he scolded us, "Why didn't

you come to the farm? I got your message but thought you understood, even if I wasn't there, my friends would welcome you."

The temperature was dropping as fast as the sun as we pedaled into the up and down streets of Riversdale. Tired and anxious for a hot shower, we grabbed the first hotel.

CAT TRAX Day 259, 86Ks, Riversdale to Swellendam. Andre and Renee met us for breakfast. Andre was preparing to operate the two video stores, one there, one in George. Renee would spend her time with the family and take substitute-teaching jobs. We parted with handshakes they wished us well in our travels we wished them luck in their future endeavors.

A quick stop for burgers, then back at it. We struggled in the increasingly steep ups and downs. It was warm, we were pouring sweat. Cat worried that due to our late start we'd be stuck in the middle of nowhere in the dark, again. After struggling,

314

even walking up three steep hills, we were treated to a long gradual down. Our hope that we'd climbed our last hill fell flat. In the final ten Ks we faced two more big challenges.

A woman with a baby in her arms pointed and told us to loop around when we asked directions for Swellendam. That led us directly onto the main street. It was nearing dusk but we had beaten darkness. A hotel sign drew us in. The price was beyond budget, again. Too late to start searching I talked to the clerk. He'd mentioned a weekend special. I asked him to give that to us. "It's the rules," he replied, "I can't break the rules, it's only Wednesday." I asked for a discount if we stayed two days. He said he couldn't. Then I asked if he knew other places to stay.

He gave me a list of B&Bs. As we turned to go, he said, "The best I can do is 395 Rand." We took his deal.

Another quote, one we'd heard on TV that morning seemed appropriate after our warm days ride and our unheated room. "Too Hot To Handle, Too Cold To Take."

CAT TRAX Day 260, A Day Off in Swellendam. Awakening to darkness, we snuggled until 8:00 a.m.. Our bodies were stiff sore and tired. We'd cycled a lot of hills. At 9:00 we walked across to a veggie market for bananas then ate them as we explored the main street. Autumn was in the air, golden leaves graced the trees. Coffee and a waffle rounded out breakfast. Not filling or fulfilling but then as Cat had said, we'd "eaten an entire pig" since arriving in South Africa. A day without bacon or sausage would be good for us.

Swellendam is the third-oldest city in South Africa. The manager at the Tourist Office, Val, was full of ideas. She shared the story of her office building. "Built in 1838 by the church, it was a school for the children of former slaves. Slavery was abolished and they wanted to help Native Africans learn to read and write. One of two clocks painted on the facade was fixed at 9:00. The kids were taught when the hands of clocks at home were the same, it was time for school." (Note, it took 30 years and a bloody Civil War to end slavery in the USA!)

Cat asked Val about the area, Three Anchors Bay, where we'd

315

be staying in Cape Town. She said, "It's a good neighborhood." When Cat asked about riding the Mini Vans into town she said, "I would never ride those, the Black people ride them." We told her we'd been riding them throughout Africa and she said, "For you tourists, it's probably okay, but for an Afrikaner, the Blacks would find it strange to see us there." Guess it would take more than ten years for the colors of the Rainbow Nation to completely blend?

CAT TRAX Day 261, 35 Ks, Swellendam to Stormsvlei. A peek outside told us the weatherman had made the right call. Heavy cloud cover threatened to bring his predicted storm.

Undaunted, we set off into cold wind, a headwind that made our lives miserable. We tucked our heads and pedaled hard, grasping the handle bars for dear life. Blasts of wind from our side left us wobbling. Perhaps we should have waited another day. We discussed turning back. Hating that idea, we struggled on.

The road to Kaap Agulhas (Cape Agulhas) turned downwind. The sign indicated, "Suidelikste Punt Van Afrika, 97 KM." I felt that if we did as some had suggested and put up a spinnaker sail we'd be there in no time. Moving onward  slowly, the wind began pelting us with drops of rain.

We had been struggling in a gale-force wind for four hours. Now we were in a full-blown rainstorm. Hunger and the struggle had tired us. Every farm became a possible shelter. Most were so far off the road that we stayed the course. Then came Stormsvlei a suitably named village. A sign read, "Wine Store." Surely that was a "good sign!" It was obvious this was not a village. It may have been in the past but those days were long past. The Wine Shop and Dried Flower Store was the sum total of it.

Soaked to the bone, we left the bikes outside and sought refuge. The woman seemed less concerned with our plight than about the mud we'd tracked in. Two couples seated at the bar were eating sandwiches. We moved past the dried flowers, taking a seat near them. The woman warmed to us as we dried, like her flowers. She had sandwiches, we were hungry. The couples Derric and

316

Sharmain, Marius and Hester began asking questions. Or questioning our sanity.

Marius told us, "Derric is an artist, I'm his agent." Derric asked, "What route are you taking to Cape Town?" When I answered the shortest most direct on the N2, Sharmain, his wife said, "No, that way is steep, scenery is boring, and, you'd pass through dangerous townships. Why not skirt the mountain, go to Betty's Bay? You can use our home." A superb offer, but our concern was to find a warm, dry place to stay for that night.

Another couple, Michael and Jane, came in. They knew the others, they'd stayed at a B&B north of there. They talked and joked then Michael and Jane went wine shopping. The others began to leave. Sharmain gave us her phone number, again urging us to stay at Betty's Bay. "It's a second home, we live in Cape Town," she said. "It would be all yours, you'd be our guests." We thanked her, but remained intent on pushing up and over, then flying down into Cape Town.

With hearty handshakes and well wishes they ducked out the door into the storm. Michael and Jane waved goodbye to them, then turned and began talking with us. They were worried about what we would do. Mary the shopkeeper said, "There is no place to stay here, no rooms!" Michael insisted, "We'll put your bikes in our rental car, drive you to Riversonderend."

Mary, who lived on a farm nearby, called her husband to see if he'd drive us to town in his bakkie. Michael seemed anxious to help, "You could leave the bikes here, we'll take your bags to town." That made sense, we'd find a ride back to avoid another gap in our Odyssey.

Mary graciously allowed us to pull the wet muddy bikes inside. Michael and Jane helped carry the few necessary bags to their trunk. We were off to Riversonderend. (River Without End) Michael mentioned, "We've been to Joburg celebrating Jane's birthday." We slipped back inside and bought a gift bottle of her favorite wine, Merlot.

In Riversonderend Michael stopped at the Jasmyn Guest House. He negotiated a good price in Afrikaans, then asked the woman to find a ride for us back to Stormsvlei the

next morning. She quickly volunteered. We had a home, a ride, and our drivers were hungry. They'd stopped in a café they liked. We joined them, even though we were full of Mary's sandwiches. It was only 2:00 p.m., way early to start drinking. However we did, to celebrate our newfound shelter and friends. What a wonderful afternoon, sipping and sharing stories of our lives. They, too, were a couple rebuilding their lives after divorce. Jane was from London, England, a big city girl. Michael was Afrikaner, and proud of it. His love was to be in the wild listening to the beasts of the jungle while sleeping in a tent. She was trying to adjust.

Oh, how we hated to see them go. Hugs, those Afrikaner four cheek kisses, and they were gone. The house of Jasmine was old and cold but the shower was hot. We walked to Vn' Desden, Beer on the Stoep, for dinner. The food was good, and the local feeling and glow that owner Desmond brought added up to a great evening. Jasmine and her husband Arman came in. She said, "We will drive you back to Stormsvlei we can leave by 9:00 a.m. okay?"

What a day, what great new friends a stormy day had blown into our lives. We studied our map, thinking about taking the extra day and skirting the two passes by looping out through Betty's Bay. The more we talked about the big hills the more Cat bought in to the beach idea. She threw the extra blanket on our already heavy load of covers, and crawled in. We huddled and basked in the glow of our good fortune.

CAT TRAX Day 262, 70 Ks, Stormsvlei to Caledon. The room

was so cold our breath formed little clouds. It was tough to crawl from under the pile of covers. Who'd think it could be that cold in Africa? We dressed in record time then went back to Desmond's for breakfast. The place was a combination butchery/bakery, and mini-market. Breakfast was the usual eggs and sausage but we topped it off with fresh-baked sweet rolls and strong hot coffee.

Desmond told us he'd been in medical research for several years. It was a good career, and he liked the work, but it was dependent on annual grants and contracts.

"One year, we'd get a $250,000 grant," he said, "Then, just as the project was in full swing, they'd cut the grant. A friend of mine quit, opened a dry cleaners. That inspired me to open this tiny bakery and coffee shop. It's been popular, business has grown, we expanded and are doing quite well."

Arman smoked as he drove us back, while Jasmine talked about their lives. We didn't quite get it all, it sounded like they were a later in life couple. He was still working but could retire. He liked the money but hated the work. Was it fear or did he just want a place to go every day?

Mary was just opening the door to the Flower Shop as we arrived. Arman tossed the bags down, shook our hands, then they hurried off to church. We got a photo of the bikes in the shop then pushed out the door and pedaled away. The unsettled weather continued. We went through rain then hit dry areas, always into a cold wind.

Desmond was out, but we stopped anyway and bought his homemade meat pies for a picnic. Out of Riversonderend the wind continued, but the rain stopped. The countryside was a patchwork of greens, browns, and golden fields under cloudy skies. There was no shelter, we just lay the bikes down and sat on the roadside, eating our meat pies.

It was 4:00 p. m. when we hit the outskirts of Caledon. The Caledon Casino was off to the left. Thinking it would be expensive, we sailed down the steep hill in to town. The Parkland Hotel had a room available. It had a tub but no shower. The gal told Cat she could use a shower down the hall. We decided to cycle back up to the Casino.

It was a tough pedal and push. Hoping the struggle was worth it, we rode in. The girl at the desk said, "Sorry, we are fully booked."

"Saturday night, you know, and we are hosting an ANC (African National Congress) Convention." Stunned, I told her we needed help, it was getting dark and cold. She started calling around, looking for a B&B. All booked. As she continued down the list a snappy-looking guy in suit  and tie stopped and listened. Hein, the Manager, stopped her and said, "We'll put them in the Painted Lady."

The Painted Lady was a guesthouse. The Casino bought it to accommodate out of area help. Hein and his assistant Edgar solved every problem before we could bring them up. "Do you want to come back for  dinner tonight?" Of course we did, but no car so no way to get there. "We'll have our driver pick you up, then take you back, when you're finished."

Edgar drove, we followed. He stopped to pick up some of the workers who were walking to "The Lady." The Painted Lady was painted mauve. She was an old, cold house. The guest room had a wall heater. Cat hovered next to it. No shower but plenty of hot water in a cold bathroom. Little discomforts meant nothing, we had a roof over our heads. Oh, and the price was right!

Benny the driver knocked on the door at 7:00. Dinner was

Ostrich steak for me and fish for the Cat. Hein stopped to make sure all was well. They'd named the restaurant The Black Sheep and the sign said, "Every family has one." I thought I'm it in my family! Another guy came out with a camera and took pictures of us. He said, "For the Casino Newsletter."

Benny dropped us back at The Lady. The room was still cold, we got an extra blanket and snuggled in. Was this Africa or Antarctica?

CAT TRAX Day 263, 71 Ks, Caledon to Betty's Bay. Man, it was a cold morning. Again, our breath made clouds and we hated to crawl from under thick layers of covers. Hein had suggested getting coffee and breakfast at the Spar Market. That would work any day other than Sunday. The clerks told us the only restaurant in town that would be open was at the Parkland Hotel. We hoped the desk clerk wouldn't remember that we'd walked out after seeing the room. We were surprised when Linda the owner met us, seated us and wanted to know about our ride around the world.

Linda was such a great gal we asked her to sit with us as we ate the fantastic breakfast. She was on her own big adventure, "I bought the hotel a year ago, and have been working, struggling with repairs and maintenance. I'm convinced it will pay off." she said, then she called out to a guy coming down the stairs, "Hey Tom, these guys are from California, too."

During intros, Tom said, "I'm from Los Angeles." I told him the only person I'd ever met who claimed to be from Los Angeles was Cat, she was born there. He laughed and said, "Well, my house is in Laurel Canyon, in the Hollywood Hills, maybe that doesn't actually qualify as Los Angeles? I own a music licensing company." We asked what that was. "I contract music to companies that do Oldie albums. My number one client and best friend is Andy Williams. I also have The Everly Brothers, and lots of other fifties and sixties artists."

Tom was a nice soft-spoken guy. He said, "I'm here on a side trip. I flew into London to book a TV Christmas Special for Andy Williams. I've been in Africa many times and usually stay at the same B&B but it was fully booked." Fate?

We were on the road by 9:30 a. m.. The weather warmed, the wind slowed, and the road leveled. Seeing Houhoek Pass off to our left and knowing there was another even higher, between there and

Cape Town, made us glad we'd taken Sharmain and Derric up on their offer of their house at Betty's Bay. It would increase the distance by about 30 Ks and take a little longer but it made good sense. Especially now that Cat had seen the height of Houhoek.

Too cold at night but the afternoon sun bore down hot and heavy! This was the ride that many had described as so "bee-u-di-fool." To us it was just another tree-lined road, but as we neared the coast it began to live up to that description. A golf course development on the water looked like California. The coastline was rough, surf crashed onto a rocky shore as we rounded the corner into  Betty's Bay. Sheer cliffs climbed straight up into the clouds.

The restaurant where Sharmain said we'd find the keys, was closed. A fellow there suggested we try The Penguin Place up the road. The lady there said, "I don't know anything about a key and I don't even know a Derric and Sharmain!" We called Sharmain from a coin phone. She told us we'd find the key hidden in the barbeque. The streets had no markers, we didn't know whether we were even on the right street. A couple of women out walking, pointed out the house.

Wow, a great looking place but no key in the barbeque. We searched around the barbeque and anywhere nearby where it might be hidden. One of the walking women came by and we asked if we could call Sharmain from her house. She knew them and said, "I will call her." She probably wanted to call to make sure we weren't thieves.

The woman returned and said, "The girl Jorika, (pronounced Eureka) forgot to leave the key. She is coming." Waiting, Cat began to shiver.

Jorika arrived a few minutes later and opened the door. She found the alarm box but couldn't disable it so it went off. She called the security company and squared things, then left us to our own devices.

Hoping that Derric and Sharmain would never know, we pulled the bikes inside and leaned them against the dining table. A warm shower took the chill out of our bones.

Jorika had given us some bad news, no restaurants nearby. Derric and Sharmain had told us to use food from the cabinets and freezer. Wonderful frozen Butternut Squash Soup with Pasta from our bags. Unfortunately, when Cat shook the salt, the cap came off the shaker and the entire bottle poured into the pasta. Pretty salty, pretty good. The wine we borrowed was great, too.

A few of Derric's paintings hung on the walls. A brochure told of his love for the land and Africa. He specialized in brilliantly-colored landscapes. No wonder his work was so popular.

CAT TRAX Day 264, 51 Ks, Betty's Bay to Strand. Oh, what a beautiful morning, oh, what a beautiful day! The sun lurked behind huge cliffs then a scattering of rays foretold its coming. We were loading up when a neighbor couple came knocking. Just checking to make sure we were okay. It seemed that every one watched out for each other at Betty's Bay. "You really should stay another day, see our Botanical Garden." Our sights were set on Cape Town a day and a half away, we couldn't stay. She helped with directions, "You can have breakfast at the Botanical Gardens, good food, and a glimpse of the gardens and plants."

The Botanical Gardens were just down the highway. We rolled in and told the guy at the ticket window we just wanted to have breakfast. He insisted we had to buy a ticket. Perplexed, again I said, "We only want breakfast, not a tour of the Gardens." He stood fast, we threatened to go elsewhere and he just shrugged. We left.

Cycling onward, we found the little store and returned the key to the house. Jorika was there, we asked about breakfast. She pointed to the adjacent Bay Café, a wonderful artistic place. The owner served, we filled up and warmed up. The cost included cappuccinos, our first in months. The wind had begun to whistle along the cliffs. A fellow diner suggested we see the penguins and pointed the way down a side road. Penguin Point was disappointing. It was a long walk to Penguin Beach and in howling wind. We stood shivering and took pictures of the signs hoping to see more of the little critters later. Of all the game animals we'd wanted to see penguins weren't even on the list. Penguins in Africa?

A looping slow decent, then we passed Pringle Bay. We began a long climb on the road between two totally different-looking hills. To the right, all rock, devoid of plant life. On the left, green, verdant covered with fynbos (fine bush). At the summit we met wind so fierce it made the steep downhill to the beach hazardous.

The coastline was brilliant, dazzling in the morning sun. The road narrowed, and it was a long drop to the water below. We saw groups of seals, one fin up, sunning in the choppy sea. Traffic moved slowly and was considerate. Our only real adversary, the wind.

We decided to spent the night in Strand. Turning, the wind had become our friend, we quickly covered ground. The Strand, at least the beachfront, was a row of high-rise condos the likes of which we hadn't seen since Marbella, Spain. Looking for any sign: Hotel, B&B or Guest House we stopped at Seeff Properties Real Estate Office. Lita greeted us, listened to our story then welcomed us as fellow Realtors. She locked the office, got in her car, and led us through small streets to Welterusten Guest House. After a quick intro to the owner, Henry, she rushed back to her office, no doubt dreaming of making a big sale. What a nice thing to do for a couple of strange-looking strangers!

Henry and Jeanette owned Welterusten, Well Rested we think? She drove up with their two daughters as we pushed inside. The eldest was carrying a guitar. "Have you been taking a lesson?" I asked. When she confirmed, I asked if she was going to be a famous rock star. "Of course!"

The room was furnished in period B&B style. They allowed us, even helped us push the bikes inside it. After a quick shower, Henry directed us to a waterfront restaurant. The ocean waves lapped under it. The wind whistled through the window. Cat had calamari, just so-so. I ordered Lambs Neck-odd in a fish place, but oh my, it was fantastic.

We talked about how different South Africa was compared to other countries on the Continent. Just walking on the streets after dark was a huge risk in some of the places we'd visited. Also people like Henry, Jeanette, Derric and Sharmain, were so outgoing and shared so easily.

CAT TRAX Day 265, 48 Ks, Strand to Cape Town. Henry was chief cook and bottle washer. He served a wonderful breakfast, just what two cyclists needed on their final days ride in Africa. He also shared some family history. His first wife died, they had a son. He and Jeanette married and had two more children, daughters. His son, just 22, was killed in a car crash a little over a year earlier. You may remember the story of my loss? My son, Ronald Jerry, was 18 when

 he died. I told Henry how that loss had changed my life, made me seek more than a "normal" life, more than a good day's business. He said, "I do dream of travel and seeing the world. First, I must get kids through school, and this place paid off."

The consensus amongst the group was we should cycle on R102, a surface road, rather than the N2. We bid them farewell and pedaled away toward the R102. That didn't last long. The road was busy and the shoulder was off and on, mostly off. After riding on a sidewalk, stopping at corners, dropping off the curb, then lifting up on the opposite side a few times, we took the next N2 on-ramp. The wide shoulder was flat, the cycling fast. We were off to Cape Town.

The closer we got to the Southern Capital of South Africa, the tougher it became to cycle. Traffic thickened and ran fast, we were harried. The on and off ramps again posed the greatest danger.

As we'd been warned, we passed Bridgetown Township, a shack town of corrugated roofs and block walls. What a striking contrast to the high-rise skyline we were beginning to see tucked under the cliffs of Table Mountain.

There were cows and donkeys strolling in the dirt streets. People walked along the edge of N2 and in the open grassy area between the highway and a fence. Joggers and cyclists shared the shoulder. Several friends had said, "People there throw rocks at cars. They may target you." The only things thrown at us were friendly waves and good wishes. Though we had survived the township unscathed,

we felt our usual anxiety when a car pulled slowly past then stopped, well ahead. Two guys got out and stood behind, waiting for us. One raised a black object and pointed it. First thoughts, a gun like we'd seen on the news. Maybe an AK 47? No, he was holding a camera with a huge telephoto lens. Denzil was a freelance photographer, Babalo a reporter. They spotted us while returning from a story. Babalo said, "You looked like you've been traveling a long distance. I was sure there was a story there!" He asked a few questions as Denzil took pictures. We gave them our card, then they were off. No promises just the thought that the story might

make the papers. Onward, three-lane on/off ramps were truly menacing. We left the N2 rather than challenging the fast moving traffic. The R102 wound its way through the heart of Cape Town, often changing names. Hungry, we stopped at a sports field. The sun was high, the temperature climbing and teams were playing field hockey. Our last lunch on the African Road.

At Beach Street, we were in Three Anchors Bay. The next challenge was finding Pat's flat. We stopped a pizza delivery guy and asked directions. He thought for a second, then said, "Up this street to the top, left one street then back down." With that, he jumped on his motor scooter and roared away. Should we trust him? The street he pointed to was up, really up. Based on nothing other than the hope that a deliveryman knew his way around, we pushed,

our thoughts flashing back two years to the day we pushed our bikes up the hilly streets of San Francisco.

At the top we drifted across and down to the next street. A construction guy told us the condos were in the building that backed up to the street. Eureka, we had found it!

The keys were at Flat #1 along with directions on how to turn on the water, electricity and refrigerator. The downside of Pat's Flat: the TV didn't work, and there was no music.

Quick showers, then a walk for groceries. Home cooked dinner of chicken, potatoes, and pumpkin.

We set the computer on slideshow and, as pictures popped up, we yelled out the names of the places we'd been. Almost like a contest.

Exactly nine months earlier we'd boarded the ferry and crossed the Straits of Gibraltar to Africa. What a huge journey, an enormous adventure. Lots of people ask us if we were ever in danger. Our stock answer, "If we were, we didn't know it!" We had survived jungles, huge trucks, robbery, theft, and lots of diarrhea. Looking back, we only remember the great moments, the wondrous adventures, and the friends we made along the way!

A local TV travel show we'd often seen since Port Elizabeth was a couple of guys driving around South Africa in an old Cadillac convertible. Stopping at tourist spots, sampling adventures like the giant Bungee Jump. The name of the show struck a chord with us: "Going nowhere, slowly!" A few glasses of wine and we decided our adventure should be called, **"Getting Somewhere, Slowly!"**

Chapter 30 The Winelands, Penguins and Cape Town

CAT TRAX Day 266, Three Anchors Bay. Home sweet home, homemade breakfast of fruit, muffins and coffee, life was good. The washing machine spun cleansing our foul smelling cycling gear.

When we opened our e-mail we were surprised to see a message from Bala, a PHD Student from India, studying in South Africa, had sent a message. He'd seen an article in the newspaper and wanted to meet, talk about cycle touring. He had a dream to take such a trip, someday.

We rushed out, bought a paper and found ourselves on page 7. As we paid another customer said, "Hey, you're Pat & Cat, the World Famous Cyclists." As we waited to pay, he said, "I'm Jewish, I don't want to travel around the world, just to New York City." Rambling on he said, "I want to see the place that's home for 2,000,000 Jews." Strange reason to want to go, but a nice enough guy, we hoped the article and our story would inspire him to open his mind.

Pat & Cat on 40 000km around-the-world cycle odyssey

Nelson Mandela's picture took up almost a quarter of the front page. He announced he would retire, stop making appearances, spend time with his family. A shame seeing a true hero fading. He'd given most of his life, including twenty-seven years in prison, to South Africa.

CAT TRAX Day 267, Another Day in Three Anchors Bay. We rode the bikes into Cape Town to Bowman's Cycle Shop. Kyle took our bikes to heart. He offered to completely go over them. He even said they'd box them for the flight to South America, the next leg of our Odyssey!

In V & A Waterfront Center, (Victoria and Alfred Streets) we bought wine to replace bottles we'd used during our overnighter at Betty's Bay. We'd invited Derric and Sharmain out for dinner at a place of their choice. A small repayment for their kindness.

She picked us up at 6:00 p.m. We enjoyed a glass of wine and tour of their home including Derric's studio. The place was superbly furnished. Sharmain was proof of the old adage that behind every successful man is a great woman. Dinner at their favorite Italian restaurant, great food, wine, and conversation.

CAT TRAX Day 268, Franschoek, TOURISTS to The

Winelands. Tough getting used to driving on the right side of the road and shifting with the left hand. The rental agent said, "Remember Sir, the left side is the right side, and the right side is suicide."

You'd think cycling on the left this past month, driving would be simple. However, we hadn't driven in more than a year. Once we were out on the street, Cat felt I was driving too close to parked cars and that led to a stream of screams.

CAT TRAX Day 269, Winelands, Simons Town. Our intro to

South African wines came in of all places, Denmark. Helja, Patriarch of our Danish Family found an inexpensive South African Chardonnay. We drank a lot of it all the way through Scandinavia.

The Winelands of South Africa are immense, and production is impressive. Once you're beyond the usual sights, if you enjoy wine you must visit the Winelands. We spent two full days exploring, sipping, and dining. We met wine lovers from every corner of the earth. Also stayed in several opulent B&Bs

CAT TRAX Day 270, Back to Cape Town. At Boulders Beach

we. visited an entire colony of Penguins. Plenty of the little guys waddling around in formal wear. The road from Boulders Beach led directly to Cape Peninsula National Park. Another must-see site, in South Africa. Strange-looking antelope called Bontebok hung out near the Park Info Center. Though we didn't see any, we learned of sushi eating baboons that harvest mussels from the ocean rocks.

We stopped at two obelisks commemorating the passage of the first two Europeans, Portuguese, who rounded the Cape of Good Hope. Bartholomeu Dias in 1488 and Vasco Da Gama in 1497.

A funicular ride provided a spectacular view of Cape Point. We were at the southernmost tip of Africa. Our memories drifted back to the people. Africans black, brown, and white. Nine tough months, seventeen countries and we were already beginning to miss Africa. All a tremendous experience now a permanent part of our lives.

Around The Cape on a rocky beach there was a monument that read, "Cape of Good Hope, The Southern Most Point of the African Continent." Almost anti-climactic, given the literal blood sweat and tears we'd invested cycling there.

We stopped at Three Anchors Bay, paid the rent and picked up our bags. We'd decided to move into the city. Cat had found a small boutique hotel near Bowman's Bike Shop. We cruised in to Cape Town and checked in to the Cape Heritage Hotel.

CAT TRAX Day 271, All Around Cape Town. As we ate breakfast, Nick, the affable owner of Cape Heritage and an avid cyclist, came in. He pulled up a chair to talk cycling. He'd traveled the world working for large hotel chains. The Cape Heritage had been rundown and for sale. Nick purchased it, applied his skills and had turned it around in a year. It was a great place to stay.

We returned the rental car and found plaid plastic bags to pack our panniers in for the upcoming flight. Also bought some necessities and picked up our airline tickets.

Next stop, the dentist. Winfred, our friendly desk clerk, guided us to the building. As we walked he told us he was originally from Johannesburg, but moved because of the crime there. "I was walking down a street in Joburg talking on my cell phone when a guy threatened me with a gun. He tried to grab my phone, and when I resisted he shot me in the leg." I told Winfred there are areas in our own home town where the same thing happens almost daily.

We were well beyond the feeling that Africa was a backward place where naked natives and hungry lions lurked in the jungles.

However, we did feel some trepidation about going to a dentist, even one recommended by a friend. Stepping out of the elevator on the 18th floor and entering the office, all fears vanished. Dr. Kevin Reed's office was the epitome of modern! The equipment was incredible. He inspected, x-rayed, shot the pictures, then shared his assessment. Cat's problems were minimal and could wait. I had a cracked filling he felt might be leaking and could cause a cavity. I

asked if he could do the work right then. He said, "Yes, we'll remove the old filling, and replace it right now, if you wish." He went to work, pulled the old filling out and had it replaced in just twenty minutes.

Back at the Cape Heritage, rain had taken a toll on the roof. Nick had mentioned his problems with roofers. We noticed a leak in our ceiling. The night clerk came, surveyed the problem and placed wastebaskets under the drips. It was an obstacle course between bed and toilet. The clerk reappeared and said, "Nick called, he wants to move you to a superior room." It was bigger and nicer-sometimes disasters lead to better things.

We snuggled down to the soothing sound of rain on the roof.

CAT TRAX Day 272, A Cape Town Tour. Last day in Africa, and we were motivated to see the places of interest in Cape Town. Our first stop, Bowman's Bike Shop. My front fork had a slight crack, but Kyle felt sure it would survive the ride from South America to California. He replaced the chains, bearings, tires, and seat posts.

The Cape Town Explorer offered an open-top City Tour. The bus wheeled quickly through the narrow streets as Melanie the guide pointed out landmarks and gave a short history of each neighborhood. One point of interest was Neighborhood #8. The Apartheid Government decided they would convert it from Colored's housing to an all white district. The residents were relocated, their homes demolished. The decision was made just as the Apartheid system collapsed. The area, politically sensitive, was never rebuilt. It was a just a vacant scar, a sad reminder of a terrible era.

The Explorer Bus climbed Table Mountain, but our hopes of seeing Cape Town from above were dashed by Mother Nature. She'd slipped a thick cover of clouds over the Table.

Chapter 31 Freedom Born, of Robben Island

The Cape Town Explorer dropped us at the waterfront. We hustled to make the noon boat to Robben Island. Disappointment, there was no "noon boat." The fellow at the ticket booth pointed out another problem. The letter Janine from Travel Club had given us was good for only one ticket, and we were supposed to have called a week in advance. We complained, he sent us downstairs. There a gal took a look, then went back inside as a woman walked out

proudly carrying a birthday cake. I took her picture then we sang "Happy Birthday to You!" The other gal re-appeared and conferred with Phyllis the birthday girl. Turned out Phyllis was the manager. She set her cake down, looked at the letter, then turned to us and said, "This letter isn't valid." As we began to lose heart, she said to the other gal, "Give them tickets." What a nice gift Phyllis had given us for her birthday.

Our boat wouldn't float until 3:00 p.m.. On the nearby waterfront we fell in love with the performance of a family group calling themselves the Abonwabisi Brothers. They sang Zulu a capella, accented by group dance moves. We watched, listened, took a photo and video then bought their CD.

The Robben Island tour guides were all former prisoners. Sideeq had been a political prisoner from 1960-63. He was funny but firm at times. He said, "I lived on the island, for a while, after getting the job, but couldn't take it. I needed to leave at night, to keep bad memories at bay. We were subjected to a very tough life. Most of us, like me, were political prisoners, because we'd resisted Apartheid Rule. Many of us were held in isolation, often for years. We were separated from our families, by rules. We were only allowed to communicate in English or Afrikaans, with visitors. Many of our families who spoke only their native languages weren't allowed visits. Also, a prisoner's children weren't allowed on the island. I, myself, and many other prisoners didn't see our children for years."

Sideeq's bus tour to the Lime Quarry held two points of great interest. The first, a tunnel where many great ideas were formulated. He explained, "That was the prisoners' toilet. Guards dared not step foot inside the Black's Toilet. It was against the law for Whites to use Black Toilets. Many of Mandela's and the other dissident's thoughts and ideals were formulated in that toilet. Mandela recognized that ignorance was deterring Black progress. It was in that very toilet cave that the idea, 'Each one, Teach one' was conceived. That was, each prisoner was required to teach their skills-reading, writing, etcetera, to those who lacked schooling."

Sideeq said, "The second and most important thought born of the Toilet Hole, became the basis for change once Apartheid ended. The words, 'Love, Forgiveness and Reconciliation,' were written on the wall. Eventually, that saved thousands of lives," He continued, "Your own CIA, famous for flawed information-even disinformation-warned South African President F. W. De Klerk that legalizing the ANC would culminate in a blood bath. In fact, their estimate was as many as a million would be killed, most of them white. De Klerk moved forward. Fortunately Nelson Mandela and the others leaders chose that path: 'Love, Forgiveness, and Reconciliation.'

Another feature of the Lime Quarry was a mound of stones. Sideeq said, "Mandela and a crowd of others were here celebrating the 10th anniversary of his release. When they came to the Lime Quarry, Mandela spoke of that time. Leaving, he picked up a stone, and as he walked  away, he said, "Each rock is different from the others, yet when placed together, they have a new strength." With that, each person, Blacks, Colored and Whites, picked up a rock, and added it to the pile."

Our second guide, Derick, was incarcerated from 1985 to 1991. He wrote in our book the exact day, April 11, 1991, when he was finally released. He was younger, and still angry. When asked, he said "You had to go along with all the rules, or you received no favors. I had a tough time deviating from my beliefs, so they cut me no quarters. I lived through my entire sentence including added days, and I'm proud to have done it that way."

Derick led us into the cellblocks. He was splendid in a harsh way. His speaking voice was strong, his language skills eloquent. He asked each in the tour where they were from. When we said, "America," he spat out his feelings, "Your country invaded Iraq. The prisoners in Guantanamo Bay, Cuba, are held without charges, without representation, or contact with their families, indefinitely. Much like it was here, before the end of Apartheid."

An Army General from Zambia accompanied us on the tour. One of his bodyguards was South African who had been imprisoned on Robben Island. He told Cat, "Many peoples from other countries in Africa, especially military men, visit the Island." Then he turned to the General and said, "We are standing in front of the cell, where my Boss was held. President Mandela, 46664, as he was known then, was held here, in Cell Number 5." There was a piece of wood

334

in the cell with the following carved onto it:
Mandela
No other man, has ever done so much, for so many!

Madiba, as he was affectionately known, appeared that afternoon at the opening of a school built with funds from his Trust despite his announcement of retirement a week earlier. What a guy!

We split up. Cat headed to the Cape Heritage, I to Bowman's Bike Shop. The guys there were putting the bikes back together.

Kyle had found another crack in the frame, probably caused when the boys pounded the modified seat post. He welded it as best he could and again said, "Looks like it'll hold up until you're back in California."

Cat called to say our new pal Nick had volunteered to take us to the airport. He would pick up the bikes in an hour. The pressure was on, and the guys worked hard getting the frames and wheels stuffed into the bike boxes. They were just taping them when Nick arrived. After we got them into his van he said "Good night, see you in the morning," and drove away. A packing frenzy, then sleep.

Our wakeup call at 6:00 a.m. wasn't required, we'd been up doing final packing since 5:00. Our busy minds were spinning. This was a *big day*. When Nick arrived at 8:00 we'd already moved the bags down to the lobby. Anxiety had us at the Airport 2 ½ hours early. We took a photo with Nick, shook hands, hugged, then pushed our bags to the Check In counter. Bags checked, boarding passes in hand, we boarded. The plane lifted off, headed for Buenos Aires, Argentina, at 11:00 a.m. Our Odyssey was moving on, after 265 days in Africa.

Life is a journey, we all choose our own paths. For us it was a bicycle Path. We encourage everyone to dream, pursue your dreams and never give up.

Africa tested the BOUNDARIES of our love for each other and our faith in each other. We moved on, into South America, Central America and Southeast Asia but those are stories for another time. Watch for them in our series, BICYCLING BEYOND BOUNDARIES.

Made in the USA
San Bernardino, CA
26 January 2017